ST. CHARLES COUNTY COMMUNITY COLLEGE

3 9835 0000809

W9-DIR-689

RED CARPET TO CHINA

By the same author

SPARE THE ROD

Red Carpet to China

Michael Croft

SCCCC - LIBRARY
4601 Mid Rivers Mall Drive
St. Peters, MO 63376

WITHDRAWN

NEW YORK
ST MARTIN'S PRESS

Copyright © 1958 by Michael Croft
Library of Congress Catalog Card Number:
59–15647

MANUFACTURED IN THE UNITED STATES OF AMERICA

TO

GEOFFREY SYKES

in memory of rougher journeys

24050

24080

Author's Note

THIS is the account of a visit I made to the People's Republic of China; it is written without axe to grind, tongue in cheek or chip on shoulder.

I travelled some twenty thousand miles on the communist circuit, where the welcome was never less than warm and the courtesy often excessive, but it would have been impossible to describe the experience honestly without appearing to bite the hand that fed me. I take no pleasure in this but I make no apology for it. The constant entreaty of my hosts was that I should give them my 'criticisms'; having done this freely while I was there I feel under no obligation to stop doing so now.

This is not a book for the political specialist, still less for the Old China Hand. I have no inside knowledge of communist affairs, and before my visit knew next to nothing about China past or present. I was not even much interested. Now I feel differently and, although this is necessarily a sketchy and selective picture, viewed from a privileged position, I hope that it will make some impression upon those who still feel as indifferent to the march of events in Asia as I did.

It is not only foolish but may prove fatal to shut our eyes to what is happening there simply because it seems so very far away—as though, by some mysterious natural law, distance served to indemnify our own prosperity. Distance has not prevented China from emerging, within a few years, into a world power of the first magnitude and ultimately, I believe, unless we do some rapid re-thinking on the political and economic fronts, it will not prevent China, still firmly allied to the Soviet Union, from gaining effective control over most of Asia, with catastrophic repercussions upon the western way of life. If I have not laboured this point in my narrative it is because I have preferred to record what I saw rather than what I thought, leaving the reader to draw his own conclusions.

I went as the representative of a British youth organisation, and as such mixed with Chinese youth of all kinds. No doubt many of them had been specially selected for the occasion, and some had been indoctrinated up to the hilt; but it was impossible not to be impressed by their approach to the task of building a new China. Their fervour and vitality made a striking contrast to the peevishness of those vociferous young people one too often encounters at home who seem to regard their own whining sense of futility as a positive, if not a profitable, virtue. I hope that this account may remind a few of them at least that there is a world elsewhere—and that what is happening in it now is going to be even more their concern than it will be mine.

I am greatly indebted to Mr. Roderick MacFarquhar for giving me the benefit of his specialised knowledge of the Chinese language and political background.

June 1958   M. C.

Chinese currency. At the time of my visit the rate of exchange was approximately seven *yuan* to £1 sterling.

The Liberation. The term refers to the establishment of the government of the People's Republic in 1949. To the communists it is an historical dividing mark, and I have used it throughout the book in accordance with present-day Chinese custom.

Contents

I

The Communist Visa

THE invitation came out of the blue.

I had just launched the Youth Theatre and was on the point of leaving for a Scandinavian holiday when a dapper, amiable young Scot appeared on the scene. His name was Andrew and he commuted aerially between Moscow, Prague and London. Would I, he enquired, be interested in going to China the following week on an international delegation?

At that time China could not have been farther from my thoughts—in point of fact, at no time had it been at all near them. I had never, even in childhood fantasies, yearned to sail down the Yangtse Kiang or to enter the walls of the Forbidden City. In a Lancashire cotton town in the 'thirties you learned to confine your imagination to more immediate horizons.

'It will be a wonderful experience for you,' said the amiable Andrew. 'Everything laid on—red carpet plus. You can go where you like and see what you like—within practical limits, of course. The delegation assembles in Prague on Tuesday next.'

Well, why not? I had always taken it for granted that the communist system would have little room for an awkward ideological customer like myself, but I had never actually studied it at close quarters. I had not even read Marx or dipped into Lenin, although I had no objection to the grim-browed brethren who had, so long as they did not expect me to stomach the same medicine. Presumably the invitation had some ulterior motive, but if I was ever to gain a glimpse of communism in the flesh this seemed as good an opportunity as any. At the same time I had no intention of being used as a stooge, however insignificant, in the propaganda and prestige game so, before accepting, I took some trouble to check the facts.

The invitation was genuine enough. Through their own Youth Federation the Chinese government had invited representatives from Youth organisations of twenty-five different countries. From Britain there was to be a Y.M.C.A. official, a member of a students' association, and an international woman tennis-player; a well-known actor was also to have gone but had dropped out through illness, which was how I came to be approached. Andrew assured me that amongst the European delegates there would be only four communists, 'so that every shade of political and religious viewpoint will be expressed in one delegation'. I was prepared to take him on trust about this but, having myself no particular viewpoint to express, the prospect of listening to those of the others was hardly an added attraction.

I had never been a delegate to anything and did not relish the idea of moving about in a supervised party; on the other hand, the red carpet had its appeal, for I had never travelled this way before. I have beaten a fair amount about the globe, first as a seaman in hard-lying destroyers, hitting the hardest-lying waterfronts in the world, from Montreal to Mombasa, from Beira to Bombay, and since the War I have shuffled round the capitals of western Europe in second-class cabins and third-class hotels; the only time I found myself an honoured guest was when the British Council grabbed me during an emergency in Copenhagen to visit a remote part of Jutland, and on that occasion the Danish hosts poured so much schnapps down my throat that I spent the night literally on the red carpet.

There was the problem of getting visas—Chinese, Czech and Russian—within the space of a few days. To the invited delegate nothing could be easier: the application forms consisted of single, stencilled sheets, and the details required were so elementary that they made most other visa forms look like police dossiers.

'Just scribble anything you like on them,' advised Andrew, in intervals of trotting obligingly from one embassy to another. 'They won't bother to read them, anyway. All you really need are your passport photos. Let me have them as soon as they're ready and I'll rush over with the forms and scratch in anything else that's needed myself.'

The only delay he envisaged was with the Czechs. 'They've still got the bureaucratic outlook. Sometimes they take as long as three months just to issue a transit visa. But it doesn't matter if you don't get it in time,' he assured me. 'The main thing is to get you to Prague. Everything will be fixed up there.'

'And how,' I asked, in my naif, old-fashioned way, 'do I get across the frontier?'

'Oh, you may have a hold-up there, but you don't need to worry about it. We'll phone through to our friends and they'll get in touch with the frontier. Our friends will look after everything.'

It seemed, if you tagged along with the friends, you could gate-crash frontiers, break through iron curtains and plough your way from Prague to Peking with scarcely a document to prove your identity and hardly a pfennig or a rouble in your pocket: 'the friends' would fix everything. I became increasingly curious to find out who they were.

The Czechs had a rush of efficiency to the head and my transit visa appeared hot on the heels of the Russian and Chinese. I spared a moment's thought for the journalist I had met the day before, a China specialist on a Right-Wing newspaper, who had been trying to obtain a Chinese visa for a year but had been persistently refused because, he suspected, of his knowledge of the language. I thought also of my long-cherished plan to tour the United States and wondered a little ruefully if I had lost my chance of an American visa for good. . . .

2

All Right in Prague

ANDREW was waiting at Victoria at 8.30 in the morning with Muriel, the tennis-player. He had tickets, baggage labels, boat and train schedules, and small sums of Belgian and German currency; he had forgotten nothing.

Muriel looked pale and miserable, the result of last-minute cholera and typhus injections, a formality with which I had dispensed at Andrew's advice.

'Have them if you like, but they're strictly unnecessary. I've been to China twice and never even got a mosquito bite.'

As we crossed the Channel on a sultry September morning Muriel gradually came to life. She was a tall, angular, dark-haired girl, with sparkling brown eyes, and a bright smile. I had read a great deal about her a few years ago when she regularly made the headlines as a stormy petrel on the international tennis-courts. She had felt then that the Press had treated her badly, but now she was a journalist herself and could understand how difficult it must have been to get a story out of such an uncommunicative character as herself.

She viewed the trip to China with casual equanimity. She was sure it would be 'good fun', and everyone had told her it was a chance not to be missed. She wasn't in the least interested in politics; sport was something quite separate, and sportsmen throughout the world should be able to get together without politics coming into it.

Dover–Ostend–Nuremberg: the tennis ran out and the conversation slowly stagnated. It was a relief to be joined by two American airmen going back off leave, until they started talking

4

about the certainty of atomic war within the next two years. The prospect didn't worry them in the least. They were stationed on an atomic gun-site near Frankfurt. During weekly lectures their colonel had told them that an atomic war was nothing to get excited about. Atomic missiles would be used in the same way as conventional ones, only with more accuracy. As for the H-bomb, nobody need get into a panic about that. They had been trying out a new kind of protective clothing that was completely immune to radio-activity.

'And if the Reds could just see what we've got lined up for them outside Frankfurt they'd feel mighty sorry they was born.'

One of the airmen was nineteen, the other twenty. They both came from Oklahoma. The day they joined the Army was the first time they had left home.

At Nuremberg the train was suddenly crowded with farm-workers and their families going back from a day at the market. We headed north-east through a landscape of hills and forests. A middle-aged German sitting opposite me introduced himself. He had been a P.O.W. at Culham for three years, captured in the Middle East. He was glad to use his English again. He was an electrical engineer who had been to Switzerland on business, and now he was going home.

'I live in the eastern zone,' he explained, adding in an aside, 'Unfortunately.'

We changed trains at Hedmachwitz and were joined by a burly young Scotsman with rucksack and open-necked shirt. He had done this journey many times. He knew all about our delegation, where we would stay in Prague, who would look after us. Yes, he was working in Prague. He frequently travelled about 'on business with foreign branches'. 'Are you anything to do with politics?' asked Muriel, and eventually he admitted that he worked for the International Union of Students.

Muriel proceeded to explain that she thought politics did more harm than good, while the Scotsman eyed her with a kind of pitying tolerance. She held forth at length about the irresponsibility of the trade unions. 'Why must they keep having all these strikes and stoppages? Do they never think about the good of the country?' The Scotsman gave her an avuncular, disbelieving smile. She said that she had suffered from strikes herself. She had been thrown out of a job as the result of the newspaper strike, although she'd been all against the strike from the start. She felt she was earning quite enough money as it was, and she didn't feel justified in striking for more.

This stung the Scotsman into life. 'I think I ought to enlighten you on a few heresies in your thinking.' This he did with a lengthy treatise on the relationship of profits to wages and of wages to the cost of living; but he could have saved his breath. 'I don't understand all that theory,' said Muriel, 'but I don't see why the whole country should suffer because the minority won't pull their weight. That's why I'm a Conservative; because the Conservatives are the only united party!'

From that point, during the whole time we were together, I could never make up my mind about Muriel. Was she really as innocent as she seemed, or had she cultivated a deliberately ingenuous mask with which to shield herself in any awkward situation? Time and again, whether with Czech, Chilean or Chinese, I watched her stonewalling her way out of a difficult argument, but the mental processes by which she arrived at any polemical position remained utterly enigmatic.

The frontier station might have been any other stopping place in the hills: a few isolated huts, cattle and sheep grazing in the distance, sunlight filtering through crimson clouds; the world at evening peace. But look a little farther down the track and three thin lines of barbed-wire curve and stretch away on either side as far as the eye can reach, and the middle wire is electrified to kill. And from the neat little huts where peat-smoke goes curling up into a friendly sky, watch the armed guards step briskly to their work; the cold collection of documents, the curt nod of official acceptance, the peremptory question or command. Nobody smiles to see you at this station; no warm face welcomes the traveller home. At the frontier men go on or turn back, die or are re-born; the tragedy of eastern Europe is summarised here.

But we are delegates, with documents in order; there is only a currency form to complete, a bureaucratic routine, and we can move on. We sit back, gazing through our window at the lethal air.

The interpreter identified us at once as we walked up the platform at Prague. 'It is impossible to mistake the English,' he said, meaning to flatter.

The delegation was housed in the Peace Hotel, a name which it shared, together with the insignia of the Picasso dove, with hundreds of other hotels from Prague to Peking at any point on the Red circuit where a delegation might stop off for the night. These hotels have an atmosphere of their own, for nobody is ever seen to pay a bill and, while everybody is being looked after by somebody else, nobody seems to know who anybody else is. There is no animation; nobody seems either glad or sorry to be there. People talk in little groups at their own tables, are provided with their wants, retire to their rooms, disappear in government coaches and cars, but what they have been doing and where they are going are questions which nobody cares to ask. This is not to suggest that there is anything furtive about their movements, only to indicate the air of unreality which seems to permeate the delegation traffic on this particular route.

The dining-room in the Peace Hotel was half-empty when we arrived. Although guests had been allotted to tables according to nationality, each table bearing a little flag to indicate the country, the members of the Youth Delegation had banded themselves together in one corner of the room. Instinctively I wanted to delay the formality of meeting them as long as possible. For one thing I was hungry; for another I did not much like the look of them. The table with the Union Jack was vacant, and I made hurriedly for it.

After dinner Stephen Tripp, a burly young Mancunian, introduced himself. He was just down from the university, and he explained, with many side glances and conspiratorial pauses, that he was very worried about his position. He remained worried about it, in fact, throughout the whole tour and, with the best

B

intentions in the world, tried to make the other English delegates equally worried about theirs.

It seemed that Stephen's father occupied an important position in Transport House and, although he had no objection to Stephen's going to China, Stephen felt that disaster might overtake the family if the Press got to know of it. He was at pains to make it clear that he had agreed to go, not as a delegate, but as an 'observer'—although the distinction was hard to find; he was greatly cheered to know that neither Muriel nor myself was a Party member, but enjoined us to be extremely discreet in whatever we said or did.

Twenty-eight delegates had assembled at the hotel; another ten were to join us at later stages. It looked like being the quaintest delegation ever to go anywhere. There were two Egyptians, a Sudanese, a Syrian, an Algerian, a coffee-coloured Cuban, a white-skinned Chilean, a young Australian from an evangelical movement who had happened to be holidaying in Paris when the invitations were given out, a Swedish priest, a Danish journalist, four communist youth leaders from Italy, Hungary, East Germany and France, three Y.M.C.A. officials from Sweden, West Germany and England, and Ricardo, a gangling young Spaniard who had also climbed on the band-wagon in Paris, despite the Spanish prohibition on travel to Red China.

Ricardo's understanding of English was limited, but he was the first to appreciate that Muriel was the only woman in the party. He followed her round Prague with a repertoire of little Spanish chivalries, and his ardour only cooled when the Egyptians, the Sudanese and the Syrian entered the lists with a variety of muscle, guile and sun-tanned sex-appeal with which he was not fitted to compete.

Hardly out of adolescence, Ricardo, Stephen Tripp and the Australian could fairly justify themselves as members of a youth delegation, but for the rest of us, with an age range from thirty to fifty, the youth tag seemed a trifle misleading; being new to the game and on the far side of the fence myself, I could hardly complain.

Prague: here at least was a symbol of my youth, for I grew up in the passionate 'thirties, when to be young was to care about places like Prague. And how desperately we cared: about Abyssinia, Austria, Spain, the Sudetenland. Not yet old enough to fight, we shed our blood in our classroom debates and carried the conscience of the world in our Sixth-Form brief-cases. And here, in this grey city of suspicion, where to criticise the government was to look stealthily over your shoulder first, where the day's work could not begin without a ten-minute catechism from the gospel of Marx and Lenin, where freedom had retreated for a decade in the shadows of Masaryk's death leap, was the tragic sequel to the years of appeasement; the bitter monument to French guilt and English shame.

Ada, my interpreter, and his student friends had only just learned to read when their country was abandoned to Hitler, but the meaning of Munich was burnt into their imagination. 'That was your greatest mistake,' they cried, 'and you are still paying the price of it!' Idle to protest, to point at the price they were paying themselves. They were the true children of the communist revolution, since from it they had salvaged what was left of their youth. 'We never knew what boyhood was,' said Ada. 'We lived in the woods in gangs. We had no school. The only lesson we learnt was how to kill and escape. We shot Germans in the back and hid in holes in the earth. We had no mother, no father, and all the love we knew was the kiss of death. There was no politics in this. That came later, when we had time to think. And then we knew who were our friends—and who had betrayed us.'

There is nothing an Englishman can say to this. The proud familiar clichés: Dunkirk, the Battle of Britain, the Arctic convoys, London could take it, carry no weight in a country which bore the thumbscrew and rack of Nazi occupation. You cannot argue about these things. You cannot measure one degree of mass suffering and terror against another, or mouth calm rationalisations in the scarred face of empirical patriotism.

'Tomorrow,' said Ada, 'you will go to Lidice, a few miles from Prague, and see the Garden of Roses. There is not much to see except the museum and the wall where our men were shot. Some of the children who were taken away were found again after the War, but even now forty-five of them have never been traced. Do you understand why we hate the Germans forever?'

Ada was training to be a doctor and worked as an interpreter in his holidays and spare time. Apart from the opportunity to meet foreigners, the job carried with it certain 'perks': decent meals at the delegates' hotels, film and theatre shows, trips out of town, and sometime, possibly, the chance of a permit to go abroad. He had a charm and warmth of manner which were at odds with his surroundings and made him seem younger than his twenty-four years. He was more interested in my ideas than he expected me to be in his, not because it was part of his job but part of his nature, and he had an ironic sense of humour which enabled him to smile where others might have been shocked.

With his blond hair, blue eyes and drawling English manner, he seemed curiously out of place in the strained atmosphere of the Peace Hotel. I wanted to find out how much of the Party line he accepted, but was never sure whether our conversation was being tapped. Only when walking together through the shabby streets of the city, and once on a coach trip to Carlsbad, was politics permissible, and then I got too embroiled in explaining the English political system to find out much about the Czech.

Ada knew nothing of England or the English way of life—or rather, nothing beyond what he had read in the *Daily Worker*, that being the only English paper generally available. If I could do nothing else in the democratic cause I could at least clear up a few misconceptions here and there, and the *Worker* was a good starting point. (Muriel and Tripp went to work in the same way, till at times it seemed our function was to proclaim the superiority of British institutions rather than to admire those of the People's Republics; I had never felt so patriotic since I was a boy. One misconception we wiped out completely was that the English are reticent about themselves.)

To criticisms of the communist set-up Ada had the stock

response: 'We know that there are faults, but from our own experience in the War we have learnt the need for national unity. That is why we cannot admit minority views. You cannot condemn us for this. You must first try to understand us.' If it were simply a matter of understanding Ada and his like, the effort might have paid off, but not all 'the friends' were as reasonable in their outlook.

There was, for instance, a meeting with officials from the Union of Youth. This is the fount from which all blessings flow to good young Czechs. They don't have to be communists to join a youth organisation, but their organisation is required to belong to the Union, for which privilege they pay annual dues and receive weekly homilies on the virtues of Marx–Leninism.

The President of the International Section, a smiling, plump-faced man in his early forties, outlined with great affability the range and scope of the Union's work, making it sound much like a comprehensive kind of Boy Scout movement, but catering for a wider age group, from seven to twenty-five, and administered by the State.

Nothing could have sounded more admirable—until question time. Whether the President had never been asked questions before, or whether he simply didn't like those he got, was uncertain, but within a few minutes he was lost, caught with his Party pants down, and the Union of Youth snapped sharply into perspective as part of the thought-control apparatus of the totalitarian state.

Littmarck, the General Secretary of the World Alliance of Y.M.C.A.s, had bided his time. A dapper, handsome Swede, well versed in conference procedure, fluent in five languages, with a gnawing neutral voice and terrier toughness in pursuing any subject that interested him, he probably had fewer illusions about communist youth organisations than anyone else present.

'We are very glad to hear,' he began, 'that the Union of Youth embraces youth movements of all kinds. In view of this, I am encouraged to ask if you would consider re-establishing the Y.M.C.A. in Czechoslovakia?'

The President was flustered. It took him several minutes and a series of evasions to get round to saying that the kind of work done by the Y.M.C.A. was already adequately covered by the Union of Youth.

'That doesn't answer my question,' said Littmarck. 'If, as you say, you have room for groups of all kinds what is the difficulty of accommodating the Y.M.C.A.?'

The President hurriedly conferred with the officials next to him. For once the delegates were very quiet. The President's smile had vanished. It seemed the delegation was going to be bogged down in ideological warfare before it had even got under way.

At last the President collected his answer: 'Within the many groups of the Union all possible youth activities are already covered, and therefore a Y.M.C.A. group would be clearly superfluous.'

That was meant to be final; but Littmarck was back before the President could call for other questions. 'Will you tell us precisely in what way the Union of Youth covers the Christian teaching of the Y.M.C.A.?'

This time the President did not bother to seek counsel's opinion. The surface charm gave way to mounting temper. 'Since you are being frank I will be frank too. In this country we have no place for the Y.M.C.A. We do not want it or anything to do with it. It can only be a disturbing influence for our young people. We want nothing to do with a movement which will disturb our unity.'

Littmarck sat back and nodded to his Y.M. colleagues with gleaming eyes. He had made his point.

I followed him quickly into the breach: 'With regard to the teaching of good citizenship, will you outline the Union's programme, and how, and by whom it is carried out?'

In the same heated tone the President snapped back that the subject was far too big for an immediate answer. I did not persist. I was fascinated by the change in his expression. The thin lips had become suddenly vicious. Behind the rimless spectacles the eyes were cold and cruel; the chubby, amiable cheeks a stony mask. Stephen Tripp nudged my arm and whispered: 'A Himmler in the making. Ten to one he's a fascist who changed sides on the quiet.'

That meeting removed any lingering illusions I had about 'the friends'. It also made me impatient to leave Prague and diminished my interest in going on to China. I half-wished I had gone to Scandinavia instead.

The real purpose of the delegation was finally revealed after we had met to work out points of procedure. The meeting was convened by Bruno Bernini of Italy and Tamas Larincz of Hungary, two big-shots in the communist youth movement, Bernini being the President of the World Federation of Democratic Youth and Larincz the Treasurer.

Their role at the meeting was ironic and the meeting itself confusing. While Larincz on his travels had picked up a handy colloquial knowledge of five different languages, Bernini could speak only Italian and French. The English delegates had only their native tongue, the South Americans Spanish, and the Arabs an erratic smattering of English and French. So it took some time to establish the fact that Bernini did not wish to be regarded as leader of the delegation nor to let it be thought that the delegation was in any way tied to the W.F.D.Y. (With that the western members could not have agreed more.) He thought, therefore, that each day a different delegate should act as President so that the delegation would retain throughout a truly representative flavour.

To be representative was one thing, but to be saddled with the job of making presidential speeches, if only for a day, was quite another. Robinson, the English Y.M.C.A. official, vehemently opposed this suggestion. He would be very happy if Bernini would continue as president—in a non-partisan sense, of course. He considered that Bernini had wide experience of this kind of thing and was obviously ideally suited to the job. The delegates who understood Robinson's proposal unanimously supported it.

But Bernini patently did not want the job, and Larincz ardently supported him. Confusion was further confounded when Shakir, one of the Egyptians, made a lengthy speech of protest which nobody listened to, so that it had to be repeated in Arabic and translated back into English by the Sudanese, and then back into French for Bernini's benefit by the Hungarian. After this nobody had any idea what the Egyptian had been protesting about at all, and while the Arabs conferred together Bernini stood up again and quietly suggested that his original proposal should be adopted without further discussion. '*D'accord?*' he enquired rhetorically, and before anyone could reply Larincz was on his feet to deal with the next item of business. Thus, presumably, Bernini and Larincz had carried all before them on a truly democratic basis at hundreds of Party conferences and W.F.D.Y. get-togethers. 'I was so pleased,' Larincz told me afterwards, 'that we reached agreement on this matter. From our point of view it would have given a wrong impression to have Bernini as President. We are sensitive to the feelings of the western delegates and we want to show that we can share responsibility with them.'

In other words, the outing had not been arranged just to have a quick peek at China. It was a major prestige effort, the first attempt the communists had made to gather under one roof 'all shades of religious and political opinion'. If this one worked, more would follow, and nobody could say it was the communists who were holding out on the west. They set great store on the venture and were determined to keep on their best behaviour. It was a pity that the Union of Youth man had been caught on the hop. It was a pity too that Budapest was to blow up on them when everything was going so smoothly. . . .

However, they felt they had got us off to a good start. Wreathed in smiles of mutual congratulation 'the friends' turned out *en bloc* to see us off at the airport. There were few formalities, no customs, no baggage check, hardly a glance at our visas. '*Le premier part est complet,*' said one of the Prague friends, handing us over to the chums from Moscow.

I had already resolved to take a different route on the return journey; I had no wish to see Prague or these particular 'friends' again, except of course for Ada: he would have been good company at any time. On our arrival the Czechs had given each of us a small sum of 'transit money', and with it I had bought him a cigarette case. He turned up at the airport with something in return, a small earthenware jug made by a local craftsman. 'Just to remember me,' he said. It was a useless ornament; it never survived the journey; and I didn't need it to remember him by. But it cost him far more than he could afford and it carried with it more peace and friendship than all the expensive hospitality of all the Unions of Youth put together.

I didn't tell him, when he gave me his address and urged me to look him up on the way back, that I would not be returning through Prague; and he didn't remind me when I urged him to come to London soon that he had no permit to travel abroad. Perhaps these things should have been explained, but in the circumstances it seemed more realistic to shake hands and say nothing.

3

On the Red Circuit

THEY flew us to Moscow in a TU.104. They were doing us proud—no western passengers had flown in this plane before.

The journey took just over two hours, flying in free air high over a brilliant ocean of white cloud. Much has been written about the inadequacy of Soviet civil aircraft, but in this case it did not apply. The TU.104 was high in the luxury class, with rubber-conditioned comforts, small mobile fans attached to the back of every seat, and the seats themselves adjustable almost to the shape of divans. Safety-belts are unknown on Russian planes and the streamline speed and smoothness with which we gained height made them seem a futile bourgeois convention.

The Peace Hotel had fed us handsomely before we left, but the air stewards were not to be found wanting. Red-carpet flying demanded nothing less than an afternoon snack of caviare, smoked salmon and chicken.

But in attending to the luxuries it seemed that the designers of the TU.104 had dealt haphazardly with one important necessity: the pressurising was seriously at fault. Coming down suddenly from thirty thousand feet, I felt my eardrums were about to be shattered for ever, crushed relentlessly by thickening densities of air, in a pain as demoralising as drills working along the naked nerves.

Every Soviet plane I flew in had a similar defect, although none with the fierce intensity of this, so that a pad of cotton wool became a permanent prerequisite for flying along the Red Route.

Moscow airport bulged with 'friends' waiting to receive us.

They swept over the tarmac in a black-coated, broad-trilbied phalanx with smiles and handshakes all round. The leaders made straight for Bernini and Larincz and then headed the party for the airport restaurant.

The tables sagged with caviare, smoked salmon, chicken and lobster, vodka and beer, Caucasian wines and Schnapps. It was all smiles and Peace and Friendship; the high noon of co-existence: 'Our ideologies may be different but our friendship must be strong. . . .' Wedged between Bernini, whose only con-versational gambit was '*Bon appétit, mon ami*', and a burly Russian official who had no gambits at all, I addressed myself to the vodka. Nobody served the food; nobody passed round the drinks; it was a case of every man for himself.

But someone had been detailed to look out for lonely souls. The Russian official changed places with an interpreter, who looked, in fact, more Italian than Russian, dark-skinned and sensitive, with deep brown eyes, enquiring and serious, behind thick horn-rimmed glasses. Igor was an excellent advertisement for the Soviet *Komsomol* for which he worked. On my return journey I was to get to know him well, but I liked him im-mediately at this first meeting.

'To friendship,' he pledged me privately, with no reference to peace. 'I love to read your great poet Burns. He has a wonderful poem about friendship. Never to forget your old acquaintances. I have read it many times.'

Half the tongues of the world babbled round us. Glasses clinked merrily as different groups toasted each other, without knowing precisely who or what they were drinking to; and I explained to Igor as best I could the significance of the Scottish New Year ritual. Then, beating time with an empty vodka glass, I prompted him through the tune which is more sentimentally British than any other in the world.

'And what about the Bolshoi?' he wanted to know. 'Did you see it in London? And what about Nina Ponomeravna? It was impossible that she should steal. She has everything she can want.' He was certain there had been a misunderstanding; the method of buying goods at the C. & A. store must have baffled her. She was a really good girl, but now perhaps she would not be allowed to go to the Olympics, as she had cast a slur on her country.

He greatly admired the B.B.C. The Russian Service, of course, was jammed, but he listened regularly to the Home Service News. It was always very fair . . . not exaggerated. And *The Times* . . . there was a great newspaper . . . very dull perhaps, like *Pravda*, but it gave the facts. . . .

For all I cared the dinner could go on all night. I was in no hurry to get to China. For the first time on the trip I was enjoying myself. It was a pity that nearly everyone on the delegation seemed teetotal, for the Russians were clearly bent upon further demolition work with the vodka. The mood was far different from Prague. They were rapidly letting their ideologised hair down.

'Everything is different now,' said Igor. 'We are going to understand each other. . . . Drink to old acquaintance. . . . A toast to auld lang syne.'

They had meant to send us on to Peking in the TU.104 but there was a last-minute change of plan. Possibly they were alarmed by complaints about the pressurising, for we were to complete the journey by ordinary passenger plane. There was room for only twenty-four, so four of the party were to stay behind until the following day.

The flight took two days, minus the eight hours lost in travelling east. For me it was two days of unrelieved dreariness, with nothing but the sun to look at above, and, below, only murky clouds, broken by an occasional glimpse of Siberian forest; with no-one to talk to, since my companion was Pablo, the Cuban, whose conversation began with wordless smiles and ended with incomprehensible shrugs of the shoulder; and with nothing to do except read earnest magazines selling the Soviet way of life to the foreigner.

Every three hours we came down to refuel or change planes,

and be rushed to V.I.P. tables where food was practically forced down our throats. This would have been more acceptable if the diet had varied now and then, but borsch, fried fish and chicken seemed to have been fixed as the standard fare all along the route. At Omsk the party broke into ill-mannered muttering when, having been fed at twelve the night before and woken up for a similar meal at three in the morning, we were again dragged out for an identical though larger meal only three hours later.

The aircraft on this run would never pass the fitness test on the fancier European flights but they seemed none the worse for that. They fly remarkably well, and are handled by some of the safest pilots in the world, who take them up and down, whether on a frozen runway at Irkutsk or a field of sand at Ulan Bator, with as little fuss as if they were running a country bus service.

Just as there are no safety-belts or luggage-racks there are no canteen comforts. The exact function of the stewardess is hard to define. Although she brews the odd cup of tea (on a primitive stove propped up somewhere among the baggage in the stern of the plane) and is glad to try out her English whenever she can, she is certainly not there to pamper the passengers—but at least it was possible to snatch an hour or two of sleep without having a succession of sticky sweets, chewing-gum, route maps and glossy magazines thrust gratuitously in one's face every few minutes in the name of attentive service. The stewardesses by and large are broad, beefy girls, possessed of considerable natural charm, but of the matronly rather than the glamorous type, and they have a lively curiosity about their passengers which cannot be entirely the product of professional training.

Moscow–Kaasan–Sverdlovsk in three-hour stages, and down just after dawn at Omsk. So there really was such a place! And the story about the gloomy lovers on the express from Vladivostok might well have been based on fact. Nowhere could look gloomier than Omsk, not even Manchester in mid-November fog.

It was a city dug out of a desert of mud, with long, black rows of flat-roofed huts stretching in uniform drabness around the

power-houses and office blocks: a monument to Russia's industrial revolution; the most essentially functional area of the
earth I have ever seen. A Gorki or a Mayakovsky might be
capable of revealing its inner soul, in the idiom of the techno-
logical institute, to the rhythm of the turbo-generator, but the
true poet of this unutterable dereliction, this organised negation
of warmth, beauty and light, would be a proletarian Tchekov.

Along the tarmac the Siberian wind bit and cut into the cheeks;
grey and desolate in the first grip of frost, the planes crouching
along the distant perimeter shuddered in the searing blast. Beyond them furnace chimneys jutted above the horizon, belching
black smoke into the freezing air.

Yet inside the airport we stepped a century back. Like every
hotel on the route it combined the amenities of the Marxist era
with the ornaments of the bourgeois. With its duck-egg-blue
walls, Third-Empire chandeliers and Corinthian columns, blue-
and-green plush divans and rococo ceilings, it might well have
been intended as a museum to preserve the relics of nineteenth-
century decadence.

Less surprisingly, perhaps, the airports preserved also the
emblems of the cult of personality. Huge busts of Stalin greeted
the passing traveller with Olympian serenity. In vast portraits
along the walls, Stalin still held his place in the constellation of
Marx, Engels and Lenin. In massive paintings the length of a
reception hall the younger Stalin stood firm at the barricades
with the earliest fathers of the Revolution. Stalin the Colossus
brooded outside every hotel or stood in oracular isolation in the
surrounding gardens. In time, perhaps, the statues will disappear, the portraits be taken down; in time, perhaps not. It may
be instead that the old myths will be re-dressed, the old legends
re-hashed, according to what suits the current book. Perhaps,
after all, that is why nothing has been removed.

Omsk–Novosibersk–Krasnojarsk–Irkutsk; the forests become
vaster, darker; the landscape bleaker, more forbidding.

Somewhere below, the toughest engineers in the world are
drilling virgin earth, a railway line is being carved across the

frozen waste, a city planted on a desolate plain; but these are heroic fantasies, bereft of meaning when there is nothing to see for a day and a night but the long Siberian winter setting in.

Down at Irkutsk with snow falling fast, icy winds whipping the midnight air, and we are on the Mongolian border, the doorstep of Genghis Khan. Mongolian frontiersmen mingle with Russian guards. We look at them and they back at us with a wild surmise. Squat-nosed, silent, unsmiling men; horse-breeders, hunters, born in felted tents, on the ageless hills, in dense pine forests; incongruous in well-fitting, modern uniforms, they hold the frontier with cold, impassive eyes and the smouldering ferocity of a lawless, vanished age.

It is said that on this route in winter no plane keeps to its schedule and the pilots themselves decide when it is fit to fly. We could not leave before morning; nobody knew just when. But at least we could sleep in comfort in hotel beds.

The beds were good enough and the rooms centrally heated, the windows double-barred, but I found sleep hard to come by. On this last lap of the journey, poised as it were at the edge of one civilisation and the beginning of another, I pondered, for the first time I think, what I might expect to find on the other side. I had travelled six thousand miles in a vacuum, on a journey which for me had no design, motive or expectation; I was about to make contact with a civilisation from which most Englishmen had been excluded since the War; but I felt no stir of excitement, no sense of approaching wonder. The prospect of a holiday on the Cornish coast would have thrilled me more. Why this should have been so I cannot say, but dozing fitfully that night on the threshold of eternal China I wished myself comfortably in my own bed at home.

Twice during the night I thought I heard shots fired in the distance, followed by the eerie baying of dogs, though this may well have been imagination. In this part of the world the senses can play sinister tricks with the mind long before the shutters have been bolted for the night.

There was one more stop, at Ulan Bator, the capital of

Mongolia, the township fashioned from necessity at the edge of the Gobi desert. We flew to it over mountain ranges steeped in snow, over Lake Baikal, chill and motionless beside miles of forest, stopping only to refuel and drink green, tasteless tea. We called goodbye as we left to the silent, frowning guards, and at last one of them smiled and called something back. 'Thank God,' growled Shakir, the gregarious Egyptian, 'somebody *speaks*!'

4

Red Carpet Down

I AM possibly the first traveller to have entered China from the north without seeing the Great Wall. After three hours' flying over the gnarled emptiness of the Gobi desert, where there is nothing to note for a thousand miles but wrinkled tracks running down to lonely oases and a solitary single-line railway fingering its way to the north, I gradually lost interest in the outposts of history and fell asleep. When I woke up we had landed in Peking.

The view confronting me from the starboard window was so startling that I wondered if we had arrived ahead of schedule on somebody else's cue. Bathed in afternoon sunshine, the airport was festooned with flags and banners. In front of the main building stood a vast crowd of young Chinese, smiling, waving and clapping. In front of them a separate group of fifty or more, their arms loaded with chrysanthemum bouquets, surged jubilantly towards the aircraft. When we stepped down the gangway they went mad with delight. A multitude of yellow hands fluttered aloft in feverish unison. Hundreds of yellow faces smiled and bubbled and the bouquet-bearers rushed in to plaster us with flowers as if we had been the vanguard of a liberating army. My typewriter was wrenched from my hand by a beaming Chinese girl, my hand almost wrenched from my arm by a beaming boy, bouquets were thrust in my face, even through the opening of my duffle coat; and while everyone waved and clapped more merrily than before we were swept along on the welcoming tide to the official reception-room.

Toasts were drunk in sweet red wine while a torrent of interpreting broke out all around. What anybody was saying it was impossible to tell. The great thing was to smile and clap and smile again as often as the Chinese did. Sometimes it seemed that they were applauding us and we were applauding them, and at other times we were all applauding each other. They have the curious convention when somebody claps them in public of clapping back, but this device also serves to terminate the applause, and if the unwary visitor fails to employ it he may find they will go on clapping indefinitely.

When everyone had said what they wanted to say we pushed our way to waiting coaches, wondering the while how far the reception was genuine, how the crowds had been whipped up, whether any of them actually knew who we were and what the whole thing was about. Looking around more carefully, it seemed to me that some of the welcoming band were a little half-hearted and some of the workmen watching outside the airport indifferent almost to the point of hostility.

It would be good to record my first impressions in compelling tones and brilliant verbal hues. The prosaic truth is that I was driven in a coach for thirty minutes down a long rural road where peasants were at work in the fields and labourers building houses and children playing, into a city of gleaming green roofs and blue walls and golden tiles and bamboo scaffolding and steel girders and red-brick office blocks and slum compounds and people swarming about the streets and a clatter of laughing, singing, shouting, yellow-skinned humanity, but to me nothing registered because it was all too vast and too different from any other city I had arrived in before. So that when Stephen Tripp asked, 'Don't you really feel you're in Asia now?' I replied curtly that I felt no such thing, because at that moment my only wish was to have an hour or two entirely alone, or long enough anyway to feel that my mind had landed along with my legs.

Solitude, in fact, was to prove a physical commodity almost impossible to come by.

The traditional picture of the contemplative Confucian gazing from the stillness of the lake or the peace of the garden into the shadows of eternity bears no relation to life in modern China. From the cradle up six hundred million people must automatically find it difficult to get away from each other's company, but since the Liberation such eccentricity of taste would amount almost to a social crime. How *could* anybody want to be alone when there are cultural palaces and play-centres and youth leagues and women's unions and evening classes for the intelligent use of leisure and when every street has its own committee for ensuring that everyone is on the best of terms with everyone else?

I readily concede that if you visit a country on such an outing as this you should never expect to be left alone. The whole object of the exercise is to meet people from morn till night; but on the other hand you are not a convivial pump: there are times when the mind demands a breathing space between the endless receptions, discussions and expeditions, when you want to sit back to try to digest a morsel or two of the huge, unpalatable hunk; when, in short, you simply want time to think. I concede also that our hosts made no attempt to force China down our throats. If you didn't want to visit a mine or a prison they would gladly arrange something else, but to inform them that you simply wished to do nothing at all seemed a gross impoliteness, an abuse of hospitality, a selfish lack of consideration for people whom you had no occasion to offend.

Let me say at once that I do not understand the Chinese mind: if anything, I was more confused by it at the end of my visit than before; I learnt very little about the Chinese character beyond its surface qualities of reticence, forbearance and reasonableness; but, political considerations aside, I grew to admire without reservation the intense courtesy, tact and generosity which graced all their dealings with me—all except one, and that, unhappily, the one which gave an ironic and ugly significance to their pæans to Peace and Friendship. That, however, was not to come till the end of the trip.

Peking encloses four walled cities, the Inner and Outer, the Imperial City and the Forbidden City. Ch'ien Men is the great tower gate which leads from the Outer to the Inner City, and in front of this had just been completed the latest of Peking's modern hotels, called, appropriately enough, the Front Gate.

Its basic features were similar to those of any good-class, large, western hotel: all modern conveniences, hot and cold, with a private bathroom and telephone to every room; a battery of lifts in excellent working order; several large dining-rooms; and a hairdressing saloon. Its differences, however, were more conspicuous. As with the various Peace Hotels on the route, nobody was ever known to receive or pay a bill. There was no reception desk as such; nobody apparently to whom the guests might address enquiries or lodge complaints. The number of staff, or 'servicemen', often seemed to exceed the number of guests, thereby, no doubt, helping to solve the employment problem. There appeared to be no single rooms—a peculiarity which applied to every Chinese hotel I stayed in: it was always a splendid twin-bedded room to yourself, so that you constantly had the feeling of waiting for someone to arrive, a nocturnal helpmeet, perhaps, to soothe the nerves of the jaded delegate with a generous flourish of oriental hospitality; but no such comforter arrived, and in the People's puritanical Republic, you felt, whatever the strength of the Friendship, there would certainly be no Peace if one ever did. A further peculiarity was that, while all the electrical and mechanical facilities worked admirably, the wireless was always either out of order or had disappeared completely without anybody ever knowing where it had gone. Nothing was left to chance in providing for the delegates' wants. Cigarettes and matches were laid on daily for smoker and non-smoker alike, the cigarettes sharp, slightly bitter-tasting, but very good of their kind. (The matches were a different matter. They tended to snap in two at the slightest pressure and, even if the stick survived, the head was likely to fly away from the body at the moment of ignition; while the boxes themselves, equally fragile, rapidly disintegrated once put into the pocket.)

I shall have more to say about Chinese food later, but at the Front Gate hotel the menu was arranged on the assumption that delegates would prefer the western type, although what that type might be the cooks were not at all sure. True, they faced the insoluble problem of trying to reconcile at once the tastes of Frenchman and Russian, Arab and South American, Swede and Italian. In the event they settled for a polygastric confection, optimistically labelled 'European food', which comprised three kinds of soup (potato, lentil and rice); an assortment of fish (the crayfish, which they knew something about, especially good), and chicken; with blancmanges and chocolate mousses as dessert.

Fortunately Chinese food was served to the interpreters and the Asian contingent and it was possible to attach oneself to their tables, although they regarded this as a further manifestation of English oddity.

The hotel service was not merely efficient, but relentlessly so. Certain things were axiomatic, as they are throughout China. The honesty of the hotel staff made it impossible to lose anything. Throw away an old notebook, cast off a worn-out shirt, and they would inevitably find their way back if the entire hotel had to be turned inside out to trace the owner. There is no tipping. That was abolished with the Liberation and, whether the staff approve the innovation or not, they would never risk degrading themselves by accepting a tip. The campaign of sweeping, brushing and polishing which went on throughout the day ensured a standard of cleanliness that was too near perfection to be comfortable. You could never be laid low by dust germs but you could easily have broken a limb by slipping on the polished floors. There was no such thing as a discourteous servant: if they were sometimes slow to carry out your wishes it was only because they had failed to understand them, not because they didn't want to. For all I know, this is a traditional virtue, but it could equally well be a compulsory, more recent one.

There is a darker side to the picture which it is impossible to define accurately without a working knowledge of the language but evidence of which I was to discover for myself much later.

The hotel staff are by implication watchdogs of the State, in which function, although they may not actually spy upon the guests, they certainly miss nothing that goes on. The problem does not arise so long as the guests keep to themselves, but if they form peripatetic relationships about the hotel they will find one or more servicemen patrolling the passages as though by telepathic invitation. To be just, I should add that, as far as I could tell, no check was kept on my movements outside the hotel, and inside it there was no evidence of telephone tapping or hidden microphones. As one of my hosts put it: 'You have a remarkable imagination if you think we have so many interpreters in so many languages that we can listen in to what thousands of foreign visitors are saying all the time.' Journalists who had spent several months in other hotels in Peking confirmed that there was no interference of this kind, but they had all been subject in one degree or another to the restrictive scrutiny of the servicemen.

5

The Face of Peking

How can you hope to describe with any degree of accuracy the most energetic, ambitious, paradoxical, revolutionary and enigmatic city in the world after one cursory visit?

The answer is, of course, that you can't; nor shall I attempt to. There were so many questions to ask you could never hope to answer them all; soon you gave up trying, because you rarely got to the point anyway, and while you were running in circles around it something else had slipped past that was infinitely more interesting. What I record here is indeterminate and vague: fragmentary impressions, assembled, as it were, on the run while hurrying from one earnest occasion to another.

Peking crashed authentically into my consciousness somewhere between six and seven o'clock on the first morning after my arrival. It awakes, as it lives through the rest of the day, in a frenzy of noise, a sustained cacophony, a series of competitive crescendoes in which street vendors with rattles, cymbals and tambourines, knife-grinders with bugles, car hooters, traffic-control sirens, water-cart bells, police megaphones, saucepan sellers, pedlars and menders armed with all the instruments of a Chinese orchestra, together with thousands of shrieking cyclists, blast and rend the gentle air as though to compensate publicly for their exceptional vocal restraint in private.

The new China joins forces with the old in this medley of noise. Everywhere is activity: private enterprise plies what is left of its wares in the bazaars and streets, and simultaneously the State hoists its gaunt edifices for the self-advancement of the People.

Everything is either older or newer than anywhere else, more beautiful or more ugly, richer or plainer. Here is a community which, within a few years, has lifted itself from its ancient trappings at a rate of technical and industrial development which has no parallel anywhere else in the world. Here is a city in which both the relics and the advance posts, the evils and the virtues, of the biggest industrial revolution in history can be seen by merely walking down the street.

In physical terms the achievement is staggering. With totally inadequate resources, antiquated equipment, Soviet machinery (sometimes of doubtful quality and erratic performance) and transport facilities which consist in the main of bicycle trucks, mule-carts, or buckets and baskets slung on bamboo poles across the labourers' necks, the Pekinese have pushed up a proliferation of schools, colleges, libraries, geological and metallurgical institutes, factories, mills, hospitals, rest centres, hotels and office blocks with a rapidity which would leave workmen in any western country (except, perhaps, Germany) gasping with incredulity. It is not enough to say that the red brick and grey stone are uniformly an eyesore; they are also an existing fact. And while it may be tempting to point indignantly to the swarming spectacle of sweated labour in its most totalitarian form, the charge would be partially invalid; the Chinese labourer was always sweated, but today he works regular hours, no longer dies from starvation and neglect, can clothe himself adequately for both winter and summer, and may even feel a latent sense of purpose in toiling for the future of the People's Republic. The latter is not an ironic afterthought; it is an everyday reality to people who have discovered the meaning of material security for the first time in their lives. Liberty? Freedom of expression? These are irrelevant abstractions. When a man has been saved from drowning you don't expect him to stand up and attack the crew who rescued him.

Peking's approach to the future is less surprising than its attitude to the past. On the surface a paradox, it summarises in

fact the excessive logicality of the Chinese mind. The past belongs
to the People just as much as the future. 'Bourgeois tyranny',
'imperialistic exploitation', have been routed and vanquished forever, but their monuments remain: buildings of matchless splen-
dour, ornaments of priceless grace and, the vital statistic which
other revolutionaries have been too revengeful to remember, they
were built by the toil of the People.

So they remain for the People's use, are preserved, repaired,
restored for their pleasure. Tien An Men, the glorious golden-
tiled blockhouse gate which has guarded the Imperial City since
the early Ming dynasty, now serves as a saluting base on days of
national rejoicing. Adjoining it stands the Imperial Ancestral
Temple, now transformed into the Working People's Palace of
Culture, where any day of the week, beneath the cypress groves
or under the purple eaves, the populace can refresh themselves
with lectures on science or drama or advanced methods of production. If they prefer to visit the Imperial Palaces they can
while away an hour in the Hall of Earthly Tranquillity at a demonstration of mining techniques or petroleum manufacture or wander
into the Palace of Heavenly Purity for an exhibition of Soviet
Economic Achievement or Solidarity with the Democratic
Socialist Republics.

For less ambitious tastes there are the Halls of Prayer in the
Temple of Heaven, the altars in Chungshan Park, the Tartar
pleasure-grounds in Peihai Park, and the pavilions and pagodas
of the Summer Palace where the worker may not only relax
in the Hall of Delight in Longevity but, if his production output is exceptional, may even rest for a whole week with other
labour heroes as a guest of the State in the Hall of Virtuous
Harmony.

If this sounds unromantic it is also admirably practical. Something, you might say, has gone from the atmosphere: but I do not
seek either to deplore or justify this; I merely report it. If I give
the impression that these ancient buildings are taken for granted
by their new inheritors, that is not entirely just. Certainly I never
met anyone on Temple or Palace grounds, apart from official

guides, who could give me one accurate detail about their history and origins (the same might apply, of course, on an off-day at St. Paul's or Westminster) but I saw thousands of citizens glutting themselves upon the visual glories of the old dispensation, and at no time did I see or hear of any damage done to the property.

Again, to be just, I should explain that the authorities have made some attempt to project the ancient architectural styles into the modern. The new utilitarian horrors are the product of necessity, not of revolutionary taste. When I arrived in Peking the Municipal Council was in the thick of a controversy with local residents for bedecking the new electricity offices with an extravagant, green-tiled roof in the traditional style—whilst thousands of people were still living in slum conditions. True, the roof made an incongruous contrast with the concrete walls beneath it, as Tudor gables would in a Camberwell tenement, but it found sufficient supporters in the ranks of the orthodox for the Council to escape without admonition. When I left, in fact, there was talk of repeating the treatment on the new Hygiene Centre.

Since I have little visual sense, it would be cheating the reader to take him on a sight-seeing tour of ancient Peking. Other writers will do that far better and soon, I hope, for it is worth the journey.

With people, however, I feel more at home, can trust my eyes further. But again, how to describe *these* people when you have no means of talking to them, when all communications are necessarily addressed in sign language, and when there are so many of them wherever you go that, even if you could speak their language, to enter into conversation with one would be to invite the arrival of all?

I can only record that to walk down a Peking street was a perpetual pleasure; a mystery and an exploration; an adventure which rarely reached the point of discovery; an entertainment set on the inner stage of an awesome reality; a comedy behind which you looked always for the tragedy you had been assured was there.

But these people didn't look like tragic heroes; the catastrophe never came; and the villain remained obstinately hidden in the wings.

If I had any preconceptions about China they had come from reading reports by journalists, most of whom had never been there, and from my brief brush with communism in Prague; the cumulative effect of which, on all official encounters, was to set up an automatic reflex action of cagey disbelief: the person was always a puppet, the performance a blind. But you could not carry your inhibitions into the streets; the streets were flesh and blood, the living truth, the way people really were. The first thing to learn was to lower your own defences, otherwise you would never learn anything.

The second thing was to smile. It may be that the Chinese are born smiling and find the habit hard to break; or it may be that they simply delight in seeing a stranger. Whatever the reason, it is a blessed practice, not to be repelled by the starched stare of western introversion.

A cynical cliché among the small western colony is that the Chinese realise a foreign visitor could only be there with government approval so there is no risk involved in making him feel at home. Since I made it very clear on numerous occasions, particularly during the Hungarian crisis, that I did not like their government's policy, without producing any noticeable change in their attitude towards me, I could only conclude that their friendliness to strangers was an inherent, not an acquired, characteristic.

Down the main street rise the new department stores and cooperatives, the offices and hotels, but resolutely wedged between them stand shops of older vintage and sterner individuality, while behind them, in a maze of alleys and winding passages, lie the markets and bazaars. In the old days, they told me, you would not venture alone off the main street after dark; now if you do so you will find nothing open after nine o'clock and encounter nothing more sinister than a tradesmen's self-criticism meeting or a game of table tennis in a back street courtyard—in which you will be invited to join. If you wanted to buy anything, they said, you would have to haggle endlessly over prices; now the prices are fixed by the State and receipts must be issued to cover every transaction. Whether or not the stall-owners like the new arrangement is a secret they keep to themselves, but willy-nilly many have entered into the system of joint State–private enterprise ownership.

Unfettered capitalism keeps alive mainly on wheels. Its guardians are the street vendors; its merchandise, food and household goods—chestnuts, cooked meats, spices, vegetables, toilet goods, saucepans, earthenware jugs, and sometimes such bourgeois baubles as goldfish, singing birds and stringed instruments. The pedlars, and their brethren in feudal decadence, the knife-grinders, porcelain menders and pedicab drivers, represent also a mobile advertisement to the China of Sax Rohmer and Hollywood imagination, for they have contrived to remain either grubbily bizarre or obstinately villainous in appearance. When the rest of China adopted the cult of the blue boiler suit they clung loyally to the individualist rags and tatters of pre-Liberation days, and they now constitute the only branch of Peking society of which it might be possible to say, however tentatively, that the apparel oft proclaims the man.

The pedicab drivers deserve a special mention, for they are a type permanently tottering on the verge of complete extinction but facing the future with a ragged insouciance which seems to generate both the will and resources to survive. Their plight is simply that the government does not approve of them, or rather of their profession. Like the rickshaw driver, whom they replaced, they are regarded as by-products of a vicious economic system, beasts of burden forced beneath the yoke by the imperialist whip, and their continued existence is an embarrassment to the new democracy. But to close down their business would merely create new problems on an already crowded labour market, so the government has adopted the simple compromise of allowing them to keep their pedicabs while denying them access to spare parts. In his brilliant *Mandarin Red* James Cameron described the state of the pedicabs at the end of 1954:

'It would scarcely be possible to imagine that vehicles so broken-down, so patched-up, so intricately held together by bits of string and old wire, could be capable of another day's service. The government was deliberately allowing the pedicab business to drop, like the pedicabs themselves, to bits. The machines were holding together by guess and by God and quite a few were *in extremis*.'

I am glad to report that at the time of my visit they were still somehow holding together, even if a journey in them was a major hazard, a creaking and groaning convulsion, a succession of precipitate stops and nerve-racking starts; somehow the destination was always reached; and in the course of the journey, bound together in adversity, it was possible, by the exchange of grunts, grimaces and gesticulations, to establish with the pedicab driver as intimate a personal relationship as you would ever be likely to achieve with anyone in China.

Naturally enough my hosts took a poor view of my predilection for pedicabs, especially since their own official cars (Czech or Russian-made) were at my disposal, and my constant assurance that an hour's drive in a pedicab enabled me to see more of their splendid city than I could observe in a whole week in a Zim saloon failed to ease their conscience in the matter. Vladimir, the Russian delegate, was positively shocked when I suggested he should join me on a pedicab expedition. 'It is impossible,' he protested, 'that a good young communist should do such a thing.'

In terms of road safety, Peking is both the safest and most dangerous capital city in the world: safe because the speed limit is fixed at twenty miles an hour, although there are comparatively few mechanical vehicles on the road; but dangerous because of the unwritten law which requires every driver to run along the crown of the road and, to prevent losing face, not to depart from it until the vehicle coming the opposite way has made the first move. In the event it is impossible for the stranger to figure out the processes by which this issue is decided; it is brinkmanship brought to the highest degree of finesse, edifying to watch, but petrifying to be involved in.

For most people the usual mode of locomotion is tramcar and bicycle, the former bringing out the patient forbearance of the Chinese character, and the latter its flexibility in the face of changing circumstance. Tramcars are never merely full: they are packed to bursting point, dense with humanity and all the domestic impedimenta which, through habit or necessity, the Chinese forever carry around with them—bundles of clothing, sacks of vegetables, crates of squawking chickens, bags of seeds, or rice or charcoal, cans of kitchen oil—and, if they have none of these on their shoulders, as likely as not they will carry a wide-eyed baby, silent and unprotesting. Yet order prevails in chaos. Nobody seems impatient or ill-tempered. There are no angry scenes, no jumping of queues, no pushing of people out of the way. The tramcar arrives and departs and the passengers squeeze tighter together till it looks impossible for anyone to get on or off again, but nobody complains and there is no commotion at all.

For the cyclist a journey through the city is a continual skirmish in the teeth of ever-impending disaster. The bicycle has become the most popular form of private transport, but this, while undoubtedly a tangible sign of the rise in the general standard of living, does not make for comfortable progress down the main thoroughfares. The face-saving determination of the motorists, mentioned above, is another detrimental factor, but even worse is the growing incursion of heavy lorries, now for the first time manufactured by the Chinese themselves (with Soviet guidance), and propelled by fervent young drivers who are so taken up with their new machines that they tend to be unaware of other, inferior vehicles moving round them. As well as keeping one eye on these, the progressive cyclist must have the other just as sharply open for the more predictable but no less egocentric manœuvres of mule-carts, Mongol ponies, occasional oxen, even itinerant buffalo, quite apart from the eccentricities of pedestrians.

All these problems are overshadowed, however, by the unfortunate fact that the bicycle frames, European-made, are altogether too high for their Chinese owners, so that a sudden emergency braking may prove more painful than the consequences of a head-on collision. Yet in spite of these multiple difficulties, serious street accidents are practically unknown.

Personal hygiene is, of course, a byword throughout China, inseparable from tidiness. Its virtues are preached by Street Committees, extolled at Youth League meetings and incorporated in the work of the literacy classes. So it is surprising, to say the least, to discover that the habit of public throat-clearing is still widely practised and generally tolerated. 'Throat-clearing' is perhaps a euphemism, but we have no word in English which describes it adequately. 'Expectoration' has only a remote relevance and none of the other synonyms conveys anything of the blood-curdling intensity with which the operation is carried out. The habit is not confined to the streets but goes on unabated in theatres and cinemas, creating a shattering distraction, to western ears, during scenes of dramatic tension or emotional delicacy.

The government meets the people halfway in the matter by posting spittoons at every possible vantage point, but there is clearly no compulsion about using them. Party members, the younger ones, especially, show some distaste for the habit, but even during perorations from Chairman Mao the air is occasionally assailed by the ferocious rattle of unrepentant addicts. Mao, it is said, proceeds unperturbedly with his theme as though he had never heard a thing.

Yet if there is no significance in this oddly anachronistic habit, there is a wealth of it in the fact that the children tumbling around you in the street look remarkably healthy and well-fed. If you remember that up until 1950 it was not uncommon for parents to abandon their babies in the gutter for want of the wherewithal to feed them, and if you have seen the shrunken cheeks and malformed limbs of the child-beggars in Calcutta and Singapore, in Port Said and Algiers, in this connection, at least, you cannot hesitate to concede the Chinese communists a very considerable point.

6

The Delegation Trade

IT is said that in Peking there are fourteen hotels devoted to the housing of foreign delegations. This is probably an exaggeration, but it serves to illustrate the point: the delegation business is a major development in the Chinese campaign to win friends and influence people. It is national advertising in its most respectable form—respectable indeed is the word, for it is that epithet above all by which the People's Republic desires to be known in the court of world opinion. Respectability is the precursor to expanding trade, to a place in the United Nations, to the evacuation of American troops from Taiwan. . . .

Respectability is a government fetish, in pursuit of which the idea of taking Taiwan by force has been dropped altogether. Taiwan will come in the course of time; the Americans will tire of holding it long before the Chinese tire of waiting for it.

More pressing than Taiwan are the problems of industrial development at home and economic rapprochement abroad. These considerations make respectability the operative factor, not on the road to world revolution, but on the saner path to world recognition—and consolidating the programme of national construction at the fastest possible rate. (Just how long that will take, and where the Chinese go from there—Asian leadership?—world domination?—is anybody's guess; but meantime six hundred million of them will have multiplied themselves into eight hundred or one thousand million, and it will require more than Solidarity with the Socialist Republics to make economic sense of that particular problem.) The Chinese have no illusions about their standing in the west. The pursuit of respectability is their long-term equivalent to the purging of guilt, a process of diminution rather than denial, a forensic conjuring trick, in which the familiar accusations—the mass shootings, the Korean 'volunteers', the suppression of freedom—will be reduced to such trivial insignificance by cumulative testimony to the prisoner's good intentions that, with any luck, they will eventually disappear from the minds of the jury altogether.

So the delegate is a vital import, whether he comes to talk business, to examine churches, to investigate intellectual freedom or, like myself, merely to look round. He may be one of many, but he is one who matters. Peking housed during my visit as diverse a collection of delegates as was ever known to man: Japan had sent a Trade Union Delegation, a Youth and Women's Delegation, a Scholars' Mission, a Writers' Mission and a Fertilisers' Delegation; from Pakistan came a Medical Mission, a Scientific Delegation and the Prime Minister, Mr. Suhrawardy himself; from India a Parliamentary Mission and a Goodwill Military Mission. There was a Burmese Women's Delegation, a Norwegian Students' Delegation, a French Film Delegation, a Singapore Trade Mission, an Italian Socialist Party Agricultural Mission, a Hong Kong Industrial Delegation, a Finnish Trade Union Mission and a Delegation of Syrian M.P.s.

Needless to say, there were also innumerable delegations from the Soviet and its satellites: journalists from East Germany; doctors from Czechoslovakia; a Yugoslav Military Mission, as well as a Women's Delegation; and, curiously sandwiched between them, a Mongolian Government Delegation. The traffic was frequently enlivened by the arrival of Song and Dance Ensembles from Rumania, Hungary, the Ukraine and Indonesia; while just before I left I ran into three Australian bishops hot-foot from the northern provinces.

In the provinces, in fact, the situation is repeated in miniature. Every town and city has at least one hotel set aside for itinerant delegations. The first people you meet when you arrive in a new hotel are likely to be a batch of Danish farmers, a group of Sinhalese Buddhists or a collection of Argentinian exporters; or

D

you may catch up with a crowd of Finnish timber merchants you last saw weeks ago at a Siberian airport, or a French theatrical troupe you had seen in action—was it really only two months ago? —in a West End theatre. The theatre groups, although not strictly in the delegation class, are given the same treatment, but I would refute the cynical notion that they are brought over solely for the prestige their visit bestows upon the People's Republic: the Chinese adore the theatre. They flock to see the visiting companies and will queue for hours in the hope of obtaining tickets although the theatre may have been sold out weeks in advance.

The remnant of the International Youth Delegation flew in from Moscow a day later than expected, having had a slight misadventure at Omsk. For reasons they never discovered, the aircraft had broken down and they had been forced to make a crash landing. The passengers had remained calm, although Henry Crabb, the religious young Australian, had held his head in his hands and cried, 'I know I'm going to die! I know I'm going to die! It is the judgment of the Lord!' Fortunately few of the other passengers could understand him and order prevailed while the pilot brought the plane down as comfortably as if he had been parking a car; then, later in the day, while the party were enjoying the hospitality of Omsk, a TU.104 had arrived, dispatched in haste by 'the friends' in Moscow; a superbly expensive piece of face-saving which even the Chinese could scarcely emulate.

Later, as the delegation wended its way about China, Henry Crabb was to establish himself securely as its most energetic member. With a flair for organising other people's movements, he had a forthright conversational style and tended to sledgehammer the smallest of small talk into a relentless cross-examination on the Higher Ethics—a method which taxed even the patience of the Chinese whom, without exception, he belaboured mercilessly on the Errors of Marx–Leninism—whether they happened to be Party officials or passers-by who smiled at him in the street. Henry Crabb was the one delegate with whom I found it difficult to get on, the one who wanted to hustle when I was content to stop, the entirely efficient member with the dedicated good intentions of the eternal School Prefect.

It may be that I, on my side, was unsympathetic to him, but it is difficult to like a young man who sets out to teach you your manners. ' You can't sit down in that outfit!' he complained when I appeared at breakfast in jeans and open-necked shirt. 'We're not in London, you know,' I murmured passively, not wishing to quarrel. 'But you're a guest,' he barked, 'and you ought to behave like one!' With considerable restraint I suggested that in that case we should all play the part properly and go into boiler-suits; the shaft was not entirely lost, for a few days later the virtuous Crabb discarded his own jacket and tie and arrived un-blushingly at dinner in a polo-necked sweater.

As for Muriel, I felt after our train journey to Prague that she and I had come as near to knowing each other as either of us would ever wish. There was no doubt, however, that in her good-natured way she did far more than myself for the cause of Peace and Friendship. On numerous occasions, as the only woman present, she was the toast of the delegation. She was interested in everything around her and the inhibitive bogey of Marx–Leninism never affected her in the least; possibly because she hardly knew it was there. 'Politics do more harm than good,' she declared whenever discussions between east and west threatened to become acrimonious and, although they might not have agreed with her, the contending delegates were generally glad of the excuse she gave them to cool down. Although Tripp was forever bewailing her attitude to international problems, she herself was more truly international in outlook than any other member of the delegation, for she dispensed her friendship on equal terms to all who would accept it.

Ironically, as it turned out, I felt most inclined to dispense mine to the Egyptians and the Russian.

Galal and Shakir were ex-Army officers, working for the Egyptian Council of Youth. Both in their early thirties, both Olympic games players, they might almost have been chosen as complements to each other.

Shakir was superbly built, bounding with animal energy, violent in his extremes of mirth or dejection, fierce in his friendships, explosive in his laughter. He had a virile handsomeness that might have earned him a fortune had he been born within the orbit of Hollywood, but there is no Hollywood type—or Saxon type, for that matter—with whom he might reasonably be compared, for his kind of physical combustion has no counterpart in polite western society. If he had been in Egypt when the Israelis invaded he would either have won the Egyptian equivalent of the V.C. or been shot out of hand because he was not in the mood for fighting.

If Shakir was energy personified, Galal was the essence of repose. Handsome in a reflective, sombre way, he applied the maximum of economy to everything he said or did. No silence was too prolonged for Galal, no pace too slow, no movement too relaxed; so that, when occasionally provoked or persuaded into action, he became, by contrast with his previous restraint, a figure of smouldering intensity, reminding me vividly of the French film actor, Jean Gabin, in his more menacing moments.

Like Gabin, he had the ruggedly sensitive features and melancholy eyes of a man who has touched the very soul of the suffering world and returned from the experience more compassionate in wisdom, more stoical in forbearance. He had the vision, I felt, of a poet, and he spoke in the sorrowful tones of a prophet, born out of time, to be buffeted forever on the waves of man's boundless inhumanity to man.

For an Army officer he seemed unusually deficient in military qualities. He hated fighting and disliked any activity which conflicted with his immediate inclinations. He valued his creature comforts and became profoundly distressed when anything happened to upset them. On the first cold day in Peking he refused to move out of the hotel; troubled by a sore throat, he retired to bed surrounded by medicines and lotions of twenty different kinds and greeted every enquiry about his health with the agonised expression of a man fighting a despairing battle against imminent death. Galal undoubtedly was not in the front rank of natural leaders of men but, for all that, he had an under-lying and formidable sincerity which convinced me it would be wiser to have him as a friend than an enemy. Put to the test, I felt the ebullient Shakir would act according to his whim, but Galal, I was certain, would act according to his instinctive loyalties. When the Suez incident began both Galal and Shakir insisted that it made no difference to their friendship with me, but I sensed that at any moment Shakir might feel moved to stick a patriotic knife in my back, while Galal would gladly have shed his own blood to save me.

They first earned my respect by producing from their baggage late one night a bottle of liqueur whisky which they had carried with them from goodness knows where. This, however, was only the harbinger of other good things: a nod from Galal or a wink from Shakir at the end of dinner betokened a firm invitation to join them in their room over a glass of cognac or a bottle of rum. To the parched traveller in a country where the main social lubri-cant is tea these clandestine offerings were worth all the cere-monial banquets in China; and the cutting off of this supply, along with other earnests of good fellowship, made it an especially sad day for me when the Egyptians had to leave the delegation and return hurriedly for duty at home.

My friendship with Vladimir was equally strange and unex-pected, but, seen in retrospect, it was also surprisingly logical. We were both in a unique situation. He was meeting an Englishman for the first time and I a Russian. He knew as little about condi-tions in the west as I about those in Russia. He was a serious young communist, making his first contact with men who hated com-munism; I was an almost solitary Englishman in a country that despised the democratic principles which all my life I had taken for granted. When the news broke from Hungary he was com-pelled to endure the opprobrium of most of the men he was living with; when the British attacked Suez I had to keep a stiff upper lip in the face of a whole nation's fury.

It was probably not by chance that he had been sent on the delegation (but certainly not, as Tripp suspected, to indoctrinate the English delegates). Officially he was to report the tour for his newspaper, *Molodoi Kommunist*, but he was also a first-class, because unobtrusive, ambassador: sensitive, good-humoured, genuinely curious, ready to listen to points of view different from his own, an altogether admirable advertisement for the New Look in Soviet policy. His dimpled cheeks and easy smile gave him a rather boyish charm, and this was accentuated by his grappling attempts to master the English language—a contest which he pursued relentlessly day after day, never yielding an inch, but gaining, as we proceeded together from Peking to Shenyang, from Fushun to Canton, many hard-won feet of linguistic ground. Perhaps because we had both been sailors in the War we thought alike about many things and I found in him, what I had least expected in any Russian, a remarkably English sense of humour, or should I say, one which coincided often with my own. While Vladimir clearly regarded the purpose of the delegation as a serious affair, he found it difficult to take the individual members seriously at all, even those from his own side of the fence. Bernini, the chief of the W.F.D.Y., he labelled derisively 'the little big-shot'. He fled from the company of Heinz, the East German communist, because he found him 'a nice boy, but he thinks so much he has no time to live'. After a reception at Shanghai in which he had sat for two hours at dinner between Mechini, of the Italian Communist Youth, and Ricardo, the garrulous Spaniard, he rushed to my table exclaiming, 'They will talk on forever—but the one is too serious, the other too stupid! I can listen no more!'

The Chinese baffled him completely. 'We shall never understand them,' he declared. 'They are very clever people. Very, *very* clever.' But he went into the same kind of coma as I did when regaled with statistics of factory output or the miracles they had wrought since the Liberation. 'I can tell you exactly what he is saying,' Vladimir would whisper in the middle of some rambling discourse by a municipal official. 'He is saying that before Liberation only twenty thousand children went to school, but since Liberation there are places for one hundred thousand!' Or else, at a reception, as the President of the local Youth League beamed his way through an interminable speech of welcome: 'He is talking about Peace and Friendship. He is saying that we all have our different viewpoints but he believes that the people of every country want to live together in peace.' I can hardly imagine that Vladimir's frivolous annotations would have won favour with the Presidium, but they were the first intimation I had that even a good communist could be told too much of a good thing.

Much time was wasted every evening in preparing the Programme for the following day. The desire of the hosts to ensure that every delegate crammed the unforgiving minute with sixty seconds' worth of national achievement conflicted insuperably with individual predilections. With undaunted courtesy the Chinese did their best to meet everyone's wishes, but since nearly everyone wanted different things there was no easy compromise; and at every turn the language barrier arose to add to the confusion.

There were four groups of Chinese interpreters, three in English, one in Spanish, one in Russian and one in French; but the number was hardly adequate to the complex needs of the delegation. The first group had to cope not only with the English delegates but also with the Swedish priest, the Dane, the West German, the Egyptians and the Sudanese, whose English vocabulary was, in the main, limited, and whose sense of grammar and syntax was often non-existent. The East German delegate relied upon the Russian interpreter; the Italians, Belgians and the other Arabs upon the French; and the South Americans upon the Spanish. Since some of the interpreters translated the trickier passages by a system of guesswork known only to themselves, the daily conferences, conducted invariably in a spluttering babel of tongues, achieved upon occasion nothing but the exhausted incomprehension of every delegate present.

Galal and Shakir generally came off worst, for while the majority, in the interests of general peace, might ultimately settle for a visit to a woollen mill or a Ming tomb, the Egyptians' limited English gave them little chance of finding out what was going on at all. They had come to China, they insisted, 'only for the Sport', but this was an activity in which nobody else seemed at all interested. 'Always it is the Politics,' they lamented. 'What is the Politics? We want only to know the Physical Education.'

Once, however, Galal brought the daily conference to a stand-still and wrought temporary havoc with the Programme. He had received an invitation from the Egyptian Ambassador to take the whole delegation to dinner. 'All invited!' he had announced. 'All to go if so desire!' All did indeed desire, but some break-down in co-ordination caused the event to be omitted from the Programme on the appropriate day. The fact only registered with Galal the evening before the dinner was due, when visits were being arranged instead to theatres and cinemas. 'No good!' he cried, leaping from his seat in a sudden frenzy that stunned everyone to silence. 'All invited to dinner. All say they go! Now they not go! What is wrong with dinner?' His black eyes bulged with indignation. 'All cards printed! Now! Dinner at six! Why is it not you come?'

While the delegates quailed and said nothing, the startled hosts rapidly amended the Programme to suit his wishes—although later, as it will be seen, he came to regret that the Programme had not been left as it was.

7

The War of Ideas

'WHAT do you think I should be most on guard against?' asked Tripp when we called at the British Legation. 'Failing to keep an open mind,' the official replied curtly. 'You will see as much of China while you are here as most other Englishmen since the War and you must draw your own conclusions. I have no intention of trying to draw them for you.'

'Always remember,' an old China Hand had warned me before I left England, 'that the Chinese never tell you the exact truth about anything, but only what they think you want to know.'

'We know we are very backward,' said the Chinese communists. 'There is a great deal which is at fault. We hope you will tell us how to improve things. Remember we are always very glad to have your criticisms.'

Here were three contradictory approaches, and it was impossible to correlate any of them. The best you could do was to take everything on its merits, ask as many questions as anybody might answer, and believe half of what you were told—that is, if you could resolve the ever-nagging doubt, which half?

In the end everything came back to Marx–Leninism. That was the issue that blighted every informal meeting, the recurrent decimal at every conference, the shadow that overlay the otherwise convincing reality and, try as you might, you could never shake off its oppressive implications. Finally you simply had to accept it and concede the fact that one way or another ninety per cent of China seemed to have accepted it too. The rest had either been shot or put in prison or were simply keeping their mouths shut.

It was not Marx–Leninism that the Chinese had in mind when they invited your criticisms any more than the Church of England would have the four gospels in mind when inviting suggestions for improving Sunday attendance. Their minds were fixed on method, not morality; on production output, not points of doctrine.

The policy of The Hundred Flowers, which was first publicly enunciated by Lu Ting-yi in May 1956 (following a secret declaration by Mao), was not aimed solely at wooing the non-Party intellectuals; it also expounded the revolutionary thesis that China could learn much from the West:

> '*Apart from learning from our friends, we must see what we can learn from our enemies—not what is reactionary in their systems, but to study what is good in their methods of management or in their scientific techniques in order to speed the progress of our socialist construction. We cannot afford to be arrogant and refuse to learn good things from abroad. We are still a very backward country and can only become prosperous by doing our best to learn all we can from foreign countries.*'

The point was rubbed home in college, factory and public building, where, alongside huge posters beseeching the populace to study Soviet production methods, appeared equally urgent exhortations that they should learn from the 'advanced techniques' of workers throughout the world; and the theme was endlessly repeated in letters of gilt on brilliant red banners hung across the main streets.

The field of production methods is completely foreign to me, so that any observations I make upon 'techniques' must be regarded as second-hand, culled from somebody else's expertise, jotted down in the hope that the reader might be able to make more of them than I did.

My first encounter with 'techniques' was at the Hsin Hua printing works in Peking. The visit was the result of an interpreter's misunderstanding, for I had asked to go to the national publishing house which bears the same name, where I wanted to find out how far the principle of The Hundred Flowers was applied in the selection and rejection of authors' MSS. As it happened, I never did get there and I doubt whether I should have achieved anything if I had. However, there was much of interest to be gleaned at the printing works.

'Our main problem,' the Director told me, 'is in finding sufficient skilled workers for the complicated work of type-setting. With your simple English alphabet, perhaps, it is difficult for you to appreciate the level of technical skill which is needed. Although we have reduced the number of Chinese characters considerably, we still use as many as seven thousand in our written work and of those two thousand are in common use.'

As I inspected the great type-setting blocks, where a long line of industrious young workers fingered their way along the tightly packed rows of metal characters, I began to understand his difficulties and also to realise why the news stories in *The People's Daily* were always at least twelve hours out of date. 'What is the normal percentage of error?' I asked.

'These are our most highly skilled workers,' he explained, 'so the error is slight; on average, only two mistakes in a thousand characters. But elsewhere the technical level is low because the average age of the workers is only twenty-six and most of them are of a low educational standard. Now, however, we are insisting upon getting entrants at senior school level, and our Trade Union is also organising its own course of general education.'

'Is that popular with the younger workers?' I asked.

'Immensely so,' he smiled, 'for they all want to improve their technique and, of course, as you will see from the posters, we go all out to show them the advantages both for their own and for their country's sake. In fact, of our two thousand workers, over one thousand attend the special courses three nights a week.

'You see,' he assured me, 'they are keen to improve because they realise they are more fortunate now than they ever were before. The average wage today is about fifty-eight *yuan* a month, but before 1949, in order simply to keep alive, they had to do one job in the day and another at night. The maximum they could earn was worth twenty kilograms of rice a month—that is, eight *yuan*—so you would find them in the streets at night, brushing shoes, selling papers or working in the shops. The biggest change, of course, has been in the employment of women. They do much of the work which used to be done by men and receive equal pay. We give special care to their physiological condition and when they are due to have children they receive fifty-six days' leave with pay. We also have our own nursery where they can leave their children for the day, or, if they like, for the whole week.'

Here, as in every State-run factory in China, work goes on in three eight-hour shifts for twenty-four hours a day, six days of the week. There have been no annual holidays since 1952, and the workers have to be content with their Sundays off and the days set aside for national rejoicing. If they were suffering under the strain they gave no sign of it in the Hsin Hua works. Everywhere was an air of cheerful efficiency; and as we toured the various departments the sudden arrival of the Director seemed to evoke no alarm or despondency. When I asked if I might smoke on the premises he flicked his finger in the direction of a corner table where two apprentices were idling the time with lighted cigarettes in their hands. 'It's against regulations,' he said, 'but we only enforce them strictly in the paper room.'

To my unskilled eye, the production output offered impressive proof of the success of the national campaign against illiteracy.* In the course of one month the Hsin Hua printed and bound an average of seven million books: children's stories; guide-books to personal hygiene (startlingly illustrated); fine art books; dictionaries; textbooks for every stage of the child's education; scientific works, and translated editions of foreign classics (mainly

* At present eighty per cent of the population are estimated to be illiterate, but the government claims that within the next twelve years it will have reduced this to a negligible figure by 'mobilising' the people. In rural areas parents are taught by their children; in the cities practically every street runs evening literacy classes in many of which adults are taught by secondary-school pupils.

Russian), as well as full-length Chinese novels. 'An average novel,' said the Director, 'sells in tens of thousands. A best-seller may go into millions.' (Lucky the Chinese writer who can supply the proletariat with the novels the government likes them to read!)

From one department a quarter of a million copies of *The People's Daily* were delivered to the citizens of Peking every morning; from another, a garish variety of government posters, advocating everything from the need to improve production techniques to the patriotic merits of practising contraception; from a third, finely-reproduced paintings of traditional Chinese scenes—*Spring Morning, Ebbtide at Evening, In the Park, By the Lake*—and delicately-coloured prints of flowers, butterflies and trees. When I suggested that the latter seemed somewhat fanciful, if not altogether decadent, in relation to the utilitarian needs of the moment, the Director replied with a wry smile of self-satisfaction: 'There are indeed some who take that point of view, but the government thinks differently. It realises that the people need things of beauty in their homes, so it is working to preserve the old art forms. We believe it is foolish to destroy our old traditions simply because they were the product of feudal days.'

He himself was mainly interested in fine art reproduction, but this, he said, was the field in which there had been the least technical advance. When I suggested that they seemed to be doing well enough as it was, and that the printing and binding of a full-length novel within a month would be thought miraculous in the English book trade, he shrugged his shoulders and said, 'That is a matter of mechanics. The other is the test of my skill.' He was not, I thought, an egocentric man; merely a perfectionist.

So, in a less inviting way, was the Governor of Peking's political prison.

This was not an establishment I had particularly wished to visit but one which had been wished upon me in an unguarded moment when the delegation was being escorted round the essential sights of civic interest.

'You must see our prison,' said the hosts, as though suggesting nothing more remarkable than a visit to a well-stocked zoo. (They took exactly the same delight in displaying their capitalists. 'Wait till you get to Shanghai,' they said. 'You will find plenty of them there; we even have some millionaires down there.')

I expected the visit to be a waste of time, for obviously the prison was a show-place, and in any case I would have no more chance of talking freely to the prisoners than I would on a visiting delegation to Wormwood Scrubs—probably less, with the interpreter standing by. In the event, my forebodings were justified; but in other respects I was in for a surprise.

Our arrival was greeted by the excited shouts of twenty or so young children who converged suddenly upon the coach from the outlying mud huts and tenement blocks with that combination of curiosity and delight which seems the characteristic attitude of children all over China to a group of foreigners. From the prison gates an armed guard duly emerged to disentangle them from the delegates as good-humouredly as an English bobby restraining a crowd of young cockneys during Trooping the Colour.

Inside the gates we embarked upon the ritual to which delegates are ineluctably treated wherever they happen to go: the sipping of tea, handing round of cigarettes, statement of aims, objects and achievements, and the answering or evading of questions.

It was soon apparent that the Governor, a tall, athletic-looking man in his early forties, had dealt with delegations before (at times on these expository occasions you wondered if the officials ever did anything else).

This was not, he remarked reprovingly to the Danish journalist, a political prison. There was no such thing as a political prison. The prisoners here had been sentenced for counter-revolutionary activities—something quite different. Nor were they all counter-revolutionaries; about one third were common criminals; but all were undergoing a similar process of reform and re-education.

Now at that time, which was a few days before Hungary

erupted, 'counter-revolutionary', like most of the Marxist jargon, was an unfamiliar term to me. Timorously, I sought elucidation.

'There are four categories,' explained the Governor. 'Kuomintang agents, members of counter-revolutionary leagues, bandits and saboteurs, and landlords and despots. Our policy is to remould them through productive work into becoming useful citizens and, to help in this connection, we give them a course of political education. I believe,' he said, blandly anticipating the question, 'this is a process which some of you describe as brainwashing.

'We look at the matter very differently. Our concern is to show the counter-revolutionary that his future happiness lies in working for the good of the people. Similarly with the common criminal; we aim to teach him first to understand the reason for his crime so that, having developed the correct attitude towards it, he may then proceed to reform himself altogether. Our work is directed fundamentally at reform, not at punishment.'

'What does the political education consist of?' I asked.

'It varies,' he said, 'according to the prisoner's intellectual development and his willingness to learn. First we try to instil the correct ideological outlook by giving him lessons in "current events". Then we study the history of the great socialist upsurge and the major political reports, with special reference, of course, to such things as the second Five-Year Plan, the plan for agricultural development in the next twelve years, and so forth.'

'And what happens,' I asked, 'in the case of counter-revolutionaries who fail to respond to this treatment?'

'In most cases we find that they do so before the completion of their sentence.'

'But supposing they don't? What would happen then?'

'I don't know,' he replied cheerfully. 'We should certainly continue with further re-education, but there have been no failures yet.'

I had been told previously that the practice of shooting landlords and nationalists out of hand had been halted two years before. Nowadays they were given a chance to reform by one to

WITHDRAWN
SCCCC—LIBRARY
4601 Mid Rivers Mall Drive
St. Peters, MO 63376

two years on the course of re-education. Under this system it seemed reasonable to suppose that the average landlord would come round to the 'correct attitude' in double-quick time, and that the nationalist might even finish ahead of him.

'On the contrary,' said the Governor. 'We are easily able to distinguish between the genuine and the artificial desire to reform. This will always be clearly manifested in the prisoner's work and in his actual dealings with his companions. Those who pretend soon reveal their pretence—and it does not last for long.'

From this I drew the logical conclusion that in some cases the death sentence was still carried out. 'How many executions,' I asked, 'have taken place this year?'

For the first time the Governor's brisk loquacity was disturbed. 'That is nothing to do with the prison,' he snapped. 'That is a matter for the People's Court.'

'Where,' I persisted, 'do the executions take place?'

'There are special grounds,' he said with sudden waspishness. 'I don't know where they are.'

Put like that, I was just as relieved as he to let the subject alone.

Doing the prison rounds, however, I could understand his irritation, for my questions were wholly irrelevant to the formal functions of the establishment. 'The prisoners are re-educated,' the Governor had said, 'through productive labour,' but in concentrating on the end of the business I had jumped ahead of the means.

Within the prison walls there was a large textile factory, and here, in low-roofed weaving-sheds, to the whir of wheels and the clanking of looms, long rows of surgically masked prisoners wound and threaded their way to ultimate redemption. Miles of yarn spun and twirled around them; wrinkled hands worked endlessly along rotating spindles; bent bodies swung from side to side like deformed puppets, and arms jerked and twitched to the grinding rhythm of the machines.

'LET THE BACKWARD CATCH UP WITH THE ADVANCED!' shrieked the banners along the ceiling, and the words were snatched up and pounded through the stifling air by the clattering looms. 'LET US ACTIVELY WORK TO-GETHER TO INCREASE OUTPUT!' sang the posters on the doors. 'INCREASE YOUR OUTPUT AND FURTHER THE CAUSE OF PRODUCTION!' cried the slogans on the walls; and in the macabre half-light of the sheds, to the roaring fury of the wheels, the prisoners strained and sweated to comply.

Outside, on the official notice-board, alongside the routine copy of *The People's Daily*, were posted photographs of model prisoners with their names, functions and production records. Some had supplemented their photographs with personal messages to the prison community: 'Through productive work for the People I have learnt the errors in my former thinking'; 'By improving my technique I have furthered socialist construction in the Glorious People's Republic'; 'Show your love for your comrades by following advanced methods of production.'

'We produce over fifty thousand pairs of socks a week,' said the Governor detachedly, 'and nearly twenty thousand shirts. These products are sent to towns all over China. They are also'— he indicated a hut opposite the weaving-shed—'on sale to visitors in the prison shop.

'The prisoners work an eight-hour day. They are allowed eight hours' sleep, have two hours for study and one hour for cultural and recreational activities.' (I restrained an irresponsible urge to enquire if the rest of the time was their own.) 'They are given one rest day each week, when they take part in informal gatherings—sometimes they see a film show—and once a fortnight they are allowed a half-hour visit from their families. They are given three meals a day, with a weekly ration of four ounces of meat, and they have baths once a fortnight. We don't pay them wages for their work but if their output is good and they show special technical skill they can earn a bonus of three or four *yuan* a month. In fact, at present more than eighty per cent have qualified for this.'

'Wouldn't it be true to say,' I asked, 'that conditions here are exceptional?'

E

ST. MARY'S JUNIOR COLLEGE LIBRARY

'It may be,' he admitted, 'that the material conditions are better than elsewhere, but the policy of governing and remoulding the prisoners is the same all over the country.'

'What are the methods of punishment?'

'They also are the same. We have four stages of punishment. The first consists of a warning. After that comes a bad mark, which counts against remission of time. For the third offence there is solitary confinement; and for the fourth, an increase of the sentence.'

'Do you still use corporal punishment?'

'That is absolutely forbidden,' he declared emphatically. 'Any officer who beats or ill-treats a prisoner in any way will himself be punished.'

'What happens in the case of a prisoner striking an officer first?'

'The officer will report the matter to the authorities. He will not take action himself. But in this prison,' he added, as I half expected him to, 'we do not have these cases of violence. The prisoners are well contented; in fact when their sentences expire there are some who ask if they can remain here because they have no work to go back to or they are afraid to face life outside.'

For all the reformative virtues of Peking prison, I found this last statement a little hard to swallow. But I recognised the point when I went into the sleeping quarters—it would be inapt to describe them as cells, for they were well-lit, bright, clean and comfortable. The prisoners slept from six to twelve in a room, which is not especially cramped by Chinese standards, on wooden beds, adequately cushioned by straw mattresses, and each supplied with as many woollen blankets as the prisoner might desire. Conditions, in fact, were a long way in advance of what many of the prisoners would have found in their own homes. When I was told that solitary confinement meant nothing more alarming than the prisoner being compelled to stay in his room—where he could read or write and go to the dining-rooms for meals in the usual way—the whole set-up sounded distinctly farcical. There was nothing farcical, however, about the armed guard standing in the turret overlooking the recreation ground, or about the four rows of electric wire running unobtrusively along the top of the prison walls.

Throughout the visit I had deliberately avoided watching the prisoners too closely, but as I passed a group playing basket-ball under the guard tower I paused, with furtive curiosity, to study their faces. What are they here for? I wondered. Which are the criminals, which the counter-revolutionaries? Are they pickpockets or saboteurs, poisoners or brave men? The serious, unsmiling faces gave no answer. Suddenly one of them turned and saw me watching him. I felt I had been caught in some guilty act myself and smiled self-consciously at him. For a moment he stared back and then, with a look of blank resentment, turned and went on with the game.

8

Habits of Thought

THE Secondary School was another crack job. It had been built nearly a hundred years before, but since 1949 had been enlarged and modernised. It catered for fourteen hundred pupils and had a staff of seventy-three, of whom one-third were engaged in 'administration'—a comprehensive definition which covered every conceivable activity from duplicating lesson sheets to sweeping the kitchen floors.

To say that schooling is compulsory in China would be untrue but not altogether misleading: it would be compulsory if there were sufficient schools for the purpose. Education was formerly the preserve of those who could afford it or who could obtain it as charity from the churches and missions. Now, given the bricks and mortar, it will become a universal reality within a very few years. I was given so many statistics on the advance in education since the defeat of the Kuomintang that it would be difficult to quote any of them intelligibly without reference to the rest. Suffice it to say that four times more children go to school than did in 1949, but in the primary schools there are still only sixty million places for eighty-five million pupils (although many schools work a two-shift system)—and the biggest advance has been in secondary education.

Secondary schools are divided into junior and senior departments, with pupils from twelve to sixteen at the former and from sixteen at the latter, although technically they are eligible to join the senior at any later age. (I came across several young men in their early twenties who had recently gained admission after working their own way through the entrance tests.)

The average size of a junior class is fifty pupils, that of a senior forty, but where accommodation permits these numbers are often exceeded. As far as I could gather, all secondary schools are residential and house not only pupils from outlying towns but many who live locally in conditions prejudicial to study. Those who can afford pay tuition fees of five *yuan* a semester while meals cost about five *yuan* a month, but are provided free in cases of hardship. The schools are mixed, but the boys and girls work in separate classes, meeting together in the evening 'for songs and dances, poetry-readings and the celebration of cultural occasions.'

'The daily life of the pupils,' said the Headmaster, 'is regulated by their own Students' Association. They have their own Youth League and arrange their own after-school activities. In this way they are encouraged both to express themselves individually and to accept responsibility as members of society.' (For a moment my mind wandered dreamily back to my own teaching days; the last person I had heard expressing precisely those sentiments was the headmaster of an English public school. Take out the Youth League and you had an identical point of view—on second thoughts, perhaps, leave the Youth League in and read prefectorial system instead.)

The Headmaster was, of all the officials I met in China, the one with whom I felt the most immediate affinity, which is the more strange, since my own skirmishes with the teaching profession have left me allergic to most of its higher representatives. He had an eminently civilised respect for the mentality of his visitors and showed no inclination to dodge awkward questions. His statements were mercifully free from both classroom and political jargon, although if he had any ideological reservations he did not reveal them. As a practitioner in the most complex, exasperating, heart-warming and nerve-wearing craft of humanity, he seemed generously endowed with the qualities of inner conviction and practical good sense which distinguish the good teacher in any school the world over. Through his gentle, unruffled manner there glowed a spirit of missionary dedication and behind the easy good humour you sensed the formidable self-assurance of a man completely on top of his job.

I guessed he would be about forty-five, although in China it is impossible to estimate the age of any adult male with accuracy, especially when he has reached middle age. (Even at seventy some of them go on looking at least twenty years younger, for the wrinkles have come imperceptibly and the hair has a perennially youthful texture.) His dark-blue tunic with trousers to match— the popular uniform of the professional classes—seemed ill-suited to his benignly sensitive face; and the stone floor and stark white walls of the study, unadorned except for the ubiquitous portrait of Mao, suggested a severely monastic retreat rather than a control centre of knowledge and ideological enlightenment.

In his opinion, the function of the teacher was to exhort and encourage, not to coerce or compel. Pupils were entitled to criticise the teacher if they felt they were not being properly treated—although that was a rare occurrence, he emphasised, and could only happen after the Students' Association had given careful thought to the complaint. The students were certainly not *encouraged* to criticise the staff—that was far from the official intention—but in cases of serious injustice 'or some such matter as excessive laziness on the part of the teacher' the students would wish to express their grievance. 'In this way,' he added, 'the students can do a great service to the teacher by enabling him to realise his failings, and their criticism will help him to become a better teacher.' While I was still musing upon the impact this admirably unorthodox scheme would make if introduced into schools in the purlieus of Camden Town or Hackney Wick, the Head went on to speak of corrective principles:

'Pupils are punished only in order to help them improve their work. A lazy or negligent pupil is given a bad mark, and this will make him ashamed of his shortcomings. The other pupils also will try to help him through the process of criticism and self-criticism. If he still persists in his fault—which is unlikely—his parents will be told and they will urge him to improve himself, for they value the opportunities he has been given. No,' he smiled rather wearily, as though at a threadbare joke, 'we have no corporal punishment. That is forbidden in the Constitution. In any case,' he added, 'the teachers themselves are opposed to it.'

From what I could see, the curriculum was much the same as that of an English grammar school, except that there was no specialisation, and Music, Arts and Crafts, Botany and Hygiene were compulsory subjects. There were, however, certain differences in nuance and approach; and there were also the two periods per week of Political Instruction.

'What is the philosophical basis in your teaching of History?' asked the indefatigable Crabb.

'Since the Liberation,' explained the Head patiently, 'we have, of course, introduced new text-books in this subject, as in all the natural and social sciences. The basic facts remain the same, but we no longer regard History as a colourful list of generals and emperors—it is interpreted as the evolutionary struggle of the peoples of the world.'

'In other words,' said Crabb, 'the subject is merely an historical extension of the Marxist doctrine?'

'Let us say,' said the Head, 'there is a difference in viewpoint and analysis of the facts.'

'In your Political Instruction do you teach any other philosophies besides Marxism?'

'I freely admit that our ideological basis is Marx–Leninism, but we also consider the western philosophies. The aim is to encourage students to develop their powers of independent thinking, and this will only be achieved if they are introduced to different systems from their own.'

'Suppose they discover that they prefer those systems to their own?'

'We should not prevent them from expressing their ideas.'

'Or acting upon them?'

'If they acted against the interest of the people that would be a different thing. We should never tolerate that. In any case, we believe that ultimately, through the process of discussion, they would form correct opinions.'

'What is your attitude,' asked Littmarck the Swedish Y.M.C.A. man, 'to pupils from homes where there is a strong religious background?'

'Every pupil has the right to his individual religious beliefs. He is not compelled to accept Marx–Leninism.'

'But the atheistic teaching at school must conflict with the religious teaching of his parents. Surely it is undesirable to subject him to a strain of this kind?'

'The School has never had complaints from parents about this. I think that they regard the problem the same as we do—the solution is to let the pupil choose for himself. You see,' he observed with winsome impartiality, 'today our country respects religious belief. We believe in tolerance and compromise, and there is freedom for religious propaganda as there is for Marx–Leninism. It is true to say,' he added, with what could hardly have been intentional irony, 'that the State *protects* religious beliefs.'

Outside on the bone-hard turf of the recreation ground the School was at play. A dozen different activities were going on at once. In one corner, boys were playing on the swings; in another, practising the high jump or vaulting the gymnasium horse. Down the centre of the field two separate games of football were in progress, and all along the perimeter, regardless of the hurly-burly around, pupils of all ages bunched together in little groups to practise basket-ball. Suddenly the sombre considerations of Marx–Leninism, the necessity for forming 'correct opinions', the philosophical basis in the teaching of History or anything else, seemed irrelevant: here was a scene of enjoyment unqualified; gay, noisy, robust, invigorating—just what a school should be, and not laid on for anyone's benefit, but demonstrably the way it normally behaved when it was let out to play. The pupils paid little attention to us until Galal borrowed a football and we began kicking in at the goal. I soon understood how Galal had won his international cap; from twenty or thirty yards out he fired the ball time and again into the net with professional nonchalance. The word quickly spread and pupils crowded round to watch. I left Galal to it, delighted that he had found at last something positive in the way of Physical Education.

From one of the classrooms came the excited din of high-pitched young voices and, wandering away by myself, I looked in through a broken window: two young boys were playing table-tennis while a hundred or more, jumping, leaping, shouting, screaming, urged them on from the sidelines with a competitive enthusiasm which you would have expected to put the players off their game altogether. Instead it seemed to have the reverse effect, for the protagonists maintained a concentrated calm which many older players would have envied. On each side of the room, oblivious, it seemed, to the fiendish clamour around, equally young children sat in almost motionless pairs, solemnly playing chess.

None of the children noticed me until the table-tennis battle was over, and then they rushed out to drag me inside. While they chattered and babbled and I spluttered to say something by way of reply one silent, serious-looking boy ripped a metal badge from his tunic and thrust it in my hand. It was a gift not to be refused, but it merited, I felt, something in return. I fumbled through my pockets, but could find nothing there. All I could do was to squeeze his hand, pat him on the head, and mutter something which was neither English nor Chinese, but which would convey, I hoped, that I was both touched and grateful. It was not a badge I would have chosen for myself, being a likeness of Chairman Mao, but it was given with a good heart and I wore it in my duffle coat during the rest of the trip.

9

On the Campus

THE novels of Maria Edgeworth lay dusty and abandoned in the cramped recesses of the room; unwanted, unmourned, the epics of Bulwer Lytton and the homilies of Hannah More, with half the silt from the turgid stream of nineteenth-century English fiction, had been washed up on the shelves around them.

I was in a remote wing of the library at Peking University with Wu-ping, a student of English. 'Why don't they burn them?' I asked. 'Or simply give them away?'

'They may be useful for future research,' she said. 'They will help us to understand your literary development, although of course we are not yet advanced enough to study it in detail.'

The prospect of some advanced Chinese student in years to come refreshing herself on the tracts of Miss More and the dainty delights of Miss Edgeworth seemed so preposterous that I thought for a moment she was joking, for she was an exceedingly jolly girl; but she was stating an accepted academic fact.

She had been studying English as her main subject for three years. Most of the time was devoted to linguistics, but each pupil made a special literary study of various novels on the approved list. They were expected to take a year over each one, during which time they discussed the subject for one period a week with a tutor.

'Is he the expert on that particular book?' I asked.

'Not always,' she said with unexpected irreverence. 'Although he always thinks he is.'

Her own special choice this year was *Wuthering Heights*, but the favourite with most of the students was *Vanity Fair*. The novel they apparently liked least was *Tom Jones*—'It is too difficult and old-fashioned for us'—a judgment which I should have thought much more applicable to the moralisings of Thackeray.

Wu-ping was a delightful girl: vivacious, attractive in a buxom way, and with a mind of her own. But her light-hearted approach to things seemed somewhat out of place on the campus, where the prevailing atmosphere was one of diligent studiousness and academic care. Nowhere have I seen book-learning more assiduously pursued. In the reading-rooms and libraries every chair was occupied, and every occupant wore a look of furrowed concentration—a collective awareness of youthful responsibility —which set me thinking back humbly, but not regretfully, to wasted afternoons in White's and evenings frittered away in the Randolph in the Oxford of ten years ago.

Foolishly, perhaps, thinking I might catch her out, I decided to question her on the compulsory course in Political Economics.

'What does the teaching consist of?' I asked.

'We are taught what is correct,' she said, as though nothing could be more obvious.

'But do you learn anything about systems besides your own?'

'We believe that the capitalist system will fail and socialism will follow.'

'What kind of socialism do you mean?'

'Marxism, of course. But you cannot export socialism. We know that every country will follow its own path and evolve its own kind of socialism.'

'But'—I hesitated to embarrass her—'don't you know that we already have our own kind of socialism in the west? In Scandinavia, for instance—and we have it in Britain.'

The question did not so much embarrass as strike her completely dumb. Perhaps it was something she had never been told before. Perhaps she knew the answer but couldn't quite remember it. Perhaps she was simply afraid of being tricked into unwitting heresy—she should have been more on her guard from the beginning. At any rate, she said absolutely nothing until we changed the subject.

We made our way into one of the women's dormitories and eventually met a group of geology students. None of them could speak English, but they were delighted to welcome me and to talk about their work and plans for the future.

When they had completed their course, they said, they would be employed in work of national development, probably in the oil and mining camps of the north-western provinces. Yes, they would expect to be away from home for long periods—for three or four years at a stretch, perhaps—living in tents and huts in the wildernesses of Kansu, Tsinghai or Sinkiang, prospecting for coal, oil and iron ore. Yes, they knew it would be a hard life, that the work was rigorous, conditions primitive, and the winters especially severe, but what of that? 'It is our great adventure,' they declared. 'We are working for the future. We shall be pioneers in building the new China.' (Did their eager enthusiasm strike a slightly chilling note? A shade too naïve perhaps, a little too ardent? Only, I reflected, to the westerner, brought up in a world too smart and complacent to be enthusiastic about any-thing.)

Marriage? Yes, they hoped to get married sometime. But that was a thing for the future. Why hurry into marriage when they had not yet started to live? Yes, they had boy friends at the University, but nothing serious, of course. No, boys did not make love to them—that would have been too serious. When a boy got to that stage it was as good as a proposal of marriage— something they could not allow. Looking round the little room where six of them lived together (some rooms were shared by as many as ten students) in double-tiered bunks packed tight against bare concrete walls, where the only furniture was a plain table and two rough benches, and their clothes and belongings were crammed into trunks and boxes under the beds, it was difficult to see how the boys had any opportunity to become even mildly serious. 'Of course it is overcrowded,' said the students, 'but what do you expect? Before the Liberation we could not have been here at all!'

We walked down gaunt barrack-like corridors and concrete stairways where washing had been hung up to dry, into the grounds of the old University. It was like stepping suddenly from the back streets of Cowley to the lawns of Magdalen Park, except that the contrast was more immediate and more extreme. Students dawdled at leisure in beautiful groves, under the shade of willow trees, or loitered along cypress-studded paths which ran down to the boat-house at the edge of a sleepy lake. On the far side of the water, pink lotus glowed in the sun; wistaria cast its blossoms on the lake, and gilt- and purple-tiled roofs gleamed through the trees. . . . But we had to move on to keep up with the Programme . . . past the playing-fields, the vast gymnasium and the massive new Philosophy building; past the ramshackle shed where the students had their bikes and shoes and suitcases repaired, past the huge canteens where overcrowding was so acute that, even working on a shift basis, the students had to eat their meals standing up; over the graceful lawns and the shale footpaths; back to the large and splendid Reception Room in the old building where the delegates were impatiently waiting and Dean Yen Jeng-ko was about to start his peroration.

'Before the Liberation,' he began, not boastfully but in relation to his problems, 'we had eight hundred students. Now there are over eight thousand. It is what you might call a headache and we know there is no easy cure.

'The University has been completely re-organised on a comprehensive basis. We have altogether fourteen departments and employ more than one thousand teachers. Many of these are American-trained and have recently returned to the University as a result of our new policy of permitting "flowers of all kinds to blossom, schools of diverse thoughts to contend".'

That statement, as he probably anticipated, set up a babble of interrogation, so much so that he invited delegates to put their questions in writing. He might have spared us the effort, for when he attempted to deal with the written questions he was still

interrupted by a barrage of supplementaries; and with French,
Swede, Canadian, Spanish and English tongues carrying on a
strident argy-bargy with each other while, in an inimitable
cacophony of their own, the interpreters laboured to serve all
parties at once, it was impossible to make out much of what he
had to say. (This unspeakable confusion was, of course, an
occupational liability wherever the delegation went, although on
more tedious occasions it provided welcome moments of light
relief.)

The Hundred Flowers, explained the Dean, had made a funda-
mental difference to the teaching of economics and political
philosophy. Although Marx–Leninism was, of course, the basis
of the teaching, it was no longer denied that there were many
rational features in the non-Marxist philosophies. Hegel and
Kant, for instance, were now accepted in the Philosophy schools,
although 'critically', while Malthus had been admitted into the
teaching of economics. Many of the lecturers were known to be
anti-communist, which was perfectly permissible so long as they
did not translate their ideas into action. 'The anti-communist,'
said the Dean, 'must accept implicitly the democratic dictatorship
of the People's Republic. Within that context he is entitled to
express the theory of other philosophies. In this university, for
instance, are several students of the American teacher, Hanson,
and the Englishman Keynes. They are free to teach what they
wish and their views will be openly debated in the seminars. So
that you see we have complete academic freedom. Only in this
way do we believe we can arrive at the truth'—and the truth, the
depressing truth at which you eventually and unfailingly arrived,
however bright the prospect had seemed on the way—was: 'to
make clear by the process of discussion why Marx–Leninism is
correct'.

This was the point beyond which there was no argument. It
was also the point which, at this meeting, suddenly sparked Galal
into life. 'That is enough!' he declared. 'We hear too much the
same. What is this Marx–Lenin? I have come not for the Marx–
Lenin. When do you answer my question?'

'What *was* your question?' asked the long-suffering English interpreter.

'I ask one hour ago,' said Galal. 'I want to know about the Sport. How is the Physical Education going on?'

But that was a question which unfortunately the Dean was not qualified to answer.

Later, when I visited Yang Hsiu-feng, the Minister of Higher Education, in the padded green comforts of the Hsin Hua Men (the Kremlin of Peking), I had the seal of official confirmation fixed upon the Dean's unavoidably disjointed declaration. A gaunt, grey-faced, ascetic-looking man, using an ear-aid, Yang was trained in an American university and was himself known to be non-communist.

'It is provided in the Constitution,' he assured me, 'that theories other than Marxism can exist. After all, if we only allow Marx–Leninism there could be no religious freedom, and we should have had to liquidate our capitalists. Then there are our national minorities, many of which have religious traditions. We have to consider their viewpoint and it would be impossible to force Marx–Leninism upon them.

'You see,' he explained, and I was to hear it echoed wherever I went in China, 'we are finding our own way to socialism. It is not a doctrine you can force people to accept, nor can you import it from other countries. It must be given time to grow according to the characteristics and local conditions of the people. This is not, as some people have imagined, an oriental heresy. It goes back to the original teaching of Lenin.'

'I understood,' I said, 'although I may have been misled, that the underlying purpose of your teaching in Politics and Philosophy was to instil Marx–Leninist ideas. I accept the fact that many of your professors are non-Marxist and that, to some extent, you have introduced western philosophy—although of a highly selective kind—and that points of doctrine can be openly discussed by the students; but supposing that a student rejects the doctrine completely or, to be more explicit, goes so far as to attack the Constitution?'

It would be unfair to say that Yang hesitated for a moment, but he paused in a curious, chuntering way and his reply did not come quite pat. It still ignored the point of the question, but perhaps not even Mao would have answered that directly.

'Our attitude is quite simple,' said Yang. 'Our students may propagate both materialistic and idealistic ideas. We say to them: "If you disagree, go ahead. Express your ideas. The truth can only be found after discussion." In the Biology Schools, for instance, there is at present a great discussion going on about genetics. We have criticised the Soviet theories and have introduced the work of Weissmann and Morgan. You see, the guiding principle, agreed upon by all democratic parties and groups, is that of dialectical materialism; but it is laid down that professors can express their own opinions and students can hold free discussions in order to arrive at the truth.'

That being so, there was not much else to ask. It was different, of course, from what one had expected. It was an enormous advance on anything that had gone before in the field of revolutionary communism—it was a revolutionary development in itself, a fantastic departure from communist policy in any other part of the world; but ultimately, in a shrewder, milder way, it achieved the same object, and what was more, it achieved it in a more durable form. If communism was going to last, these might prove its firmest props, not the revolver and whip but the limited discussion and open debate as the sorting house of 'the truth'.

'Remember,' said Yang, 'that the political aspect is a secondary part of our programme. Our main task is to raise the general level of science and culture and to train people for the work of developing our various fields of construction. Of course, a few articles in the Constitution cannot solve our problems. Everywhere our students are working under difficult conditions. Look at the problem of overcrowding, for instance. We are often blamed by the public for this, but until our national economy develops it will have to continue. We cannot improve things overnight. You will have seen that we are a very backward country. To catch up with the west will take us many years, but our heritage is poor and we have received little help from our forefathers.'

The last comment, I thought, was a masterpiece of euphemism even by Chinese standards. But as for taking so long to catch up with the west, I was not so sure. Looking at the new grey and red-brick Institutes of Iron and Steel Technology, of Metallurgy and Geology; at the Academies of Physics and Geophysics, the Colleges of Medicine and Economics, of Engineering and Aeronautics and Mechanised Agriculture, which were punctuating the skyline in every city and town with formidably increasing frequency; and watching the boiler-suited students crowding into them, cramming the libraries and lecture-rooms, bubbling with pride in their work, eager and aglow to go forth into desert and wilderness, to play their part in forging the image of a new China, *their* China, I had the uneasy feeling that Britain had somewhere missed the boat; it might be later than we thought, and before long we might discover that it was not the Chinese but we ourselves who would have to catch up. . . .

F

10

Brief Encounters

THERE were in Peking at this time, apart from diplomatic staff and delegates, only four Englishmen: Andrew Condron, the Marine who stayed in China after the Korean war; Alan Winnington of the *Daily Worker*; and two right-wing journalists, Arthur Boyd and Percy Dryden.

Condron interested me most, but I was never able to find him. Many hard things had been said about him in the British Press by reporters he had never met—and some harder things by René MacColl, whom he had—so that nowadays, it seemed, he kept a cautious distance from anyone who might feel impelled to report on him. Only Cameron, said Boyd, had done him justice by confessing that he did not know what to say. He was working in a factory outside Peking, but the Americans he had been living with were gradually returning home, and on the rare occasions when Boyd came across him he sensed that Condron was longing to go home too.

The same in a different way could have been said of Boyd. He had been in China for two years, and the strain of being isolated in alien surroundings had begun to tell.

A tough, compact little man in his late twenties, he had been subject for too long to the extreme frustrations and restrictions inherent in his peculiar situation, a solitary Englishman amongst people with whom he could have no personal relationships, with whom, in fact, even formal contact was difficult to establish because of his inability to speak their language. Living on these terms, even the hardiest recluse would become a shade depressed, and by nature Boyd was no recluse; so that, although at his best an urbane and helpful host, he was frequently too restive to make a very comfortable companion.

Fervently anti-communist himself, he reported China with remarkable objectivity, so remarkable, in fact, that Chou En-lai was moved to comment that he regarded him as 'a serious reporter'; which is the highest compliment that any Chinese communist could have paid him. There was so much to admire about Boyd—his mental toughness, his integrity, and the brilliant clarity of his reporting—that I constantly regretted my inability to get on with him; but I hope that one day he will write his own book on modern China, for no other western reporter has seen as much of the country and few would describe it with his uncompromising honesty.

For the long-term resident an insoluble problem is that of finding female companionship. It is physically impossible for an Englishman to enter into any form of private liaison with a Chinese woman without setting up a whirl of woe and worry all round. If he visits the lady in her home the matter will undoubtedly be communicated at the double to the leader of the Street Committee; if the lady visits him in his hotel, the room will be infested with a swarm of servicemen before she has had time to sit down. Percy Dryden once succeeded in escorting a woman unobserved, as he thought, over the threshold of his room in the Peking Hotel; but throughout the evening he was assailed at rapid intervals by a battery of servicemen irrepressibly eager to collect his laundry, brush his shoes, tidy his desk and, when the lady still remained, to replace one unwanted pot of tea with a succession of others. There seemed to be no sinister implications behind this curious carry-on; it was all based upon the not altogether facile assumption that any native woman consorting with a westerner would automatically be defiled—a belief inherited from associations in the earlier part of the century and systematically embodied in the prevalent puritanical dogma.

In any case, by accepting his invitation Dryden's guest had laid herself open to 'social rebuke'—or serious admonition from her Street Committee. She would undoubtedly be treated as one in need of correction, and if she persisted in the offence would be letting herself in for a torrent of criticism and self-criticism hardly designed to add to her enjoyment of life.

The social rebuke, or fear of it, has been the strongest police weapon in the campaign against vice and corruption. It has proved a more effective deterrent to prostitution than any system of fines and imprisonment, a safer keeper of the nation's chastity than any edict or promulgation, although, as Dryden told me, there was still a small black market in sex: 'But only the Japanese can break into it.'

Both Boyd and Dryden were emphatic that there was no censorship of their dispatches home: 'Any interference,' said Boyd, 'is much more likely to come from the other end.' At the same time there was nothing very startling to write home about: there may be 'leaks', but there are certainly no 'scoops' in a communist country. The journalist has to make the best he can of the material he is given, chiefly in the form of hand-outs, official statements and reports in the Hsin Hua news-sheets. He can, of course, report the passing show in any way he pleases, but this rarely adds up to a hard news story. Except in the case of a major calamity, such as earthquake or flood, he is unlikely to find out anything of national significance until weeks after it has happened; even then he will only know what he has been told and will have to guess the rest.

Part of the regular routine for Boyd and Dryden was to 'cover' the arrival of foreign V.I.P.s, but since one or other of these arrived nearly every day without expressing anything more sensational than a desire to maintain peaceful relations with the People's Republic, they regarded the whole procedure as a singularly pointless chore. For me it was a different matter, and I was delighted when, early during my stay, they asked me to accompany them to the airport for the arrival of U Nu.

The occasion was a mixture of carnival and crusade. The airport was bedecked with bunting and flags. Huge red banners, proclaiming eternal faith in Sino-Burmese friendship, streaked the sky. Thousands of Peking citizens stood four-square around the tarmac chanting slogans and waving flags. The usual reception party stood poised and alert with bouquets, ready to sweep down upon the honoured guest as soon as he stepped out of the plane. On the near side of the tarmac representatives of the various Leagues and Federations waited in long, serried ranks, while behind me, next to the entrance, stood an assembly of brown-robed Buddhist monks, diplomatically invited for the occasion in honour of U Nu's own religious beliefs. Their faces looked strangely haggard and grey against the general background of colour and jubilation.

While the incoming plane circled the airport, a party of blue-uniformed, peak-capped government officials suddenly brushed past us to take up positions on the nearby platform. Dryden pointed them out as they went by: Teng Hsiao-p'ing, the squat, bullet-headed General Secretary of the Party; Liu Shao-ch'i, a leading theoretician, second in command to Mao, and the jovial, steel-jawed Chu Teh, legendary hero of the People's Army. Then, smiling, unobtrusive, slightly stoop-shouldered, more aged than I had imagined him, like a devout but benevolent monk emerging from devoted study in the cloisters, the Founder of the People's Republic, the architect of Modern China, the one statesman of undisputed genius in the contemporary political arena: Chairman Mao Tse-tung himself.

At that moment, I suppose, I should have been mentally recording impressions, searching for something of import and significance behind those care-worn eyes and that surprisingly blotchy complexion, but my mind was on other things; here was I, I reflected, standing within two or three feet of the rulers of the largest totalitarian state in the world; I had entered the airport without a pass or document of any kind, nor had I at any time been asked to produce one; there may have been, for all I knew, security police dotted all around me, but wherever they were they could not have prevented me quietly slipping a time-bomb under the platform where the upper hierarchy of communist China was now disporting itself; true, the consequences would have been distinctly unpleasant, but there was no denying that the

opportunity existed. 'That's just another of the amazing things
about this country,' said Dryden in a whisper. 'You can't ask a
woman to have a drink in your hotel without being snooped upon
by the entire staff, yet you can wander round on an outing like
this and nobody takes a scrap of notice what you do. They're
genuinely not worried. It makes a royal arrival at London
Airport look like an exercise in a concentration camp!'

While I was still musing on this a small, lean, grave-faced man
detached himself from a group of journalists and approached me
with outstretched hand. He muttered inaudibly, shook hands,
looked at me searchingly for a moment, smiled, shook hands
again and passed on to talk to Dryden while I was still wondering
whether to address him in English or not. Too late I realised that
I could have done so without the risk of misunderstanding, for it
was Chou En-lai. His face looked less youthful and more severe
than the newspaper photographs suggested, but the salient
features—the black, beetle-browed eyes and finely curving cheeks
—were unmistakable. 'He has a special thing about journalists,'
said Dryden. 'He always makes a point of shaking hands with
them even if he hasn't seen them before.'

As the plane touched down, the same frenzied activity as had
greeted the arrival of the Youth Delegation broke out all round,
only on a much vaster scale. U Nu and his family were besieged
in an ecstasy of welcome. The government officials converged
upon him. The people waved and clapped and shouted. Broad-
backed, beaming, towering magnificently over his diminutive
hosts, U Nu was escorted by the reception committee along the
rows of cheering crowds. '*Ho-p'ing wan-sui!*' they shouted.
'Peace for a thousand years!' 'Long Live Sino-Burmese Friendship!' 'Long Live Asian-African Solidarity!' 'Long Live Peace!
Long Live Friendship!' It was a bizarre, endearing and strangely
disturbing spectacle, but nothing about it was stranger than the
conduct of the Buddhist monks. Normally, I imagine, un-
emotional men, not given to displays of jollity and exuberance,
they waited with patient solemnity for U Nu to approach them.
When at length he did, their grizzled faces burst into expressions

of fervent acclamation and, with arms raised, in husky, trembling voices, they gave him what I took to be the Buddhist equivalent of Three Rousing Cheers. Obviously moved by their ovation, he walked away from the official party to talk to them privately. The cheering and shouting died down and for a few minutes the afternoon became convincing and real.

Then he was escorted away; the leaders disappeared in a fleet of fast cars; the crowds dispersed to make the long journey back to town by whatever means they could. I had the impression that for many of them this had been just another outing; they would have cheered as gladly, I felt, if the visitor had been Sir Anthony Eden or even, perhaps, Mr. Dulles. The important thing to remember—and it was what your home-bred cynicism tempted you continually to forget—was that, at least, they were cheering for peace.

A less agreeable occasion was the dinner with the Egyptian Ambassador.

As mentioned earlier, this had been arranged, after minor complications in the Programme, for the general refreshment of the delegation by Galal.

It was an event which the British delegates embarked upon with some trepidation, for, although we could hardly have guessed that within a few days British troops would be engaged upon 'police action' in Egypt, recent expressions of sentiment on both sides had not exactly been couched in the honeyed phrases of Peace and Friendship. My own feelings in the matter were nebulously bipartisan: it was obvious that in the course of time Egypt would have complete control over the Canal, whether gained legitimately or not, so it seemed logical to cut our losses and yield it with a good grace, instead of being pushed out from within or forced to pull out by external pressure; on the other hand, I took no pleasure in contemplating my country's dis-comfiture in the rejoicing hands of Nasser. Moreover, I still re-garded the Canal with a fondly nostalgic sense of possession, based on nothing more substantial than various wartime journeyings through it and a number of nights spent in and about Port Said—although this was a sentiment I could hardly express to Galal and Shakir, to whom, illogically, I found myself defending the British case with all the Front-Bench platitudes which at home, a few weeks earlier, I had most vehemently rejected.

So we argued, respecting each other's instinctive patriotism, with tolerance and goodwill; and we went, determined at all costs to be tactful, to dine with the Ambassador.

It was not, as dinners go, much of an occasion. There were, including our Chinese friends, nearly fifty mouths to feed, and resources were obviously limited. The dinner was held in the International Club, a lugubrious establishment, better suited to a Convention of Funeral Directors than to an ambassadorial binge; nor was it actually a dinner, but a cheerless cold buffet, to be washed down with small quantities of Chinese beer. Tedious and dreary from the start, it ended up as a minor diplomatic disaster.

'I have great pleasure,' said Hassan Ragab, the Ambassador, a spruce, wiry, ex-military man, who did not look on the surface a trickster, 'in welcoming so many friends from so many parts of the world. To celebrate the occasion I have arranged to show you some films of Egyptian life, for I am sure you will all be interested in the various problems of my country.' In that assumption, of course, he was correct, and we sat back expectantly on our green plush divans while the lights of the International Club were dimmed and the projector began to whir.

To the dismay of the western delegates there flashed across the screen a film purporting to tell the history of the Suez problem. To say it was a film of 'Egyptian life' would be as accurate as to describe Cairo Radio as a vehicle of impartial information or *The People's Daily* as an independent newspaper. It was red-hot anti-British propaganda, designed to horrify and appal, with all the evils of imperialist exploitation laid on with a trowel. It started with imperialist atrocities during the building of the Canal —Egyptian slave-labourers cowering from the sadistic lash of their British oppressors, women and children starving to death on the Canal banks, and maimed bodies being carted away for mass burial—and finished with bloated British shareholders and Jewish financiers plotting the overthrow of Nasser, who appeared in person in the last reel triumphantly driving through the Cairo mobs on July 31st after abrogating the Canal Treaty.

It may be that in some respects it touched the fringe of truth: there *had* been oppression; there *had* been injustice; there *had* been little regard for native life and limb. This was an historical argument which not even a Waterhouse or a Hinchingbrooke could refute; but it was not remotely relevant to the immediate issue and, more to the point, having accepted the Ambassador's invitation in good faith, we felt entitled to something more palatable in the way of hospitality.

Some of the western delegates, notably the Danish journalist and Littmarck, the Swede, who disapproved of British policy in Egypt but equally resented being taken for a ride in Peking, were for getting up and walking out. Crabb turned his back on the screen and carried on a loud conversation with the Belgian behind him. Tripp stood up in great agitation and proclaimed to Abou, the Sudanese, that, having championed Egypt's cause at innumerable students' meetings during the past six months, his sympathy for it had now been considerably weakened. For my part, I felt there was little to do except sit it out and avoid falling into the same trap again; certainly nothing would be achieved by walking out—and, after all, one had a native pride in standing up to criticism—what else was democracy for?

Suddenly the show was over, although there were supposed to be two more films to follow. It was difficult to tell what had happened, but the lights had come on, the Egyptian delegates were in earnest conversation with the Ambassador, and Bernini, the delegation's President for the day, was making a speech of thanks in French. I had no wish to hear him or to speak to the Ambassador, so I slipped quietly out with Vladimir. He seemed unable to understand my annoyance, since he regarded the whole evening as a huge joke, so I tried to explain it by comparing the Ambassador's manœuvre with the treatment given to B. and K. at the notorious Labour Party Dinner. He still did not see the point. 'But that was very funny incident!' he roared. 'Very funny English dinner! In Moscow we thought that was very great joke. And here in Peking, Ambassador is very serious man, trying to show brutality of Fascist British to all peace-loving peoples. But no need for bourgeois Englishman to be serious too. Good bourgeois English should laugh at very dull propaganda dinner!'

It was a salutary attitude, but one I could not easily share, still less could Galal and Shakir. I did not suppose they had been a party to the deception, but it never occurred to me that they might actually resent the fact that it had been practised.

Later that night Shakir invited me to join them for a glass of cognac. He poured it out silently while Galal sat back contemplating the ceiling with troubled eyes. Shakir passed me the glass without a word, then sat down abruptly with frowning face and shifted uneasily in his chair; I had never known him so quiet before. The atmosphere was distinctly uncomfortable, but I could think of nothing to say that might improve it; trivialities would be intolerably banal and I had no intention of discussing the evening's contretemps unless they made the first move.

After long moments of nervous silence Galal spoke. Looking at me with an expression of the utmost misery he began hesitantly, 'I tell you something, Meeck' (his inability to pronounce the short English 'i' was one of his many linguistic idiosyncrasies), 'I tell you this for true. We did not know of feelm. Nothing about it. That is my promise.'

His melancholy eyes were charged with an intense sincerity which made further protestation unnecessary, but he was determined that I should know exactly what had happened. 'After Suez feelm I told Ambassador we would have no more feelms. He said there were two more. I said No. First feelm was enough. You have cheated me already. He said No, he had not seen feelm. It was not his fault, but information officer who said it was feelm of "Picnic on Suez". I said No. It was wrong picnic. We would have no more feelm!'

Shakir suddenly leapt from his chair blazing with indignation.

'I tell Ambassador it is disgrace to all!' he cried. 'It is insult to our friends and to all delegation! You must think we are filthy cheats —swindlers—who lie to you about dinner to make propaganda. But we did not know. I go to Embassy again tomorrow and tell Ambassador he has betrayed us.'

It was useless to reply, to insist that I knew it had nothing to do with them. They were not to be mollified. Galal rolled his eyes, bitterly reproaching himself for having arranged the invitation. 'It was all bad . . . all very bad,' he muttered inconsolably. 'We have not come here for Suez Canal, but only for the Sport and the Physical Education.'

The Chinese ordered their entertaining differently. Every night there were receptions in the government houses and hotels; every newly-arrived delegation had to be wined and dined, and Chinese etiquette forbade any skimping of resources or shoddiness of service. The outlay on this wholesale carousing must have exceeded the expenditure of even the most profligate feudal emperors. Setting off of an evening through the slum compound in front of Ch'ien Men you wondered, ungratefully perhaps, just what passed through the local inhabitants' minds as they observed yet another coach-load of guests en route for another long night of guzzling at government expense.

I experienced a number of these receptions, but the pattern was invariably the same, so that ultimately I turned up to them in a spirit of earnest duty rather than anticipation. The first one, however, was a completely novel experience which merits some detailed elaboration.

In terms of concern for the entertainment and welfare of the guests it would have been hard to beat. Leading citizens of Peking, representing every professional and cultural activity, had been invited: for the Danish journalist there were two members of the Hsin Hua News Agency; for the Swedish priest, a Chinese fellow-churchman; for Muriel, two national tennis champions and leaders of the All-China Federation of Women; for the Y.M.C.A. officials, their opposite numbers in Peking; while I myself was luxuriously treated to two leading actors, two theatre directors, the director of a dancing school, the producer of a choral and dance ensemble and, for some obscure reason, a leading political cartoonist. These people were amongst the most delightful chaperons I met during my stay in China: intensely interested in my own Youth Theatre; passionately eager to hear news of the English theatre and, especially, of modern developments in Shakespearean production; almost pathetically optimistic that one day soon one of our great classical companies would perform for them in Peking; and all aglow with a spirit of artistic dedication and humility which I was forever unable to reconcile with the ideological fetters they had elected to wear. The only hindrance to our better relationship was that none of them could speak English, and the young female interpreter assigned to us for the evening seemed to be in much the same case—or, to do her justice, was having, perhaps, her first practical experience outside the classroom. The result was that the conversation rarely got beyond the stage of monosyllabic starts and awkward, gesturing stops, a limitation which in this most admirable company was a matter for real regret.

These and fifty or so other luminaries of Peking life were awaiting us in a solemn semi-circle when we arrived at the hotel. In single-line formation we were introduced to each; to each a handshake, to each the only Chinese word we knew, '*Ni-hao*', which to us meant simply 'hello', but when repeated consecutively several times over by the Chinese, which it invariably was, conveyed also the illimitable depths of warmth and gladness they felt in having the opportunity to make your acquaintance.

These amiable ceremonies over, we were seized and swept away for social pleasantries, while a squadron of waiters hovered around with trays containing succulent shreds of chicken and duck, and an assortment of savouries and other spicy delicacies of indefinable origin but quite irresistible flavour, to be taken with glasses of yellow rice-wine, banana wine (both served hot) and grape wine, which is the national variant of *vin rosé*, but of syrupy taste and comparative innocuousness.

After some thirty minutes or so on the savouries the dinner proper began. It is not generally known that a truly Chinese meal bears little resemblance to those served in Chinese restaurants in London; nor, contrary to English supposition, do bird's nests, shark's fins and hundred-year-old eggs form its basic ingredients. The latter are dishes of great luxury which I came across only once (although the 'black' egg, which has been preserved for a mere six months in a coating of lime, is a favourite offering) and it is not perhaps generally realised that, though many of the dishes and tit-bits are of exquisite taste and fragrancy, a number of others may prove unutterably repulsive. Thus, my first real gastronomic engagement in Peking was in the nature of an exploration rather than a fulfilment: I toyed hopefully with what turned out to be dove's eggs, sea slugs and duck's livers, and clutched gratefully at the more familiar straws of fried chicken, prawn salad and crayfish *sauté*. In total, however, it was not a meal I greatly enjoyed, and as one sequence of dishes followed another, I realised with an acute sense of disillusionment that my palate was not, and probably never would be, attuned to the often-sung delights of the Chinese kitchen.

Equally disappointing, though less unexpected, was the liquor situation. It seems that, as a general rule, the Chinese drink only during the course of meals, and then they do so less from intrinsic pleasure in the exercise than from a desire to participate adequately in the game of drinking and proposing toasts. I use the word 'game' in its literal sense, for it is a pastime which starts with leisurely formality and finishes as a competitive scramble in which all who have the stamina are at liberty to join. It is played in rounds of variable duration, with the arrival of each fresh course in the earlier part of the evening, working up to a free-for-all in the later stages, as those who began as onlookers pick up the rules and rush to the fray as serious protagonists. The Chinese, in their tolerant wisdom, have appreciated that westerners, schooled on decadent distillations of barley, rye and hops, and Russians brought up on vodka, need some coarser stimulant than the gentle local wines in order to compete on level terms, so they have invented from the juice of their native sorghum a drink which they call *bai-gar*. It is impossible to convey in words the full barbarity of this potion. At the first tentative sip it seems no more harmful than an exceptionally dry sherry, but as the liquid flows down the throat it suggests a closer affinity to paraffin diluted in vitriol. Nothing I have tasted before, not even Egyptian 'rum', not even Algerian *ẓibib*, not even the Jungle Juice of Lourenço Marques or the Black Death of Reykjavik, can match the corrosive ferocity of this particular concoction.

It was introduced by Liao Cheng-chih, the President of the All-China Federation of Democratic Youth, a stout and roisterous man who was one of the few Party officials I met who actually seemed to *enjoy* drinking. He was proposing the first of many toasts to our closer friendship and understanding: 'We agree on the need for that. We disagree on ideology only. Let us drink to our friendship,' he held his glass exuberantly before him, 'in our strongest Chinese wine! But,' he roared, to the general acclamation, 'this wine is only eighty per cent proof—our friendship must be one hundred per cent!' Taking my cue from him I drained my glass in one rapid gulp, like schnapps—and recoiled a few seconds later feeling that my stomach was on fire. Vainly I tried to restrain the waiter who rushed to refill my glass, and next minute we were all on our feet again drinking to the better friendship of young people throughout the world. Since it was unthinkable to insult the President—or risk losing face—by changing to a weaker potion, the only thing to do was to go on firing the stuff down the throat by the glassful—a somewhat lethal method which had, at least, the virtue of brevity; and which also, by the end of the evening, had served to condition me for the rest of the trip to the rules and rigours of the toughest toasting game in the world.

With the heroic exception of the President, the Chinese left the *bai-gar* severely alone and confined themselves to discreet sips of grape-wine. '*Gan-pei*' is the rallying cry of the serious drinker ('Down the hatch!' would be a fair colloquial equivalent), and '*Sui-bien*' the token response of more abstemious guests—and the table where I had been placed was emphatically of the *sui-bien* type. True, my theatrical friends clinked their glasses at every opportunity, but very little of the contents seemed to pass their lips. 'We are artists,' said one of them when I asked why they abstained. 'Therefore we drink little.' 'We are singers,' said another. 'We must be careful to protect our throats.' The latter, however, in a rush of *noblesse oblige*, eventually decided to toast the singers of England in a glass of *bai-gar*—with disastrous consequences. His olive complexion turned a vivid crimson; his cheeks expanded like tennis-balls; and his eyes, suddenly blood-shot and ghastly, looked about to drop out of his head. With muttered apologies he staggered off to the lavatory, where he remained during the next several toasts, returning at length to drink nothing but orange juice.

During his absence I explained to the table at large that in England artists had the reputation of drinking more than most other people—an observation which was thought most amusing all round—until, with misplaced jocularity, I added, 'Of course, English artists are all decadent bourgeois types.' Then there was a numbing silence; friendship, even one hundred per cent proof, did not permit jokes about the Book.

No meeting, of course, was ever complete, no friendship went far beyond formality. The personal element could never enter into it because there were too many inhibitions on each side and, even if they could be overcome, there was always the language barrier or the interpreter standing in the way of direct communication.

One morning, however, there was a meeting with a difference. It was nothing very much—casual, inconsequential, unfruitful, but it stays in the memory with a warmth and poignancy which other encounters, of weightier significance, were never able to evoke.

I had set out with Galal and an interpreter on a tour of the Temple of Heaven. Galal did not stay the course for long but suddenly complained that his feet were aching and sat down outside the Hall of Prayer for Good Harvests, refusing to go any further. I made my own way through the Temple grounds, mingling with the crowds, looking in at one building to watch an exhibition of advanced techniques in coal-mining, joining a crowd of students in another to study a demonstration of glass-blowing. It was a relief to arrive at the Circular Mound Altar, where the only techniques on view were those of the craftsmen and architects who had built it five hundred years ago, in three concentric terraces, bordered with marble balustrades and supported upon three hundred and sixty magnificently carved pillars which symbolised the degrees in the celestial circle.

The Chinese were too interested in the buildings and exhibitions to take much notice of me, the solitary westerner present, until, coming out of the Imperial Vault of Heaven and stopping for a moment to whisper, according to custom, along the Echoing Wall, I had the uncomfortable feeling that I was being followed. I walked on slowly down the temple steps and then stopped on the Triple-Sound-of-Voice Stone and looked suddenly behind me.

About ten yards away a boiler-suited Chinese youth stopped too and stood watching me rather shyly. He was by no means disturbed at being caught out, but on the contrary broke into a bashful smile and, when I smiled back, ambled towards me, beaming delightedly, and took my hand in his. He was about twenty-one, big and broad by Chinese standards, with a relaxed, easy gait and strangely tousled hair which gave a touch of the gamin to his robust good looks and cheerful, honest eyes.

For a moment, in fact, I wondered if I had stumbled upon someone the Street Committee had missed, a Peking *ragazzo*, a lad of life who refused to conform to the 'correct attitude'. With profuse smiles and nods of cordiality he led me away by the hand to admire the gardens and altars, babbling happily the while and smiling regretfully whenever I reminded him that I could not understand a word he was saying.

After proceeding all round the Temple grounds in this fashion we arrived back at the Hall of Prayer for Good Harvests, where Galal and the interpreter were waiting. Now at least, I thought,

I can find out the young man's name and thank him for his company—but it was not so simple as that. After a few minutes, the interpreter had to confess that he himself could not understand the dialect in which the young man was speaking. This was the cue for uproarious laughter all round, during which, with a great deal of gesticulation, shouting and nodding of heads, we all did a sort of communal rock 'n roll down the Temple steps. At length the interpreter reported that the young man came from the province of Kwangsi, which was 'somewhere in the south'. After further parley and pantomime he discovered that, far from being a vagrant, he was a teacher on holiday, although what he actually taught could not be ascertained.

For some time we lingered together on the Temple steps in a spontaneous kind of chummery, compounded of smiles, hugs, hoots and shrieks of laughter, which nobody seemed to enjoy more than the young teacher. I could not find out anything more about him and I was certain I should never see him again. When we moved away he followed us towards the Temple gates, not walking beside us but always a few yards behind, with his relaxed, easy stride, smiling and shyly waving his hand whenever we turned round. I never knew what to make of this meeting, but I remember that when eventually he disappeared into the crowd the Temple of Heaven seemed a colder, less joyous place.

11

Two-Faced China

'MEES-TAIRE CROFT,' sang the nasal, high-pitched voice at the end of the telephone every morning. 'You WILL be ready at nine o'CLOCK to go to the steel rolling MILL' (or the Agricultural Co-operative or the Dramatic Academy). 'Are you altogether READY? Please HURRY!'

It was Pan, the first and fondest of my interpreters, for whom I was invariably unready and could rarely force myself to hurry, an entirely selfish tardiness which Pan accepted with outward good grace, although inwardly it must have driven him to distraction.

He had been an interpreter for less than a year, after graduating at the Foreign Languages Institute, but he was in many ways unique. He had more linguistical defects than any interpreter I ever met, but remained sublimely indifferent to them all. While his colleagues laboured feverishly to render some Chinese discursion into precise syntactical English or ferreted out the colloquialism most aptly suited to the needs of the moment, Pan brushed all difficulties aside with an airy wave of his hand and a short phrase of such comprehensive abstraction that it might have meant anything; or, when completely stumped, as he almost always was by the technical jargon of works managers and factory foremen, he would dismiss the operative part of the exposition with a shrug of his shoulders and the categorical negative: 'Oh, I don't know what! He's saying something about the mechanical workings—it is not at all interesting.'

He was a slightly-built, delicate-looking boy of great sensitivity and a radiant sense of goodness. Communism for him had a deeply emotional significance, for he had grown up in a dank slum in Shanghai where his father had died of tuberculosis and his own boyhood had been blighted by years of malnutrition. His mother was still alive, and it was a great comfort to him that he earned enough as an interpreter to send her a regular weekly allowance. In all Party matters he was a rigid adherent to the Book, but he had a nice sense of irony, and even where the Book was concerned did not object to leg-pulling.

For some reason he took a proprietary interest in my welfare and generally tried to get himself assigned to me on my private expeditions. Never having met an Englishman before he seemed to regard me as the embodiment of John Bull, an assumption which gratified him so much that he was forever pinching my arm or squeezing my shoulder, as though to confirm his discovery.

As our acquaintanceship developed, his conception of me took subtler, more fantastic and sometimes less flattering forms. 'Big-John-Bull-Englishman' and 'Big-Strong-Muscle-Englishman' were his original appellations for me, from which I rapidly became 'Big-Magnificent-Winston-Churchill-Englishman', but, unaccountably, at the Trades Exhibition in Canton towards the end of the tour, I degenerated suddenly into 'Very comical curious Englishman', and on our last day together dwindled ignominiously into 'Most-Unusual-Charlie-Chaplin-Englishman'. On what visual grounds Pan based these startling analogies I never discovered, but he always presented them with an air of intense gravity which was, I suspected, the most important part of the joke, and they provided a blessed relief from more serious matters between us.

Politics naturally came first. It falls to the interpreter, by dint of day-long propinquity, to hear his charge holding forth *ad infinitum* on the evils of the communist system. It is said that interpreters are warned to stay out of controversy, but they cannot always help themselves: they are not wood, or stones, but men; and sometimes, on these occasions, they were stung into defending China's policy with a directness and empirical sense of conviction a hundred times more persuasive than anything coming

out of the mouths of the Party leaders. This was especially true
of Pan, who was too emotionally convinced to argue the case by
chapter and verse and too impulsively patriotic to keep out of
a political wrangle; he defended the Chinese attitude to Taiwan
with a succinctness which even the State Department might have
envied. 'But it is Chinese country,' he protested when I tried to
explain the American case. 'Only the Chinese can decide who
should govern it. America is a long way off. It is not here. It
should not be in Taiwan.'

'But,' I answered patiently, 'America is afraid of war. She is
afraid of Russia, afraid that China will help Russia, afraid that if
war starts your country will let Russia dominate the Pacific. You
must remember,' I explained, 'what the Americans suffered at
Pearl Harbour. They dare not take a similar chance again.'

'But we are all afraid of war,' he cried. 'China wants no war.
We have our people to feed. We have had years of war. How
can the Americans think we want *more* war? China wants only
peace.'

'So do the Americans,' I insisted. 'That is why they stay in
Taiwan. Not for Chiang Kai-shek, but because they have to protect their own interests in the event of war breaking out.'

'But,' he laughed derisively, 'that is stupid talk. We all have to
protect our interests. But China does not go to Long Island to
look after *her* interests. China stays in China! Why cannot the
Americans stay in America?' And that, I had to admit, overlooking the niceties of Tibet and the goings-on along the Burmese
border, was a statement of compelling if not altogether irrefutable
logic.

Where Pan was outwardly soft and vulnerable, Shen Yueh-
feng, the senior interpreter, seemed dour and inflexible—until you
got to know him. In my case this was not until the end of the
trip, but it was a discovery worth waiting for. He indulged in
none of the affectionate gesturings of the sentimental Pan and did
not welcome the social intimacies of the late-night chat and the
lunch-time cigarette. Yet he devoted himself to ensuring that the
guests in his charge wanted for nothing and accepted their whims

and tantrums, their changes of plans and inclinations, with stoical if sometimes icy forbearance. The one thing he could not easily accept was the smug sarcasm in which they couched many of their passing observations on the regime; in the face of this, Shen became quietly sardonic and generally gave back as good as—or better than—he got.

He was a wiry, sharp-featured young man from Canton, and like most Cantonese something of an individualist. He liked wearing western-style suits and soft shirts; and in assimilating the English language, he had caught also some of the idio-syncrasies of the English character and outlook. He understood the difference between reticence and modesty and the English distrust of intellectual reasoning. He appreciated English scep-ticism about communist show-places and, where I was con-cerned, he realised from the start that I was more interested in talking to people than in studying statistics of social and industrial progress. Consequently he enquired anxiously each day if the Programme was to my liking and, even when I insisted on being taken round the slums and back streets instead of the new housing estates, he dutifully accompanied me, watching without com-plaint as I photographed the squalid hovels and alleys which still exist behind the department stores and towering office blocks.

'I take no pleasure in showing you these,' was all he said, 'but I realise why you want to see them. I only ask you to be honest when you write about them. Remember that they are not things we are proud of.'

Whereas I regarded Pan as a pleasant but slightly pathetic figure, I respected Shen for his honesty and bluntness of bearing. He refused to flatter or kow-tow to his guests. Having noted their wishes, he did his best to carry them out, but he did not regard himself as anybody's drudge, and he expected the delegates to treat him with the same consideration as he showed to them; nor was he above reminding them of their manners when he thought it necessary. He was the only interpreter I ever heard losing his temper, and then with some justification: we were somewhere outside Nanking, heading south for Shanghai, when we passed a group of labourers squatting in a circle beside the railway track in the throes of earnest discussion. 'Look!' said Ricardo the young Spaniard. 'The local trade union! They are so busy with self-criticism that they have no time to get on with their work!'

'Coming from you,' said Shen heatedly, 'that is not a very funny remark. I believe that in your country the people have no time for any kind of criticism!'

I believe it is wrong to assume that the interpreter is little more than a police spy, an affable informer, although it may well be that this is sometimes the case. When I taxed Pan and Shen about this they pointed out with some asperity that they thought western visitors had got police on the brain. 'Do you think,' they demanded, 'that we could possibly talk to you as we do if we felt you did not trust us?' It was as much as they could do, they pointed out, to carry out their ordinary duties—and act as guide, courier, cultural adviser, general factotum and sometimes wet nurse to the delegates—without also dabbling in security work.

It was obvious also that they made no attempt to steer conversation into approved channels or to alter the gist of what was being said. True, there was never any proof of this, but one was constantly on the look-out for the awkward pause or hesitant expression, but when these occurred it was invariably to avoid something which might prove offensive to the guest—Chinese opinion of the attack on Suez, for instance; my impression was that they were far too preoccupied in following the sense of what was being said to attempt deliberately to alter it and, when misunderstandings took place, which was seldom with Shen but frequently with Pan, they were the result solely of an inadequate grasp of English. (On the other hand, of course, the mere presence of the interpreter automatically inhibited the range of conversation wherever one happened to be.)

My third interpreter, with whom I had the least satisfactory relationship, was Little Wang, an attractive but serious-minded girl, with a steely Marxist outlook, who regarded me with ill-concealed disapproval, not because I criticised her beloved ideology but because I did not always take it seriously.

'I wonder,' I remarked with attempted flippancy, watching a group of Peking students playing basket-ball, 'if they are as keen on Marx–Leninism as they are on their games.'

'They must be equally good at both,' she snapped tersely. 'Marx–Leninism is as necessary for the healthy mind as games for the healthy body.'

Clearly there was nothing to be gained by discussing the contemporary situation with Little Wang. Conversationally we kept at a formal distance from each other until, very late on the tour, she thawed out a little and, to my immense surprise, she even seemed genuinely sorry when I left.

It was Little Wang who took me to see the Great Wall, in company with Galal and Abou. The latter was a large, black, bouncing man, a school inspector in his native Khartoum, who had been educated at Ruskin College, Oxford, and had a profound respect for English institutions, especially since the English had cleared out of the Sudan.

We made a curious little party: the tight-lipped Little Wang, who, I was sure, regarded the Wall as a feudal anachronism which should have been demolished at the Liberation; Galal, who complained incessantly of the cold—the temperature had dropped suddenly—and was not interested in the Wall anyway; and Abou, who was only going to look at the Wall out of politeness to his hosts.

We drove for forty miles or so through the brown-tracked Yenshang Hills, lowering and inhospitable in the grey morning air, down jagged precipices and pot-holed tracks, until there at length it was, twisting and winding into the hills on either side, the most enormous fortification in the world, the most enduring monument in the history of mankind.

It should, I felt, have evoked feelings of awe and wonder, amazement and admiration—if only at the prodigious feat of engineering it represented or the recollection of the millions of slaves conscripted to build it. As it was, there was too much of it: like a gigantic Hollywood epic, it dominated the screen, but its very grandiosity dulled the imagination. 'Yes,' you thought. 'It is indeed a wall—a wall to end all walls. But what is the point of a wall?' And indeed, with this wall there seemed less point than with most, for despite its gaunt durability, its turrets and embattlements, it could have been stormed and scaled at any given point by an invading army which really knew its business.

When I put this point to Little Wang she bristled slightly and displayed her only flicker of feeling about the entire structure. 'We do not consider it in that light,' she said. 'We are not interested in the military background. But we remember that the Wall was built with the sweat and blood of the Chinese people, who died by their hundreds of thousands in constructing it. *That* is why we preserve the Wall—to commemorate the exploitation of our people and at the same time to show the genius of their labours.' That was the measure, limit and sum total of her interest; she did not even know, although the facts were in the guide-book for all to read, that it had been built twenty-three centuries ago to ward off the Tartar hordes, nor that it ran in all to a length of fifteen hundred miles; and she certainly didn't care. To her it was another remnant of feudal oppression in the dark night before history began.

So we strolled along the parapets and climbed the towers and took photographs of the Green Dragon Gate—where carved indelibly into the stone on either side runs the giant slogan, 'Long live the People's Government!'—and smiled at the sombre soldiers lounging on the ramparts and the families of sightseers out from Peking for the day, until very soon, in his plaintively inevitable way, Galal began to complain of his feet and, abruptly halting the party, declared, 'Now I think we have seen Wall. Better go back to hotel.'

With a distasteful sense of duty, however, Little Wang insisted that we should first visit the Ming tombs. So we branched off the main track and bumped our way past a congestion of cars and coaches to observe the pavilioned relics of the most lavish period in China's history. It would serve no purpose to record the visual details. The significant fact was that everything had been preserved as it was—and not merely preserved but repaired and re-decorated—the tombs, the pavilions, the magnificently carved eaves, the feudal dragons and phœnixes, the gigantic stone gargoyles, the pagodas and parks—all in a state of gleaming preservation for the enjoyment and edification of the People.

'Like the Great Wall,' said Little Wang when I gave her the cue, 'they were built by the People. They are the product of our people's skill and the monuments to their toil. It is only since the Liberation that the people have been able to enjoy them. These visitors'—she pointed to the crowds sauntering around the pavilions—'they were not even allowed to enter the grounds before the Liberation; now they may come whenever they wish for their own recreation.

'But that is not all,' she continued. 'Under the Kuomintang there was no care for things of beauty. These buildings fell into decay. The Kuomintang would spend no money on their upkeep. They looted the riches within, but they allowed the walls and the pillars to rot. When these grounds were opened after the Liberation, the gardens were like a wilderness and the pavilions were falling to pieces. . . .'

She was a good propagandist; she knew how to sell the goods (although she could not tell me the names of the emperors who were entombed within); but I had seen enough of China by now and heard enough of the ways of the Kuomintang from neutral observers to admit the validity of her point.

Of all subjects after Marx–Leninism, the one which I personally should have most avoided broaching with Little Wang was that of love; but the hot-blooded Abou felt no such constraint.

'There is one thing,' he said with troubled curiosity, 'which seems very wrong. I have never seen people making love in your country. I go to the Summer Palace, to Chungshan Park and to Coal Hill. This afternoon I come to the Ming tombs and there are thousands of people enjoying themselves. But there is never boy and girl together. What have you done to cause this? Why do young people never make love?'

For once Little Wang laughed; she thought Abou was joking.

'But it is not true,' she said. 'Boys and girls are often together, but they cannot always find time for making love. Even at the week-ends they have their work to do.'

'But I *never* see them together,' said Abou. 'In the gardens I have looked especially to find them, but they are always apart. And in the streets I see boys walking hand in hand together, but I never see them holding hands with a girl. It is unnatural for things to be so. It is terrible to keep them apart. You have done many wonderful things in your country, but this is something to your shame. You have forgotten love.'

Little Wang still could not take him seriously, but however hard she laughed and protested that boys and girls carried on together much the same in China as anywhere else in the world, it was difficult to believe her, for everyone coming to China comments on the same phenomenon. It is, no doubt, one of the direct products of female emancipation: the girls have not yet learnt to trust themselves with young men, nor have the young men, freed from the tyranny of the parentally arranged marriage, learnt the finer arts of courtship or the amorous advantages to be gained in public pleasure-grounds; where exactly they do their wooing, how the first move is made and how the pace is determined, would have been interesting to discover, but Little Wang did not venture to explain, and even the forthright Abou was too timorous to ask.

'It has been my greatest disappointment,' he repeated. 'All the time I have been in China I have seen no love. I have heard nobody talk about love. You tell me about your great industrial programme and your factories and health schemes and you show me your old monuments and your temples, but never do you show me love. I think your women must be afraid of love so they dress themselves in these terrible clothes deliberately. They try to look so awful that the boys will not be interested in them.'

At this point I suggested, with crude jocularity, that they were too concerned about production to have time for reproduction, which set Abou roaring and bouncing about in the car, but brought from Little Wang a withering glare of contempt.

She sat tight-lipped and sullen for the rest of the journey back; and I felt doubly ashamed of myself because I knew I had deliberately meant to offend her.

12

Peking Nights

THERE is an extraordinary misconception amongst English
people that, despite the strictures of Mao's regime, China
is still a country in which, when evening comes on, all the
vices in the calendar burgeon forth illicitly down sinister alley-
ways, in smoky dens and doss-houses, to the accompaniment of
eerie, wailing music and mysterious oriental smells.

Anyone setting out with ambitions in this direction would be
well advised to terminate his journey in Hong Kong or head
straight for Tokyo instead, for since the Liberation China has
been cleaned up with a truly comprehensive efficiency.

The high mark of this achievement is to be found in Shanghai,
where later I took some pains to investigate the methods thought
appropriate to the operation. In Peking I was content to examine the results, the most conspicuous being that night life in
the western sense of the word has simply ceased to exist, or, to
be more exact, is conducted with a propriety in comparison with
which a Sunday night in Cheltenham would seem like a Neronian
orgy.

To say that there are no bars, no cabarets, no dance-halls, no
speak-easies, honky-tonks, clip joints or dives is only to hint at
the complete social paralysis which grips the city after about
eleven o'clock, when the theatres have emptied and the last over-
laden tram has gone clanking home. After that hour a walk
through the streets is a darkling communion with yourself; you
may stumble at street corners upon cigarette-sellers and vendors
of chestnuts and noodles, vegetables and sesame cakes, or pedlars
of soya sauce and biscuits and old clothes, but their wares have

been packed up, their stalls shuttered, and they are preparing to lump their way home; or you may hear, from the building sites and factory yards, the endless *Wei-ho Wei-ho* of the labourers as they sway and bend in ghostly form beneath the great arc-lights that blaze all night long, beaconing the path to China's immeasurable destiny; but you will not encounter—unless it be a restless fellow-spirit from licentious foreign parts—a solitary prowler in search of nocturnal pleasures.

If you bear in mind that the first sign of aberrant activity by the local residents would almost certainly be spotted and reported at once to the nearest Street Committee, it should not be difficult to appreciate the aseptic thoroughness with which the new morality is maintained. That it is a reformation of phenomenal range and rapidity cannot be disputed, nor that it is an entirely admirable improvement upon the vicious immorality it has replaced; but it seemed a pity that, in destroying the weeds of the old regime, the government should have wiped out the garden altogether.

But if there is not much activity late at night there is a wealth of it earlier on, although again it has little in common with the fictional conception of the exotic and mysterious orient.

The bazaars, of course, remain, and the brilliant fairs, and the little street tables where families squat around, eating supper or drinking tea, but these no longer provide the centre of social attraction. The focal point has shifted elsewhere: to the huge department stores where, hour after hour, crowds of workers wander enquiringly around, sometimes to buy, more often just to look; to the Hall of Sino-Soviet Friendship where, every night, people queue in their thousands for an exhibition of Economic and Cultural Achievement in East Germany or of Ten Years Socialist Construction in Bulgaria—does it matter if they sometimes have no idea what they are queueing to see?—it is something to do, a break from routine, a place to go; or else there are the vast new gymnasiums, the festivals of sport, the skating-rinks, the swimming-pools and stadiums.

The latest of these had just gone up when I arrived in Peking.

It was called, with characteristic exactness, The Working People's Palace of Sport, and its name did full justice to the scale on which it had been built and the remarkable facilities it offered.

Compendious enough to incorporate the Empire Stadium and Olympia together and still leave room for a tennis-court or two in the wings, it comprised: eight indoor basket-ball pitches; a recreation-room, where twenty-four games of table-tennis could be played in comfort simultaneously; a central arena, with a seating capacity of five thousand, for concerts, wrestling, boxing and acrobatic contests; two gymnasiums; an underground swimming-pool two hundred and fifty feet long; and all the peripheral necessities of the modern games-player, from rest and relaxation parlours to rooms for massage and medical treatment.

Surprisingly I was given no statistics about the numbers of people availing themselves of these facilities and no comparisons were made with recreational conditions under the Kuomintang; perhaps none were necessary because, as far as the mass of the people were concerned, they did not exist at all. Although not myself a devotee of the sportsdrome, I would say without reservation that the Peking Working People's Palace of Sport is giving more pleasure to more sports-lovers per night than any similar institution elsewhere in the world.

Then there were the cinemas, where Socialist solidarity was further strengthened by the predominance of Soviet feature films. In Peking I saw only one home-grown product, an adaptation from an ancient popular romance, which had exquisite charm but moved at such a tortured pace that both then and subsequently, when I saw it again in Shanghai, its effect was so soporific that I never knew exactly what it was about.

More interesting were the coloured documentaries which pre-ceded it, beautifully composed films showing the gardens of lilac and peonies in Fengtai, the autumn chrysanthemums in Peihai Park and the glistening brilliance of the goldfish ponds in Chung-shan Park. They had been specially dubbed, either for export or for the benefit of English-speaking visitors, and their enchant-ment was marred only by the commentator's continual reminders that, until the Liberation, the parks had been the private preserves of feudal landlords. When, in the last reel of the goldfish film, he smugly reiterated, 'So now you can see the people wandering at leisure among these beautiful ponds which after the Liberation were taken out of the hands of the reactionary classes,' Shakir sitting beside me growled under his breath: 'Maybe soon they will liberate the goldfish too!'

It is the theatres which stay open latest (even the last lights of the restaurants are dimmed by ten o'clock), and it is here that something reminiscent of night life may still be found, although the connection is largely tentative.

To the Chinese, the theatre does not denote merely an enter-tainment, still less a fashion parade or social jamboree; it is a functional necessity, a place where they spend a goodly part of their lives, may die or be born in, a joyous communion, a bedlam, a mystique, a mirror giving transcendent expression to the throbs and stresses of their collective soul. They do not simply go to see a performance; they go time and time again until they know every gesture, every inflexion by heart, until they have shed their own identities and become themselves participants in the action.

But while the play is so intensely the thing, the accessories per-taining to it have been shrugged aside. The audience sit packed closely together on wooden tip-up seats. The walls in most theatres have a barrack-like bleakness; the foyers are grey passage-ways, drably lit, starkly utilitarian. There are, of course, no bars. The thirsty spectator may help himself to a glass of hot water from one of the taps in the foyer or may even purchase a glass of orange-juice in the gloomy refreshment-room, but there the amenities end. Yet if the conditions seem a trifle Spartan by West End standards, to the Chinese, intent only upon enjoying the performance, they represent the height of upholstered luxury.

My first theatre visit was to see a Song and Dance Ensemble which had recently returned from a tour of the Middle East.

These ensembles are something of a communist speciality, but this one was more special than most. In the course of their tour the artistes had visited Egypt, the Sudan, Ethiopia, Syria and

Afghanistan, and had taken the trouble on the way to study the folk culture of those countries and learn some of the national songs and dances. In honour of our delegation they sang Arabian love-songs in the original languages and performed complicated Egyptian dances with a precision and sinuosity which amazed the Arab delegates. 'Singing not so good as Egyptian,' declared Galal, deeply moved, 'but movement of dance altogether correct . . . all details exact.'

More surprising, however, than the apparent verisimilitude of the performance was the revelation it gave that Chinese women did actually understand the fundamentals of sexual allure.

For the Afghan folk-song '*You are so good that I have given my heart to you*', they wore tight-fitting flowered dresses and vivid brocades, slashed generously down the sides; and in the plaintive Syrian lyric '*If I continue to love you it is sin, But please let me look at you once more*', their gently swaying hips conveyed a catalogue of tingling suggestion which, applied to their native opera, would have fetched out every Street Committee in Peking. This was demure modesty, however, compared with what they did to the Egyptian dances. In a moaning ecstasy, they abandoned themselves to the rhythms of the music, and their bodies swirled and vibrated as though in fevered anticipation of gaudy nights to come—or as though they had found at last a release for their own pent-up desires and yearnings.

The rest of the evening was taken up with imitations of birds and animals and excerpts from Peking Opera. The former type of entertainment does not normally appeal to me, but here it had a novel—and ear-splitting—fascination. Using only the *panhu*, a Chinese form of the violin, one artist produced an extraordinary evocation of 'Birds Singing in Solitary Hills', while another, playing the *sona*—which vaguely resembles a horn with bellows attached—ran through the vocal gamut of an entire aviary.

The impact these noises made upon the senses served to lessen the shock of the final assault when the orchestra let loose on the most beloved of all Peking operas, *The Riot in the Dragon King's Palace.*

It should be said that a Peking Opera orchestra does not merely play; it rends, flays, batters, belts and hammers out sound; it vaults from one mountain top of crescendo to another; it turns normal noise into a state of enduring silence and the fiercest stridencies of western music into feeble pipings in the tranquil air. With its joss-gongs and beating bells, its cymbals and drums, its *er hu* and *yang chin*, it gives a sustained climactic intensity to the action it accompanies and is as much a part of Peking Opera as the tumblers, acrobats and dancers engaged in the surrealistic conflicts on the stage.

The Peking Opera is only one of many distinctive Chinese forms, and has itself absorbed many other local forms and features since it reached the imperial court in the middle of the eighteenth century as a traditional peasant art; but the discordant fury of its orchestra, the grotesque brilliance of its actors and the processions of emperors, warlords, dragons, generals and traitors who, in mighty beards and gorgeous robes, forever surge and battle together upon the seething stage are its hallowed and immutable trademarks.

In *The Riot in the Dragon King's Palace*, the protagonists are the black-bearded, purple-robed Dragon King himself and the diminutive little king of the monkeys who has travelled to the Dragon's palace to try to secure his magical iron staff. The action culminates in a fight between the monkey and the aquatic army of crabs and shrimps on the rolling waves of the ocean palace.

This fight is said to be one of the classic moments in Peking Opera, the touchstone of acrobatic dancing and, for the actor playing the monkey, the point at which genius becomes distinguishable from skill. On this occasion the actor was Chang Cheng-wu, who stands in the same relationship to the part as Gielgud to Hamlet or Olivier to Henry the Fifth. I had no means of appreciating the true subtlety of his performance, but as he leapt and jumped over the advancing waves, duelled with a dozen soldiers at once, contorted himself into a rubber ball to bounce and hang suspended in the air, and dived and glided unscathed along the points of twenty swishing swords, I was content to take

H

it on trust that I was watching one of the greatest artistes of the Chinese theatre, if not—although the Chinese would never have suggested it—of the theatre anywhere.

After the performance the company were waiting to receive us on stage and, as at a reception, we passed down the assembly line, Ni-haoing, shaking hands and applauding each other with fervent enthusiasm. Communication was made difficult by the sudden disappearance of the interpreters and the arrival of a variegated batch of other delegations, until the whole of the vast stage was filled with grinning, bowing acrobats and hand-shaking delegates; but nobody could say a single word that meant anything to anybody—although Vladimir had fastened upon one of the Egyptian dancers and was laboriously trying to make himself understood in a mixture of Russian, English and sign language at once. At length Chang Cheng-wu appeared in the opposite wing, robed in a bath-towel, and a further riot of hand-clapping broke out in which Chang heartily held his own. Then the big, blond Danish journalist, Carl, who was President of the delegation for the day, delivered himself of a speech of thanks in totally unfathomable English, and everyone clapped again more loudly than before. As we trooped off the stage down into the auditorium, the clapping gathered force behind us and rose in still louder bursts as we made our way into the street.

'Ah,' said Vladimir, seizing me excitedly by the arm. 'They were so gay . . . the Egyptian dances . . . yes? It was great surprise . . . not like Chinese women we have met.

'I am told,' he said, expressing a problem which had been on his mind ever since he arrived in China, 'they are all innocent till marriage. And many young men, I believe, never marry at all. Intelligent girls are . . . how you say? . . . grabbed quick by young men and married at once. . . . Very bad system. In Russia is not so. Our women very much enjoy their life.'

He had heard a sad story from his interpreter the previous day. 'He tell me of passionate old man who try to seduce young girl. But this make all people very angry. All go to court. Judge ask what they think and all say, "Shoot old man!" '

He shook his head sorrowfully. 'That is terrible thing. In Russia is not so. In my country is better understanding for old man.'

The People's Government have raised the status of the theatre to a level of importance almost akin to that of productivity, and the demand for actors far exceeds the supply. The actor is classed as an intellectual and, although his salary is a mere pittance by Hollywood standards, it is princely by comparison with the average worker's: in the State theatres he can earn as much as ten pounds per week and may even double this in the privately-run companies.

Chinese drama, or what the actors call 'the dialogue play', is still in its infancy; to be exact, the first dialogue play was performed as recently as 1902. These plays are deeply rooted in revolutionary idealism and mirror the social and political tumults of the time: the struggle for female emancipation; the revolt of young people against patriarchal despotism and 'arranged' marriages; the developing political consciousness of the petty bourgeoisie, and the embryonic struggle of the peasants against the mandarins and landlords. They are didactic plays rather than proletarian, closer to Ben Jonson than Karl Marx; their voice is that of Sun-yat-sen rather than Chairman Mao; their passions and protests belong more to the missionary college than the communist youth federation; but for all their occasional bursts of dramatic excitement they seem turgid in development, repetitive in situation and one-dimensional in their picture of humanity. Yet, under the Kuomintang, when, unless he were a privileged official pet, the actor was a despised creature, forced to grovel for a living, to act in one of these plays was to run the risk of arbitrary imprisonment, torture or even death.

With the Liberation, the drama has become a vehicle of Party policy. In the interests of the proletariat, only plays with the requisite ingredients of 'socialist realism' are likely to reach the stage, and then they must not only illustrate 'the life of the people', they must also provide an exercise in 'correct thinking'. (Even scenes in the traditional operas have been 'revised'. 'We have to bring them up to date,' say the Chinese, 'so that they do not show the ordinary people in an unfavourable light or seem to uphold feudal conceptions.')

In one respect, however, the proletarian drama would win favour in the contemporary American theatre, for it has evolved its own Method. It postulates that the habits and utterances of the illiterate, inarticulate and generally under-privileged are fertile dramatic material; although there, perhaps, the resemblance ends. When the writer has been 'commissioned' or given a theme, he departs for a period of anything from a month to a year to the village, mining camp or co-operative in which his play is to be set. In time he is joined by the company, who settle down to a detailed study of their parts by joining in the work of the community. At the same time the original script is exposed to the criticism of the workers, and by the time the company return they have already identified themselves thoroughly with the characters and situations they are to represent.

As an approach to acting this obviously has much to recommend it. It bridges the gap between the proscenium and pit; it induces in the artist a healthy respect for his raw materials; it stimulates the kind of group consciousness which the commercial theatre and the star system have dulled. But what the Method gives with one hand the Party line takes away with the other. The outcome is resolved before the conflict begins and, although at its best the end product may serve to illuminate the external forms and pressures of the age, more often it emerges as a mere charade, dutifully holding up to nature the dichromic mirror of Marx–Leninism.

Nor has the Method noticeably improved the general level of acting. Of the many paradoxes in modern China none seemed so odd as this: that while the young operatic actor can command his body to assume the myriad shapes of his imagination, too often the young dramatic actor appears to grope his way across the stage as though he had never learnt the use of arms and legs, lips, eyes and hands; at times, in fact, he gives the impression that he is acting in a strait-jacket.

Understandably, the proletarian drama has achieved no conspicuous success with the people whose lives it is supposed to reflect, although it has not yet been subjected to the kind of critical onslaught which was then being made upon socialist realism in Russia. 'We know our plays have many faults,' said Huan Liang, a young dramatist I met in Peking, who had just returned from ten months in a geological camp, 'but we are still learning our craft. The workers complain that we do not show them as real people but too much as mechanical puppets, and we are trying to correct this. In my new play, for instance, I have introduced a love story between an engineer and a female geological student, but this is a difficult theme to handle when my main concern is to show the workaday problems of the camp.'

With his sombre, taciturn features, determined jaw—with dark blue suit and peaked cap to match—Huan was a rugged representative of the new school. He had profited from the government's drive to popularise the dialogue play, for he came from a peasant family in the north and had won a scholarship to study in Peking—where there was even a course for illiterate writers who had shown some skill in dramatic invention.

He took me one night to a performance of *The Family*, a pre-Liberation play by Pa Chin, who is to the Chinese theatre what Shaw was to the English or, more properly, perhaps, since Pa is a revolutionary of passionate humanism, what O'Casey was to the Irish.

This play is probably the most popular in all China. I was constantly running into it in theatres, film studios and dramatic academies; but on this first encounter its immediate effect was to lull me to sleep. True, at the time I felt desperately tired—for the past month I had been straining too hard to cram a volume of observation into a mere paragraph of time—but the play itself was also much to blame. During the first act any hint of dramatic movement was effectively concealed by an hour of exposition—and with three more acts to come, in a language no more exciting for a foreigner to listen to than it is to read—the prospect was not one to stimulate the receptive faculties. Despite the unfaltering efforts of the faithful Pan who sat beside me, oblivious to the rest of the audience, translating the dialogue line by line in pinging, high-pitched tones that were a great deal more dramatic than any being used on the stage, I gradually felt myself dozing off. Sometimes I caught a momentary glimpse of the stage, only to see the same motionless actors in the same stationary positions, expounding their emotional problems in the same relentless monotones. I tried to force myself awake by shuffling and shifting in my seat. I pinched my fingers together, moistened my eyelids, rubbed my cheeks, but to no purpose. From time to time I heard the ferocious rattle of someone in the audience clearing his throat, while Pan's voice pinged imperturbably on: 'Now he is saying that they must FIGHT against their grandfather!' . . . 'She will RUN AWAY from home IF she is made to marry that ODIOUS old MAN!' . . . but the sounds came to my ears as through a distant haze.

Then abruptly, sometime after the second interval, the stage burst into dramatic life. The odious old man in question seized the servant girl he wanted for his concubine and stubbed a lighted cigarette on her naked wrist; and from that point the play moved forward with an angry intensity that made the discursive preamble seem doubly pointless and kept me awake and absorbed throughout.

It was easy to understand why it had become a revolutionary classic. It is a passionate protest against the domestic tyrannies of 'feudal society' in the early part of the century, indicting the evils of the concubine system, the grim tradition of binding the feet and the savage repressions which parents inflicted on their children. It is a play of deep humanity and stark horror in which the claustrophobic pattern of bourgeois family life generates tensions and antagonisms of a neurotic nastiness which even O'Neill might have envied.

There is the grandson who runs away from home when the servant girl he loves has thrown herself in the river after being beaten by his parents; there is the daughter beaten to death by the lecherous old man she has been made to marry; the despotic grandfather himself, who dies of a heart attack on hearing that one of his grandsons has run him into debt through consorting with prostitutes; and, dominating the household after his death, there is his malevolent concubine, who immediately asserts her authority by throwing out the eldest brother's wife—who is about to have a child—on the ground that 'the blood she will shed will act like a curse on the dead man's spirit.'

Thereafter the unhappy wife, whose husband is too feeble-minded to stand up to the concubine, is transported to what appears to be the coldest house in the district—bleak, windowless and snowbound—and here, with a gale howling outside, she dies in a scene which, even in Chinese, I found poignantly moving. Her epitaph, spoken by one of the grandsons, summarises the theme of the play: 'It was not entirely the concubine's fault—it's the rotten system we live in.'

If this play is a fair representation of middle-class life in the old days—which even the non-Marxists admit it to be—it is difficult to regard the new order of the Street Committee and the Social Rebuke as a change for the worse.

To my surprise, at the end of the performance there was little applause. The actors took two brief curtain calls, without smiles or ceremony, still maintaining the tragic expressions they had worn in the last act, while the audience, after perfunctory applause, bolted for the doors. When I asked Huan the reason for this he replied, with the only flicker of humour he had shown all evening: 'Perhaps after sitting so long they begin to feel tired.'

For virtue-loving delegates the Peking night offered additional and peculiar attractions.

'A party is being thrown for you,' announced Shen in his most methodical English manner, 'by the young people of the city. All delegates are invited to turn up for seven p.m.'

The party was held in the Hall of the People's Consultative Assembly; and the scene that ensued on our arrival was a convivial riot, a fantasy of real Peace and genuine Friendship, which defied the laws of ideological analysis and simply had to be taken spontaneously, uncritically, the way it was, precisely for what it was.

As the coach came to a halt outside the Hall hundreds of young Pekinese swept down the steps, shouting, cheering, clapping and leaping about in a rapture of enthusiasm. It was some minutes before we were able to force our way out of the coach and begin manœuvring up the steps. Eventually someone hacked a path through the welcoming throng, but suddenly the doors of the Hall jerked violently open and a battery of hundreds more young people raced frantically through them.

When comparative order had again been restored I proceeded to inch my way along. '*Ni-hao! Ni-hao!*' shouted hundreds of jubilant voices. '*Ni-hao! Ni-hao!*' I shouted back—and with that a kind of delirium came over the group surging round me. They grabbed my hands and bobbed feverishly up and down like boxers sweating off surplus weight on the morning of a big fight. Somebody identified me as English and the cry went up 'Hello-hello-hello! How-do-you-do! how-do-you-do! how-do-you-do!' In a tumult of shouting, skipping, jumping and heaving I was dragged, tugged, pulled, pushed and finally half-carried inside. Off went my coat. On came a chair. A dozen pairs of hands thrust me into it while beaming faces hemmed me in on all sides, but I could respond with nothing more constructive than a zany-like prolongation of the *Ni-hao–Ni-hao*–hello–hello–how-do-you-do theme.

Relief came with the arrival of a chunky, bespectacled girl who spoke excellent fourth-year student English: relief, at least, to the extent that I was able to communicate intelligibly with my expectant admirers—but what was there to say? What *can* you say on such occasions to a hundred different people at once which is not absurdly trite or utterly meaningless? You can, of course, tell them what you think about Marx–Leninism or, better still, ask what *they* think about it, but this did not seem the most appropriate moment for digging in that particular field. So there is nothing for it but to ask the first routine questions that come into your head and try to look interested in the routine answers.

But I discovered that they were too shy or too polite—or just too plain curious—to do anything except pass the conversational ball back to me with the same enquiring clichés, until I returned to the point from where I had started and looked dazedly around, trying to seem as overjoyed at having made their acquaintance as they abundantly were at having made mine.

For the occasion, those who could afford it had shed their boiler-suits: the girls had put on flowered blouses, a few—especially daring—*cheong-sams*, slit to an inch above the knee; and the boys either high-buttoned tunics, grey, brown or blue—the Chinese equivalent of naval Number Ones—or double-breasted suits. They had also laid on a western-style dance band which manfully ploughed its way several times over through a repertoire of three Strauss waltzes, two Gershwin tunes—imported from Moscow after the visit of *Porgy and Bess*—and four or five foxtrots of nondescript origin.

The Dancing is notable for the spirit of determined optimism in which it is carried out rather than for any flashes of technical dexterity. The western style, of course, is completely alien to their own and they approach it on a principle of whimsical propulsion, whereby the feet of the female dancer are saved from permanent mutilation only because she holds her partner as far away from her as is physically possible without losing contact with him altogether.

From the Dancing we proceeded to the Entertainment in which the younger artists of the Peking Opera companies, together with student acrobats, jugglers, equilibrists and dancers, provided a magnificent impromptu cabaret. Not a word was said all night about productivity or the advancement of 'techniques', and nobody made any speeches about Peace and Friendship; until Tripp, tugging my sleeve during one of the songs, observed darkly, 'It worries me to see all this frenzied enthusiasm. If they can get so excited over this, what would they be like if the government wanted to prepare them for a war?'

It was impossible, of course, to say; but the question could never be ignored, a lingering hangover which hit you at the end of every delegation party. But there was no point in spurning the party for fear of the consequences; it was even possible that some little good might be done by going to it with a good grace.

'How does it come about,' I asked the chunky girl in the middle of the last waltz, 'that so many people are here?'

She laughed in surprise. 'But there are not many enough. There were only tickets for two thousand, so only a few could be allotted to each college. But thousands more were crying to come. All the youth of Peking would have come if there had been room.'

'Why,' I asked, 'should they be so excited by our visit?'

'Because,' she replied simply, 'they are happy to see you.'

13

Breathing Space

A PAGE FROM MY PEKING NOTEBOOK

22 October

I HAVE caught Galal's cold so I am staying in bed—it's a good chance to catch up with my notes and try to *think*. Some of the delegates have gone to a handicraft producers' co-operative; some are gadding about the Zoo; some are at a timber-processing mill; one or two are just lying about the hotel.

Next week we leave for Manchuria: a depressing prospect. At the discussion on the Programme yesterday the Egyptians refused to go. 'For one,' said Galal, 'I have not finished my work on the Sport! For two, I do not like the weather north! For three, I am not interested in the north!' He is exclusively interested in the Sport. I wonder sometimes if he actually realises there has been a revolution around these parts.

The morning suddenly becomes, as it were, *mouvementé*.

Three servicemen arrive to clean up the room. I indicate I would like some fresh fruit but they don't understand. One dashes out while another produces pencil and paper for me to illustrate my wants. I sketch a rough approximation to an apple. Joyous recognition: he rushes away to get it.

The third serviceman carries on dusting. Lying back in bed, I spot three flies on the ceiling: a remarkable collection—you don't expect to see even one. I point them out to the serviceman. We count them solemnly together, one by one. He registers three distinct expressions: first, a mental note; then mild surprise; then righteous indignation. He rushes away for the swatter,

113

stalks them methodically round the room, and finally bears the dead bodies away in a large ash-tray.

Grinning with delight, the other two servicemen return, bearing before them enormous plates laden with every imaginable kind of fruit from pears to pomeloes but not, curiously, with one single apple.

They retire, and are followed in by the laundry boy. I get out of bed and put the dirty clothing into the bag provided for that purpose. I also give the boy a pair of blue socks which found their way into my bag by mistake a few days ago. They are socks of great age, holed and threadbare, and seem unlikely to survive the rest of the trip; I presume the owner had meant to throw them away but was thwarted by the efficiency of the service.

After various gesturings I succeed, as I think, in convincing the laundry boy that the socks are not mine. I am over-optimistic.

A few minutes later there is a knock at the door. Enter the laundry boy plus a very sprucely dressed young man in a double-breasted brown suit whom I don't seem to have seen before. He asks hesitantly, 'Do you speak English?'

When I assure him that I do he asks, '*Parlez-vous aussi francais?*'

'*Très petit peu,*' I murmur apologetically.

As though disbelieving me, he embarks upon a rapid speech in what sounds like very competent French in which he makes repeated references to a *chemise*. Eventually I infer that, apart from the mystery of the blue socks, he is under the impression that I have also mislaid a shirt. Earnestly I assure both him and the laundry boy that my shirts are all correct. I try to explain in my inadequate French that I was only concerned with the socks. I am not a collector of other people's socks and am only anxious that this particular pair reach their rightful owner. If they look at the socks in my bag they will see that the blue pair belong undeniably to somebody else for they are only half the size of my own.

The young man is still not satisfied. He must needs know the *colours* of all my other socks. Solemnly I bring out every sock

I possess, calling out the colour of each as though cataloguing them for sale. At last the young man appears convinced. He goes into brief conference with the boy, and then announces triumphantly, '*Peu-être appartiennent-ils à l'Italien.*'

'*Oui, oui. Certainement.*' I nod in vigorous agreement and lead them to the door. They bow courteously and move down the corridor with quiet determination towards the room of the unsuspecting Bernini.

I am scarcely back in bed before Liu arrives. He is the official in charge of the day-to-day running of the Programme. He works in the international section of the Youth Federation and this is his first big assignment.

He is a charming young man about twenty-eight or nine, with an infinite desire to please. He knows that I'm not especially enamoured of the official Programme and prefer to get about on my own, and he's very willing to help. But today he is embarrassed at having to report a failure.

In a fanciful moment the other day I told him I would rather go to Tibet than Manchuria, never expecting he would take me seriously. On the contrary, he has been to some pains on my behalf.

'We understand fully, Croft,' he begins (he is the only official who calls me by surname in the English manner), 'that you have not come simply as a delegate but also as a writer. We approve your interest in Tibet and we should like to send you there. But we are humbly sorry,' he folds his hands together in mock-supplication, 'and we ask to be forgiven. Our Federation does not have the money for such a long journey.'

Hastily I assure him that I quite understand the Federation's difficulty; after stumping up the fares for the far-flung members of our little delegation it is hardly to be expected that they will have any surplus cash to throw around on individual jaunts to Tibet.

'You must understand, Croft,' he insists, 'that we are very ashamed we cannot help you. But money is a terrible problem to us. We should like you to go to Tibet, though, if that is your wish, and if you can afford to pay for yourself we will arrange a passage for you.'

I make it very clear that I no longer have any wish to visit Tibet and gradually shift the discussion to the proposed visit to Manchuria.

'I feel,' I explain, 'that I should find more interesting material for my writing in Peking. Is it not possible for me to remain behind and catch up with the delegation later on in Shanghai?'

The distressed, unhappy look returns to Liu's face. 'Oh, Croft,' he sighs. 'Why have you not told us this before? It could have been arranged to suit you exactly. But now the Programme is arranged for the train. We have booked all the tickets. We have arranged two special coaches for the delegation. It would be very difficult to make a change.'

'But isn't it possible to change my ticket,' I ask, 'so that I could travel on later by myself?'

'This is our problem,' he says. 'This is something we cannot do. We can *cancel* tickets without trouble. But we cannot *get* them. Every ticket must be booked a long time in advance for we have six hundred million people but very few trains; so always, you see, we have a queue. I am deeply sorry, Croft,' he folds his hands again and prostrates himself. 'Infinite apologies. In this way we are very backward and we ask humble forgiveness.'

He withdraws with a succession of extraordinary genuflections and muttered mock pieties.

He is followed in shortly by Shen with the information that the doctor has asked to see me: in the surgery on the first floor.

Down we go, where I explain that I am suffering from nothing more serious than a common cold. If he can fix me up with a strong inhalant I assure him I shall be all right by tomorrow.

The doctor is not of the same view. A dapper, smiling young man, he motions me to strip completely and stretches me out on the surgery table. He then begins a comprehensive overhaul of my entire body. Having assured himself that the upper part of the anatomy seems in order he moves down to the stomach and begins pounding and digging the flesh with his fists. I notice detachedly that his finger-nails are black with dirt. When there is nothing else left to test he writes out an extensive prescription in Chinese and proceeds to dispense it himself. Suddenly he breaks off and suggests I should have a penicillin injection, which I firmly decline. At length I return to my room armed with four kinds of pills and two bottles of medicine.

Percy Dryden is waiting when I get back. He leaves for Melbourne tomorrow to cover the Olympic Games. I have been reading copies of his dispatches home during the two months he has been here and I am greatly impressed by their extreme honesty and objectivity. I am rather surprised that his paper should print them.

He has just come back from Port Arthur, where no other English journalist has been since the war.

'From what I've seen the Chinese know exactly where they're going and nothing will stop them getting there. It may take longer than they intended—at present they're trying to run before they can walk—they haven't got the capital equipment to develop their industry at the rate they expected—they're hopelessly short of everything, especially mechanised transport—and they've had a disastrous harvest this year which has knocked their economy sideways—but, having seen what they've done in the First Five-Year Plan, I have a feeling they're not going to slip far behind in the second.

'What nobody in Britain yet seems to realise is that if they complete their industrial transition by 1967, which is the date Chou En-lai has fixed, they will have an army of somewhere round a hundred million black-coated workers, the most colossal cheap labour force in the world, backed by government subsidy, manufacturing goods which could undercut any other market in the world. When that happens, embargoes and blackballing in the United Nations will seem pathetically out of date.'

With that sobering thought he takes his leave and is followed in by a girl from *China Youth*. She is pleasant, fresh-featured, smilingly self-possessed, in no way abashed at finding me abed, as though all her interviews were conducted in similar circumstances.

She wants me to write an article for her paper, describing my impressions of China, a prospect which fills me with dismay; but I feel I should oblige in return for hospitality given. The paper is the organ of the New Democratic Youth League and has immense influence. I point out that I will only write on condition that any criticism I make will be published in full. She assures me that it will be, but I am not convinced, and long before she goes I have changed my mind.

While she is here it seems a good opportunity to check on one of the more unsavoury pronouncements in a recent edition of *China Youth*. Large numbers of educated young Chinese, apparently, have been neglecting to instruct their parents in habits of 'correct thinking'; worse, in some families, parental misdemeanours, such as failure to take a responsible part in the co-operative or persisting in a 'feudal' attitude towards private business profits, have not been reported by their children to the police in the approved progressive manner. 'This,' says *China Youth*, 'shows that many young people are themselves deficient in ideological understanding. They must revise their habits so that they can contribute their full share to the advancement of the people's interests.'

'Do you seriously believe,' I ask the young girl, 'that it is a good thing to encourage children to spy on their parents in this way?'

Far from blushing with shame she could hardly sound more virtuous. 'We teach our children to be truly patriotic,' she says, 'because we believe that the happiness of the family comes from working for the happiness of the State.'

'In England,' I explain, 'we have a different attitude. We believe that the happiness of the State depends upon that of the family.'

'But if the family are not behaving correctly we consider it is the duty of their children to report them.'

'Doesn't that,' I suggest in my naif, old-fashioned way, 'tend to ruin family life altogether? After all, unless the children have been treated unjustly, or unless the parents have committed some very serious crime—and perhaps even then—the children must feel an instinctive loyalty to their parents which is deeper rooted than any feeling of patriotism.'

She brushes my silly old bourgeois scruples aside. 'In our country we have learnt from our own experience that patriotism is the most important instinct of all, although not all our young people have yet been able to realise this. For this reason we have constantly to remind them of their duties in our newspapers and discussion meetings.'

'So what happens to the parents,' I ask, 'after their misdeeds have been reported?'

'They are made conscious of their shortcomings and afterwards they feel glad that their children have helped them to improve their behaviour.'

'Don't you think they would be more likely to be somewhat angry with their children?'

'Some may be angry, but not very many, because they will realise the wrong they have done.'

'But what about the obstinate ones who don't?'

'They will have to pay the penalties given by the Court.'

'And what happens to family life after this?'

'I don't think this situation arises very often so that the problem is a very unimportant one.'

'Have you,' I ask, 'ever felt compelled to report any unpatriotic actions of your own parents?'

'They have never behaved unpatriotically,' she assures me—which I can well imagine—'but if such things did happen I should naturally do my duty.'

'Isn't it also likely,' I persist, although the discussion has long since passed the familiar futility point, 'that many children who, for some reason have a grudge against their parents, might exploit this particular form of patriotism to serve their own selfish ends? Wouldn't that, don't you think, be very likely to happen amongst young people who lack the correct ideological understanding?'

'It is true,' she admits, unhesitatingly, 'that some of our young

I

people have behaved badly in this way. There have been cases, for instance, of children inventing crimes for their parents because they wanted to secure their parents' houses. But these incidents are brought to light in the People's Courts and the children are given further education accordingly.'

There is an answer for everything; no eventuality, it seems, has been ignored; whenever was virtue so viciously solemn or patriotism so synthetic? I wish the lady a cordial farewell and she smiles radiantly on her way.

In the afternoon I am visited by Tamas Larincz, the Hungarian, who is Treasurer of the W.F.D.Y., a stocky, thick-set young man who is desperately determined to make the delegation a success and has been studiously careful to avoid communist sales talk. 'If you don't try to sell me the English system,' he says, 'I shall not attempt to sell you ours,' and his jet-black eyes and rosy cheeks positively glisten with goodwill to all men. I am still not sure whether he is biding his time to spring some kind of propaganda trap, but I know that, when attacked, he can defend his dialectical position in five different languages and this seems as good a time as any to challenge him.

I outline the gist of my conversation with the *China Youth* girl. 'Is this an attitude you support?' I ask him. 'Do you personally believe in this kind of patriotism?'

I don't expect a straight answer but, at least, he sees that it's a significant question.

Hunching his shoulders, he broods deeply upon it. 'This is a very delicate issue,' he admits at length. 'I would not like to answer immediately.'

'Let me put it more simply,' I say. 'Ignoring specific cases, do you believe in the principle of children telling tales on their parents?'

The question neither disturbs nor defeats him. He simply refuses to answer it; either this particular chapter of the Book is not very explicit or else he's uncertain of the current form. 'I think you should speak to several people about this,' he says, 'and find out their feelings in the matter.'

He goes out and returns a few minutes later with Liu, who listens patiently while I repeat the question. His reaction is equally thoughtful and almost identical: 'I couldn't say what should be the general rule, although I think such cases are rare. I suggest you speak to various other people and if their answers still do not satisfy you I think you have good grounds for criticism.'

I may or may not put the question again. I can't wait forever for someone to have the guts to answer it.

Now Muriel returns from the Zoo to bemoan the activities of Tripp. He has done nothing but worry about being on the delegation and now he's worrying her too. 'He says that when we get back home we'll find it impossible to get jobs. If employers know you've been to China they will automatically suspect you're a communist. He's sure that will happen to us.'

I reassure her that it will not, but wonder the while if the depressing Tripp may not actually have a point.

My cold has been pampered long enough and I decide to go to tonight's Social Evening. It's being given by the students of the Foreign Language Institute and I want to meet some of the English-speaking types.

As it happens they also want to meet me. There are over three hundred in the English faculty and the opportunity to try out their vocabulary throws them into a state of abandoned enthusiasm. I am mobbed immediately on arrival, thrust into a chair and pelted with a non-stop volley of questions on subjects as commonplace as cricket and as recondite as Anglo-Saxon Grammar. When I let slip that I am a Shakespearean producer of sorts, the beaming faces break into expressions of idolatrous ecstasy: 'What Shakespeare plays have you produced?' 'When is your company coming to Peking?' 'Have you done *Romeo and Juliet*?—we had it in Peking last year!' 'Please, please recite some Shakespeare for us!'

They have arranged among themselves a concert for our benefit, each faculty singing songs thought appropriate to the countries represented on the delegation. The English faculty

rather oddly choose *Swannee River*; their passionate earnestness
to please compensates for the grinding havoc they make of it and
then, especially to please me, they prevail upon one of their
number to recite, 'Shall I compare thee to a summer's day?' He is
a smiling, elegant youth, wearing a raffish bow tie and double-
breasted fawn suit and he jauntily sports a long cigarette-holder,
but the stresses and rhythms of the Shakespearean sonnet utterly
defeat him: he speaks the first few words of each line in a nasal
monotone, ignores the cæsura, and hits the middle syllable with
the sharp ferocity of a Chinese gong: 'Shall-I-compare-THEE!!!'
Then, having flattened out the rest of the line, he takes a tremendous swipe at the end syllable: 'to-a-summer's-DAY!!!!!' It is
dreadful to listen to, but also fresh and exhilarating because, for
him and his classmates, it represents at least a means of friendly
communication.

It also sends them wild with desire to hear Shakespeare spoken
in his native tongue. I am impelled on to the platform and,
through the mental fog that always engulfs me on these occasions,
struggle to remember a few lines from the canon that might suit
the general taste. Unfortunately, the only sequences that come
to mind are from the more war-like moments of *Henry V*. I
summarily dismiss 'Once more unto the breach' and the rhetoric
before Harfleur, toy with the monologue on kingship and the
sombre beauties of 'all those arms and heads cut off in battle',
and finally settle in desperation for Crispin's Day. From the
delirious applause with which they receive it I can only conclude
that the meaning has escaped them completely, an impression
which is quickly confirmed when they crowd around in almost
trance-like adoration, murmuring, 'Thank you—thank you for
the beautiful music of Shakespeare.'

In the circumstances I abandon hope of ever talking to a
Chinese student alone; but that apart, this has been an evening
with which I can find no fault.

Back in the hotel, Muriel calls me into her room, where I find
Tripp groping on all fours under the bed. 'He tells me the rooms
are all wired,' she says, 'so I've asked him to see what he can find.'

Having emerged from beneath the bed he starts poking under the carpet. 'I don't know what to make of it,' he says. 'I can't somehow believe they would tap us but, at the same time, I feel convinced that they do.' Suddenly he jumps up, claps one hand across his chest in Union debating style and declaims with measured deliberation to the empty spaces of the room: 'Friends, and all who may be listening in, I am about to make a speech! I want to explain that for the rest of the evening we three people in this room will be talking about entirely personal matters. I invite you therefore to switch off your machines, take a rest from eavesdropping, and go to your beds. We are enjoying our stay in Peking and, although it may be the practice in other communist countries to spy on their guests, I had expected something better of the People's Republic of China!'

In the passage outside I stumble upon Vladimir and Carl, the Danish journalist, embroiled in political argument. Their understanding of each other is impeded by the fact that they're both speaking in English and, whereas Vladimir's vocabulary is merely limited, Carl's is practically non-existent. Carl is a big-boned giant of twenty-five, with a sharply Danish sense of humour. Despite his inadequate linguistic resources, he delights in telling the communist delegates what is wrong with their political system.

The present exercise would be farcical if it were not so serious. I gather they are discussing the Russian Revolution but cannot fathom which aspect. Carl maintains that Britain and France intervened in it because 'they had lost a partner, understand you?' while Vladimir speaks continually of 'the burden on the shoulder of Russia'. 'That,' says Carl, 'is only speak-word— what say you?—propaganda.'

He proceeds to paste Vladimir with all the iniquities of the communist system from Lenin onwards: 'You make great mistakes—ha!—what say you?—terrible things—but you no admit them—all long, Russia do killing—Stalin like Hitler, very bad— terrible cruel man—Cold War—no think of other side—all wrong—many years Russia make war only.'

Vladimir listens calmly: perhaps the words hurt less in Carl's basic phrasing than they would in Russian. He condemns British support of the White Army during the Revolution and refuses to budge on the need for violence in the 'twenties; but on the Cold War he admits: 'Great fault lay with Russia. Now we know that is so, but that also is past. Now we want to go to future in peace.'

'But not so,' cries Carl. 'Look what happen in Poland! Czechoslovakia! Hungary! No peace there. Look what you do. No need you be there. No need Russian armies there. Why stay you then? Cause trouble only, not cause peace for future.'

'Who causes trouble in Formosa?' demands Vladimir angrily, while I intervene to suggest that probably nobody wants to cause trouble anywhere but, until each side can trust the other, trouble is bound to come. 'That,' says Vladimir with emphatic gravity, 'is the big thing. Perhaps it is really the only thing that divides us—mutual distrust.'

Bernini passes by in the corridor and mutters a perfunctory '*Dormez bien*'; and Shakir, after listening in to the argument for a moment, shrugs his shoulders and moves rapidly off. 'Politics! politics!' he calls back from his doorway. 'Communist! Democrat! Tory! Why not you all stop talking and talk some little sense?'

It is as good a cue as any for bed.

14

To the North

THE following afternoon just before five o'clock I called to see Arthur Boyd. Apart from the Legation officials he was my only reliable source of information on events in the outside world. He switched on his radio and we waited for the B.B.C. news from Hong Kong.

The announcer's voice crackled excitedly through the air: 'Riots have broken out in Budapest . . . police have fired on demonstrators in Red Square . . . armed workers have attacked Government offices. . . . Kruschev has ordered the return of Russian warships *en route* to Poland . . .'

It was October 23rd. Next day I left for Manchuria and it was another two weeks before I caught up with the news.

From Peking to Shenyang takes thirty-six hours by train. For the delegation two special coaches were provided, with sleeping-car, dining-car and a personal staff of attendants and cooks who were to stay with us throughout the rest of the trip—opulent luxury compared to the cramped compartments and Spartan facilities offered to the ordinary passengers. While I regretted being unable to study travelling conditions in the raw, conversely I was glad to be denied the opportunity.

There was a ceremonial send-off with officials and representatives of this and that committee, and a throng of beaming young people chanting songs on the platform.

I retired to my compartment, but suddenly Vladimir rushed in in a state of great excitement. 'Come and see!' he insisted, tugging me by the arm. 'It is something incredible! Wife of my interpreter is outside. She will have child in few days' time but,' he roared, shaking me furiously by the shoulders, 'there is nothing to see! NOTHING! IT IS FANTASTICAL!'

While I smiled and shook hands with the charming Chinese lady in question, Vladimir dashed back into the carriage, reappeared with his suitcase and pulled out a set of finely-lacquered Russian spoons. 'From Russian boy with two fine children,' he cried admiringly, 'to Chinese girl who will have big fine child in very quick time!'

Galal and Shakir also turned out to see us off, Galal somewhat the worse for wear after hitting the cognac hard at a little party he had thrown the previous night. They planned to rejoin the delegation at Tientsin. The Y.M.C.A. party had already departed, forming a delegation of their own, which would catch up with the main body in Shanghai.

No purpose would be served in elaborating the details of this journey. I learnt nothing from it of Chinese conditions and very little of the Chinese scene, for one paddy-field glimpsed from a moving vehicle is much the same as another. I saw, of course, something of eternal China in the armies of labourers toiling down distant, dusty roads under the bamboo yoke and in the long files of mule wagons and bicycle carts hauling their overloaded way endlessly to hidden destinations; but the only human interest in the journey was generated by the delegates themselves.

Ricardo, the gangling young Spaniard, came of a wealthy family in Madrid and had once been thrown out of his home for openly advocating the overthrow of Franco. He had a smattering of four languages but was difficult to comprehend in one, and it was some time before I realised that he was as much anti-communist as anti-fascist. He belonged to the February the First underground student movement, which aims at reconciling all anti-fascist elements, including Catholics, in an attempt to get rid of Franco.

'But by peaceful revolution only,' he said. 'No violence. We have shed enough blood already.'

He had come to China on a bogus passport and with little clothing save what he stood up in. If the police learnt of his trip he took it for granted he would be sent to prison on his return. 'But what of that? All my friends have been in prison. That is the honour of the Spanish student. Without it we lose our self-respect.'

He made several attempts during the course of the journey to renew his wooing of Muriel but ran into stiff competition with Baghdadi, the Syrian, who described himself as a *fonctionnaire* and brought such a polished intensity to the function in hand that, despite the protective safety of numbers, before we reached Shenyang he had given Muriel some distinctly uneasy moments. His French was so enchanting to listen to that I once endeavoured to sustain a conversation with him; he spoke to me with laborious simplicity as to a child, but the effort proved too exhausting for both of us: all I could gather was that he had formerly been an Army officer and was now a government inspector of Physical Training. This was not the only occasion when I found myself cursing my stupid linguistic insularity; everybody, it seemed, except the English, could get along competently in two languages at least.

Except, perhaps, for Pablo, the Cuban. The only people he could talk to at all were Ricardo and the Spanish interpreter. There was also a Chilean delegate but, for some reason, he boycotted Pablo and hung continually round the French-speaking contingent. Since Ricardo buzzed ebulliently to whichever group the fancy took him and the Spanish interpreter spent most of his time in the interpreters' cabin, the coffee-coloured Pablo was probably the most silent delegate ever to visit China. But he seemed happy in his isolation. He leaned back in his seat, curled his long legs under him, smiled amicably around, and from time to time sang plaintive little Cuban songs in a rich baritone voice which everyone applauded and which made him seem a very pleasant fellow if only you could have got to know him. I never discovered what he was doing on the delegation; he never asked questions at any of the conferences; when toasts were being proposed at official dinners, he tended to contribute a song instead of a speech; and he seemed to take perfectly for granted everything that happened to him.

The Belgians, French and Italians showed themselves as insular as the English, for they fell into closed little groups of their own and showed no desire to move outside them. Bernini, however, was in a class apart. Whether it was through the majesty of his office as President of the W.F.D.Y. or a preoccupation with the global aims of communism, he remained strangely aloof from all except his lieutenant Tamas and the East German communist, Heinz, speaking only when spoken to, surveying the passing landscape with the vacant disinterest of a man too deep in thought to notice it was there.

Or perhaps too bored. As the journey progressed I decided that was it. Bernini had done it all before. It was a wearisome chore for him. I took to watching him when we stopped along the route. At every station there was a welcoming party of Youth Leaguers and Young Pioneers hustled up for the occasion to greet us with song. There was friendly waving and smiling all round and everyone tried to look as if they meant it. But Bernini never succeeded. A glassy smile would cross his saturnine features; he would wave his hand mechanically, as though from memory, and continue going through the motions with diminishing effort as the train pulled away, but I felt certain he was hardly aware that we had ever actually stopped. It may be that the strain of being a professional delegate on the strenuous communist circuit would do this to anybody, but I should have expected him to take his duties more seriously. 'Bernini has many hands to shake,' chuckled Vladimir confidentially. 'But he not always know which hand is which. He think himself king of all young communists. But not for me. I think him VERY BAD king—like stupid kings of *your* country.'

Lest I should seem to paint Vladimir as the nigger in the communist woodpile—and because this account may be duly read in Moscow—let me state categorically that, whatever mocking shafts he may have levelled at other members of the Marxist fraternity, and whatever strictures he might have passed on the Stalinist era, he never uttered one word which could have been taken as a criticism of the present Russian set-up. That is not to say that he enthused about it; he remained as reticent on the subject as a loyal Englishman might about his own government when travelling amongst foreigners who disapprove of its policy.

In the course of the journey he finished reading my novel, *Spare the Rod,* and gave me the most potent criticism of it I had ever had. 'It has very bad fault,' he said. 'You give your hero no private life. You should show his own problems, not just those of school and teacher. You do not show wife or girl friend. This is hero without love. I am sure also you have much more to say. This is novel, not of end, but only of beginning.'

This was rather the opposite to the socialist–realist analysis I had expected, but there was a more damning comment to come. 'You make your hero think too much. Always you say what he thinks. You state every thought. This is very dull to read—not good writing. In good writers the thoughts are always implied.' However, there was a saving clause. 'Your teachers are very real and they save your book from great dullness. It seems to me that all teachers must be same, for in Russia are also very bad teachers and—how you say?—sour. It seems to go with teaching. But your inspector,' he continued, 'is not real character [he was in fact the only entirely fictitious character in the book]. He has only one side—how you say?—all white character. This is very bad—as in bad Russian novel. Such characters are very poor. We have many such in our novels but these belong to bad writers. You see,' he explained, 'although I speak English like schoolboy I can read everything in books. I write all new words in little notebook and so I increase vocabulary every day.'

Aldington and Maugham were his favourite English authors. 'They are crazy for Aldington in Moscow,' he told me. 'He is great idol of all young students. He is writer of great feeling, of strong ideas.' I told him about Aldington's recent book on T. E. Lawrence and its reception in the English Press, but he had only heard of Lawrence as 'famous English spy'. When I explained that this was not how most Englishmen regarded the hero of Arabia he was considerably puzzled. 'I think you have very strange government,' he said, 'to fight for Arab country with English spy. But very strange Englishman also to live like Arab. Not good for Arabs, not good for Englishman.'

'Somerset Maugham also,' he said, 'likes to show himself as spy. But this is writing of—how you say?—poseur. I have read all novels of Maugham and am sure such man was never spy. He is not type of man for spy. Would be shot, very quick,' he added grimly, 'in war with my country.

'But he is very fine writer,' he declared, 'very, *very* fine. It is very pleasant to study English through his novels. His language is so beautiful and he has very pure style. But he has also very great defect—it seems to me it is greatest of all. He writes without heart. His novels are all from head—all brains. It seems to me he does not like humanity very much. He is cold writer. For this reason,' he concluded surprisingly, 'I do not like him so much as Hemingway, who is writer of great feeling and truth, but not yet popular in Moscow.'

From Maugham we turned to Galsworthy, also popular in Moscow.

When I explained that Galsworthy's social criticisms bore little relation to the contemporary English scene, Vladimir replied, 'We do not read him for his ideas but for his dramatic qualities. He is true dramatist of situation. In same way,' he said, 'we like your imperialist Kipling. He was real poet. With such poetry there are no frontiers.'

'Not even,' I suggested whimsically, 'the North-west?'—and promptly wished I hadn't, because, having missed the point, he insisted that I explain it in detail.

'It is a pity,' he said, 'you cannot speak our language, for we also have such poets. There are many who cry for patriotism, or for war, or against war. They are—how you say?—hysterical. But we have some also who write great verse of humanity, for the soul of our people is deep. But poetry is not universal like novel.

You cannot read poems in foreign language. You can understand words but not between . . . strokes—do you say?—not between lines. One poem by your Kipling,' he added, 'I know very well. I learn it from my teacher. It is when he talks to his son and tells him—how you say?—to grow up into a man. That is poem of good feeling, written from heart. Very, *very* good poem.'

15

In Manchuria

I was in Manchuria, or what, for emotional and understandable reasons of their own, the Chinese now call North-east China, for ten days.

It is, I suppose, mile for mile, the densest industrial area of the earth. It has been ravaged and exploited, plundered and despoiled, first by the Japanese invaders and after them by the Russians but, since 1949, with gigantic aid from the Soviet—an ironic compensation for the estimated £500 million worth of looting and dismantlement during their post-war occupation—its productivity has multiplied four and five times over. It represents not only the industrial heart of China but also the lifeline by which the Second Five-Year Plan will stand or fall.

For students of industrial development, perhaps, a crowded week in this part of the world would amount to an experience of almost poetic intensity; for me, it was a journey into caverns of ever-thickening darkness which I entered with reluctant acquiescence, and left with a sense of exhausted futility.

To say I was unmoved, however, on this heaving industrial ocean is not to say I was unimpressed; only that I had no means of measuring the significance of what was going on. I could register abstractly the fact that China was now building her own jet planes; that the Anshan Iron and Steel Combine was producing nearly three million tons of pig-iron and two million tons of steel products per year; that metal turning lathes and planing machines, now being produced for the first time in Shenyang, were (according to Crabb, who claimed to be an expert on the subject) 'as good as anything produced by America'; that the out-

put of the automatic seamless tube factories, the first of which had
opened only a year ago, was nothing short of miraculous; that
stainless and rolled steel had not been produced at all before the
Liberation; that it was a remarkable achievement for a country
as scientifically backward as China to be producing up-to-date
turbines and transformers, locomotives, twenty-four-row sowing
machines, refrigerators, X-ray equipment and electrical sterilising
machines. I could believe all this and more, and take it on trust,
as they proudly insisted you should, that in every town except
Harbin, they were now developing their own industrial plants
without technical assistance from the Russians; but what it all
amounted to—or might amount to when they complete the process of transition in another ten years or so—I could only begin
to guess. But even if they were running too fast too soon, and
neither their machines nor their economy will stand the pace—
a possibility which they themselves refused to acknowledge in
public—I had the sharply uneasy feeling that, sooner or later,
the gaunt chimneys belching black smoke into the skies of Manchuria are going to provide a more formidable threat to western
prosperity than any ideological edict issuing from Peking.

To suppose, as some commentators have done from afar, that
the rigours of the totalitarian yoke have induced a spirit of rest-
lessness among the workers is wishful, if not dangerous, thinking.
In Manchuria at least, possibly, of course, only by contrast with
the conditions they had suffered under the Japanese, they seemed
more than contented with their lot. It is true that many of them
look dog-tired, for, although they keep rigidly to an eight-hour
day for six days of the week, there are no annual holidays, and
they are subject to the continual strain of increasing their productivity 'in the cause of national construction'—with all the
accompanying palaver of factory slogans, labour heroes, model
workers, wall newspapers and workroom statistics to spur them
on; nor is the day's work over when the factory siren sounds, for
then there are literacy classes to attend, lectures on 'Current
Events' to listen to, trade-union meetings and sessions of criticism
and self-criticism to take part in.

On the other hand, working conditions compare favourably with the average in England. The new factories are centrally heated in winter and air-cooled in summer. There are clinics and recreation-rooms; well-run nurseries and canteens which serve meals a great deal more nourishing than many I had in the delegation hotels. Many factories run their own operatic and dramatic ensembles, and in every town there are Palaces of Culture and Sport where the air of abandoned enjoyment hardly suggests that the workers have anything particularly pressing on their minds.

Everywhere new housing estates were going up in feverish profusion, although I was told that, despite heavy appropriations, the authorities could still not afford to rehouse all the workers from the dank hovels of pre-Liberation days. Even so, they seemed to be accommodating a fair number. The new red-brick tenements were neither more ugly nor less habitable than similar establishments I had visited in Brixton and Camberwell, albeit they were a great deal more overcrowded.

I spent a moderately instructive afternoon in one of these in Shenyang (or, as it was formerly known, Mukden), talking to two young housewives, Mrs. Chen Yi-hai and Mrs. Wang Shu-mei.

Mrs. Chen lived on the first floor with her four-year-old son. She saw her husband only at week-ends because he slept in the steel mill where he worked, outside town. Her flat consisted of a single living-room-cum-bedroom and a kitchen and lavatory which she shared with the family next door. 'This,' she said, 'is the allowance for a family with one child.' When I enquired about a bathroom she explained that baths had to be taken communally in a separate building.

With its whitewashed walls and concrete floor the ill-lit living-room could hardly be called inviting, but she had done her best to brighten things up. Flower-prints, family photographs, pictures of birds and animals—and of course, of Chairman Mao—were pinned to the walls, and she had allowed herself the luxury of brightly coloured pillow-cases and a brocaded green coverlet for the bed. Chinese lanterns and red-and-green streamers hung gaily from the ceiling, but she denied that they had been put up specially for my benefit. 'When I first came here a year ago,' she said, 'I put them up to celebrate my new-found happiness, and they have been there ever since.'

'Don't you feel lonely,' I asked, 'with your husband away all week?'

'Not really lonely,' she said, 'though sometimes I feel sad. But there is always too much to do to be lonely.'

I saw her point when she explained that she belonged to the Street Committee.

'There are many things to do,' she said. 'I organise crèches for the children of neighbours who are out at work, and I try to educate other housewives in hygiene and cleanliness. Some days I go out to nurse sick people, and other times I have to visit disorderly tenants and tell them to improve their behaviour.'

'What happens if they take no notice?' I asked.

'I have to report them to the leader of the Committee.'

'And then?'

'Then she will rebuke them and persuade them to show more respect for their neighbours.'

'Supposing they still go on misbehaving?'

For a moment she seemed to hesitate, but then the reply came pat: 'Such cases are very rare. There have been none in my experience.'

The most surprising thing about Mrs. Chen was that she was a fourth-year pupil at the local primary school, which she attended two hours every afternoon for lessons in Chinese, mathematics and 'General Culture'. She had received no education as a child and now she was trying to catch up. Her neighbours apparently were equally industrious: some attended the same school; some went to evening classes; and those with large families received visits from the teacher in their own homes. When Mrs. Chen completed her course it was her ambition to become a teacher herself in one of the literacy classes.

The interview finished on an abrupt and painful note.

She had explained in some detail how she budgeted her husband's monthly income: twenty *yuan* for his food and pocket-

K

money, six *yuan* for rent, sixteen for herself and her son, six for milk and eight to be put in the bank—and then, when I enquired how this compared with family spending in the old days, she suddenly broke down in tears.

It seemed that my question had reminded her of pre-Liberation conditions, and of her father, who had died of sickness and hunger. He had never known what it was to be happy, she said, to have regular wages and enough for clothing and food for the family. 'He was the slave to a cruel landlord, who beat him and stole most of his earnings. I shall never forget what he suffered.'

She lifted her young boy from her knee and tried to wipe away her tears. Pan murmured soothingly to her; but I could think of nothing to say, for while I felt instinctively moved by her grief some mean political whisper within warned me that the tears might be merely a trick.

Mrs. Wang lived on the floor above in a less tidy, undecorated room where the homely smell of oatmeal and baking seeped through from the kitchen.

She was a duskily handsome woman with sparkling brown eyes and a trim figure neatly enhanced by tight-fitting slacks and a gay flowered blouse. She also belonged to the Street Committee but her main interest seemed to be less in welfare than in the discussion of Current Affairs. Her greatest enjoyment, she said, came from reading the daily newspapers and discussing the world situation.

Since she volunteered this information cheerfully I felt no compunction in taking her up on it.

'What do you think should be done,' I asked, 'to improve relations between China and the western countries?'

I could have saved my breath, for though, as she said, she had never been interviewed before, she could beat the professionals at their own game. 'I have only just begun to study,' she apologised, 'so I can say nothing of international affairs. This is something I do not yet understand. All I know is that China wants peace with all the world.'

She did not belong to the Party, but her husband was a member of the Youth League and she was studying hard to gain membership herself. Previously she had lived in a slum with her husband's parents and family. Her father had been beaten to death by the Japanese in the mines and her mother had died of T.B. She stated these facts dispassionately, as faded memories which bore no relationship to the delights of the new life she had discovered.

Later, when I saw the damp and primitive squalor of the slums, I could understand better how she felt and could appreciate the jubilant impulse which had caused Mrs. Chen to go to town on her decorations.

As China possesses the longest wall in the world, so it can boast one of the largest holes.

The open-cast coal-mine at Fushun is nearly four miles long, half a mile wide and six hundred feet deep; and within five years, they say, it will have been dug a further seven hundred feet. With the aid of pneumatic drills it now produces ten thousand tons of coal a day, an output nearly five times greater than in 1949, with substantial by-products of synthetic petroleum, cement, and—a recent discovery—*Han yaa*, a medicine for the treatment of blood disorders. Under the Japanese and Kuomintang, they said, the mine was so badly mismanaged that casualties from fires and floods were high; now they rarely occurred, and three days were set aside each month for the repair and examination of machines.

The miner, with an average wage of seventy-five *yuan* per month in the open mine (eighty in the three closed mines), is approximately twenty per cent better off than the administrative worker. A trade-union official expressed this improvement succinctly: 'Nowadays nearly every miner is a married man. Before, only twenty per cent of them married because the womenfolk knew that they would never earn enough to bring up a family.'

I tackled this official on the question of holidays. 'The country is backward,' he said, 'and we feel that production will fall disastrously if we restore annual holidays. This happened in 1952, but production went down by five per cent, and since that time we have given up holidays. The workers do not raise the demand because they realise the country's needs.'

'But surely,' I said, 'if they are given no rest at all their output is bound to suffer anyway.'

'I agree,' he conceded dubiously, 'that holidays are necessary, and perhaps in the Second Five-Year Plan we shall re-introduce them. But meantime we have made very big improvements in welfare and canteen facilities so that the miners don't suffer from the strain.'

The main function of the trade union, it appeared, was to criticise the municipal administration. 'For instance,' he said, 'last year the miners needed more houses, but the city bureau refused to build them. The union complained, and so the houses were provided. Then there are commodities. Sometimes the miners are dissatisfied with the quality of goods in the shops, but we complain to the government and the quality is improved.'

'Has any issue arisen when the miners have threatened to strike?'

'That is unlikely to happen so long as we look after their interests and so long as they realise their duties in the cause of national construction.'

One miner who genuinely realised this was Liu Yung-tang, who had worked in the Dragon and Pea-hen—the biggest of the three closed mines—for fifteen years.

I made my way to his home through a maze of wooden and straw hovels, down bumpy lanes where labourers tugged and hauled dilapidated carts laden with stones and bricks and children squatted over crude sanitary fixtures on patches of waste land. He was not expecting me and, despite the inhibiting presence of Pan, I think his family and myself equally enjoyed meeting each other.

With his wife and young son he lived in a small room in a Japanese-built house and shared the kitchen with another family. His two eldest sons were strapping lads of sixteen and eighteen who worked in an ammunition factory and slept in one of the town dormitories. When I called, the evening meal was being prepared on a little table propped up on the bed.

Yes, said Liu, he could certainly do with a holiday, but he didn't worry too much about it because working conditions were so much better than they used to be in the days when nobody even mentioned holidays. Now he worked a regular eight-hour day and he could go down the mine without wondering if he would ever come up again alive; he could bring up his young son properly, buy two suits of clothing a year, and even invest some of his wages in national bonds.

'Is Mrs. Liu happy about this?' I asked.

Yes, Mrs. Liu, a buxom, beaming woman in her early fifties, took time off from kneading liver balls on a wooden board to confirm that she was very happy. It would have been difficult indeed to imagine a housewife who could possibly look happier, with her young son bustling about the kitchen to help her, her elder sons coming in from work, greasy, begrimed and affectionate, and a stranger from a remote country suddenly arrived to sample the pleasures of her board.

No, she had no problems besides looking after her family, although living in such a tiny room always bothered her. Yes, she took an active part in the cultural performances in the town and she also belonged to a women's organisation which specialised in sanitation and hygiene work.

She went to evening classes with the rest of the family three times a week, and she was gradually learning to read. Some nights they also went to film-shows or they might invite other families to visit them—'to play games amongst ourselves and study the newspapers'.

'Do you take any interest in politics?' I asked her husband.

'Yes,' he said, 'but not in the big things. They are too big for me. I think only of my mine and what I can do to improve it.'

'Do you belong to the Communist Party?'

'Yes. I qualified for membership in 1952.'

'Do many of your workmates belong to it?'

For some reason he replied that they did, but Pan assured me privately that this was impossible—'There are fifteen thousand miners in Fushun, and it cannot be imagined that even one half of that number have been admitted to the Party!'

However, we did not venture any further on the ideological front, and the meeting developed into a gay family party, typified by Liu's interjection when I asked the eldest son if he had yet started courting: 'No,' said his father, while the rest of the family hooted with laughter, 'but he's trying hard to.' As our smart Molotova car pulled away from the cramped but happy home, Pan turned to me and said, 'I think you have enjoyed for the first time your meeting with the Chinese people.'

'Yes,' I said, 'I think I have only met them for the first time.'

There could be no conflict of feeling about the merits of the Old Miners' Home at Fushun. Its purpose was solely to provide for its occupants, in the evening of their lives, the ordinary material comforts and consideration which had been denied them for longer than most of them could remember.

It accommodated one hundred and fifty men who were too old or too worn out for further employment and who had no homes to return to. They were given State pensions which covered all their wants and they lived in conditions of comparative luxury, two to a room, with central heating, spacious windows, cheerful wallpaper and an overall atmosphere of relaxed comfort and well-being.

Without exception they had suffered terrible hardships under the Japanese, the marks of which they would carry to their graves. They were the only men I met in China who looked a good deal older than they were. Listening to their stories of the occupation, I wondered how some of them had survived at all.

Huan Liu was a typical example. He was only sixty-three, but with his lined and battered face, punched-in cheeks and tight-drawn eyes he looked nearer to ninety. He spoke with a stammer and his shrivelled hands twitched continually beyond his control.

When I asked him about conditions under the Japanese he

winced and trembled as though from a blow. As he spoke of the gruesome conditions in the mines, of the floggings and barbarities and the slavery of the fourteen- and sixteen-hour day his voice rose sharply in anguished recollection.

'When we had no strength to lift our picks,' he said, pulling back his sleeve to show the scars and wounds on his arm, 'we were whipped and beaten with spiked clubs till our bodies were covered with holes and our backs dripped with blood. We were treated like dogs, like horses'—his voice rose higher, half-strangled with pain—'like cattle—not like human beings. Every day we saw our workmates beaten unconscious, to be kicked and trampled to death, and every day we fought to keep on our feet because, for every dead man, there were twenty more waiting to work to keep themselves from starving.'

There was no need to look at his wounds to believe him implicitly; his pathetic, broken figure told its own tale. Pan, who had accompanied me, was moved almost to tears, and for some minutes, ignoring his official duties, he talked tenderly to the old man in his own language. 'I have heard of such sufferings before,' he told me, 'but it is the first time I have seen them face to face.'

When we rose to go Huan shook hands and thanked me for calling to see him. Then he added something else which Pan chose not to translate. When I asked him what had been said he tried to brush the matter aside. 'Oh, he just made some sentimental remarks,' he said. 'Not very interesting to you.'

'Even so,' I said, 'they were meant for me to hear. I should be glad to know.'

'Very well,' said Pan, 'but it was not my wish to tell you. He said that without the help of the Communist Party he would not be alive today. From his own experience he believes that socialism is a good way to go.'

Tsing Ching-shan, a bald-headed, withered little man of seventy-five, told much the same story, but he had not been so broken by his sufferings. He had a hearty sense of humour, with twinkling eyes, and was remarkably lively in his movements. His room was the tidiest and most cheerful in the home. The walls were covered with pictures of innumerable children and richly coloured scenes from Chinese Opera, with a multi-coloured quilt on the bed and goldfish bowls and large pots of chrysanthemums on the window-sill.

He had started in the mines as a boy of six, looking after the mules and gigs, and had never once been outside his native Fushun.

When I asked if he had met any foreigners before, he suddenly winced and jumped from his chair, in a state of great agitation. Apparently he had taken my question as a joking reference to the Japanese and it took some time for Pan to persuade him that this was not what I meant. When the misunderstanding had been cleared up he asked me to excuse his behaviour and then surprised me by saying that the Home had recently been visited by a Japanese Trade Union Delegation.

'I should hardly have thought they would have been welcome,' I remarked.

'It was a different matter,' he said. 'They were people who wanted peace, not war. We had no grudge against them.'

'Do you separate the men who ran the mines from the Japanese people in general?'

'You cannot compare the two. Our old taskmasters were beasts, evil men who were amused by our suffering. They were only interested in themselves, but they did not represent the people. The real Japanese are like the people of every other country. They want only to live in peace with all the world.'

'Do you,' I asked, timorously—and idiotically in the circumstances—'take any interest in political matters?'

The question had to be repeated because at first he could not understand it. When at length he did he shook with laughter.

'Nobody has ever asked me that before,' he said. 'I've never given the matter a thought. I can only say I want the general prosperity of the whole country.'

So I left politics alone for the rest of the afternoon and joined Huan and Tsing and their friends in the games-room where they taught me to play mah-jong and told me stories about their early days in the mines, and of the changes they had seen from the start of the century onwards, and of the furore there had been one day in 1913 when a peasant, digging his land, had struck unwittingly upon the surface of the huge vein which was to be opened up as the Lung Fung open-cast mine, and of the coming of the Japanese in 1931, and of the joy of the Liberation . . .

'In 1949, when the Home was opened,' the Director told me, 'many of these men were too weak even to climb up the stairs. They had worked many years as slaves, receiving no pay and only enough rice to keep them from starving. They lived herded together in huts, eighty and ninety to a room, with neither fresh air nor fuel, in a space barely sufficient for twenty. In Europe I don't think you have anything with which to compare these conditions, and though we might still seem backward today you must compare everything with our past standards—and remember that in China there is much in the past which can only be left to the imagination.'

There was nothing backward, however, about the Liberation factory at Changchun. It represented China's first attempt to produce its own motor vehicles and had been officially opened two weeks before I arrived.

The Director admitted that it had been built 'with considerable Soviet help' and that a number of Soviet technicians were still working there. In addition, over five hundred Chinese employees had been sent to Russia to study 'special techniques'.

The target was to produce thirty thousand Liberation lorries a year, but at present technical and economic difficulties had restricted the number to ten thousand. Even so, here was an achievement about which you felt the Chinese had every right to be proud.

The place had been built on a large scale. It had thirty-four workshops which covered every aspect of production except tyre manufacture, glass-work and upholstery, with special electrical and hydraulic power units and a direct connection with the main-line railway.

'Because this is our first motor factory,' said the Director, 'we have to study at the same time as we produce. We have over eighteen thousand workers, who have come from all parts of the country, eighty per cent of whom are under twenty-five.'

Their influx along with their families had brought into being what was practically a new town, with a population of over forty thousand. Tenements, dormitories, schools, canteens and shopping centres had been built around the factory, although, as always, there was the sharp contrast with the outer surroundings of tumbledown huts and gloomy compounds. Even more striking was the contrast between the shining five-ton vehicles sliding off the assembly line at the rate of twelve a day and the Mongol ponies and broken-down carts being used for internal transportation.

Within the workshops, despite the giant banners exhorting the workers to study advanced techniques and the rousing messages from labour heroes urging on the production effort, there was no evidence of any great sense of urgency. It may have been that the requisite tempo had not yet been established, that neither men nor machines had clicked into gear, or simply, perhaps, that there was a shortage of raw materials, but groups of men stood staring and smoking in quiet corners with time on their hands and, well before the lunch break, a crowd had gathered near the canteen with paddy bowls—and some with packs of cards—in their hands, nor did the arrival of the Director seem to disturb them. For a moment I could almost have imagined I was back in England.

16

'Far from the Heart of Culture'

OF all the relics of bourgeois frivolity, a copy of the *Yellow Book* was the one I should have least expected to find in the functional hinterland of Manchuria.

Yet there it was, solemnly and conspicuously displayed as 'An Interesting Volume of Lu Hsün's Youth' in an exhibition arranged to commemorate China's greatest modern writer. Beardsley, Burne-Jones, Gibbings, Dalgleish: what had these hot-house plants to offer to the dour apprentices of proletarian art? In which exotic corner of the hundred-flowered garden were they likely to be tended and admired?

The question was as incongruous as the presence of the *Yellow Book* itself in the bleak showroom of the Fine Arts Institute at Shenyang. It was just another freak, a bizarre manifestation of Chinese logicality, of the mental elasticity which persuades them to preserve even the most decadent ornaments of a despised society if by so doing they can illuminate some aspect of their own. Even the Dean, who knew something about western art and must have regarded the Beardsley crowd as ideologically beyond the pale, took the situation perfectly for granted.

I had not come, however, to gaze on the faded leaves of English romanticism, but to examine the communist claim to be sponsoring an artistic revival. What they were doing in Manchuria would be a pointer to the general rule—and undoubtedly they were doing a great deal.

The Institute had formerly been a comprehensive university which had undergone many shifts and changes during the Civil War and years of occupation. Since 1953 it had enjoyed a status of its own with departments of painting, sculpture and textile design. It was one of seven such institutes throughout the country and had its own secondary school attached, at which pupils could specialise in the Fine Arts from the age of twelve.

'Last summer,' said the Dean, 'a whole class graduated from the secondary school although competition was extremely keen, with over one thousand candidates from a very wide area competing for eighty places.'

When I questioned the advisability of this kind of specialisation at school age, the Dean assured me that it was additional to and not in lieu of the general course of education.

'If the pupils fail to gain entrance to the Institute they can still take the University examinations, in most cases with successful results. The same principle has been applied to music, dramatic art and dancing, where most of the large institutes have their own secondary schools. This is a system which basically we have copied from the Soviet, although our teaching methods are entirely our own.

'Each institute,' he continued, 'has its own characteristic. Here we specialise in oil-painting and etching, with a special department in commercial design where the students produce all kinds of domestic requirements, including labels for bottles and canned goods.'

Surprised by the emphasis he placed upon the latter, I enquired how the serious student regarded work of this kind.

'It serves the people and gives enjoyment,' he replied abruptly. 'A painting will last forever—a canned beef tin is gone tomorrow.'

'But our students also learn to paint tea-sets and vases and other things of beauty for the home.'

'Even so,' I pointed to a portrait of Mao and a series of Increase Your Output Posters on the wall, 'it seems a pity they should have to expend their talents on this kind of thing. Don't they regard this as a decadent form of painting?'

'Our point of view,' he said conclusively, 'is that they should be trained to paint both things of beauty and household necessities.'

We were joined by the senior Professor of Sculpture, and I raised the question of Marx–Leninism dictating the artist's choice of subject.

Both Dean and Professor were taken aback. It seemed a possibility that had never occurred to them; but far from dodging the issue they were eager to pursue it.

'In class,' said the Dean, 'we teach the formal methods of painting. In his own work the student may paint as he likes.'

I mentioned such esoteric western forms as surrealism, cubism, dadaism. 'Are there any Chinese equivalents for these?'

'We have never had such forms here. Our artists want only to paint for the people.'

'But surely the artist paints to please himself. Look at Picasso' —I deliberately chose the one western artist whose name is revered in the People's Republic. 'Much of his work means nothing to the people.'

The shaft went home, for the Dean and the Professor went into an animated huddle, the outcome of which was the edifying statement: 'We agree that many people do not like some of Picasso's work, but we believe that there are many more who do.'

'On the contrary,' I said, 'I believe that very few of the *people* have any notion what most of Picasso's work is about—they complain that it means nothing except to Picasso.'

'Picasso's early work is of the highest quality. It has a universal meaning. He is a painter with diverse talents.'

With that statement I could hardly disagree, so I tried another tack. 'What are the prospects for a young painter who is entirely subjective, who insists on painting merely to please himself?'

My insistence on this theme sent Little Wang, my interpreter for the day, into a fit of giggling, and even the stern-featured Dean seemed momentarily amused. But he was not to be shaken into any original statement. Perhaps he had said what he thought; perhaps he didn't think; perhaps he didn't want to. 'The artist may paint as he wishes,' he said, while Little Wang went on giggling unaccountably to herself. 'We have adopted the policy, "Let flowers of all kinds blossom." The artist must choose for himself.' As though to prove his point, he led me into the library, where, in the well-stocked western section, almost the first books I saw were recent editions of illustrated works on Stanley Spencer and Henry Moore. 'You see, although we cannot afford to purchase many books like these, we like our students to know what is being done by the leading artists of our time—whatever their ideology. I presume that the same policy applies in your own country. The teacher is merely the guide, but it is left for the student himself to decide which way he wants to go.

'In China, at least, the young artist has no need to starve. He can work in publishing houses, in textile firms or for the government. If he is really talented and wishes to work for himself, his paintings will be reproduced and published in book form. He can earn from eight to thirty *yuan* for each reproduction—and there may be as many as a hundred paintings published in one book.

'For the sculptor,' said the Professor, 'the position is even better, for he is assured of work by the government. All the sculptural work in China is on a big scale—collective work on public buildings and monuments—and for a long time yet the demand will be far greater than the supply. When he has gained some reputation in this way the young sculptor will then be able to set up on his own.'

The Dean and the Professor were eminently practical men, their feet firmly planted on the ground and their eyes fixed on the future; only once did they make any reference to conditions in the past. This was after I had visited their museum and admired their Ming vases and Ching urns and a collection of ivory and walnut boxes which had been carved, they said, before the birth of Christ.

'In these you see our best traditions,' said the Dean. 'For centuries they were shut away for the private enjoyment of feudal owners, but now they are openly displayed to give pleasure to all the people.'

In the main studio, in an atmosphere of intense quiet and application, twenty students or more were at work on the head of a bearded old peasant, while others worked individually on paintings of beetles, birds and fish in the style of the great classical master, Ch'i Pai-shih. In the etching-room another group were laboriously fitting stone tablets into place on an antique machine. And in the textile-design building students who had come back in their spare time were executing original and brilliantly coloured floral patterns for curtains, bedspreads and clothing. I began to regret some of my earlier remarks. There was no denying the liveliness and vitality of their work; whatever its proletarian limitations, in terms of beauty and craftsmanship the little I saw had more to commend it than many of the peculiar creations I had seen masquerading as art in the fashionable London galleries.

The Liaoning People's Cultural Institute stands about five miles outside Shenyang, beyond the new housing estates and grey-brick technical colleges, down a road so undeveloped that driving along it became a feat of skilled navigation. My visit had been arranged at short notice and, far from receiving the red-carpet treatment, I was left mercifully free for the early part of the evening to make my own way about while the Director conducted a rehearsal.

In that wintry Manchurian night the bleak corridors, the gaunt, concrete walls and broken windows—blocked up with faded pieces of newspaper—gave me an initial feeling of having entered a singularly depressing provincial workhouse; but the evening turned out to be as warm and refreshing as any I had spent in the more spacious comforts of Peking. The austerity of the dormitories—uncarpeted floors, sparse, shabby furniture, shared kitchens with cold water only—contrasted sharply with the radiant cheerfulness of the artists and their families, whose intensity and dedication to their work were of a kind I had never encountered in the theatre before.

The Institute was one of eight which the government had set up in the major cities since 1951. It housed 470 artists, of whom over half belonged to the dramatic group, and the rest to the Song and Dance Ensemble. Different groups might be performing as many as five plays at a time, one in the town itself and the others in villages and factories in the Liaoning province.

After watching a rehearsal of Pa Chin's *Family* (where the acting was of a demonstrably higher standard than when I had seen the same play in Peking) I wandered down the corridor, and was suddenly arrested by the sound of a baby crying. Little Wang beckoned me after her into a nearby room, where we found the baby, only a few days old, lying beside its mother on a wooden bunk.

The mother gestured me to sit down. She explained that she was the wife of one of the musicians and was herself a singer in the Ensemble. She was a large, middle-aged woman with a handsome peasant face. She had never met an Englishman before, and she wanted to know all about the opera in London and the English singers and the 'national ensembles'.

I did my best to oblige until eventually her husband arrived. He was equally excited when he knew I was English, for he had just been rehearsing a Mozart opera with the Ensemble. I expressed my surprise at finding Mozart in Manchuria and he said that the musicians would like to play more western music but they found great difficulty in adapting themselves to the instruments.

A lean, bristle-haired young man looked in and asked if I would take tea with him and his wife on the floor below. He was leaving in the morning to join a company in a north-eastern village where they were to prepare for a play about life in an agricultural co-operative. He himself was primarily a stage manager, but he also acted occasionally and his wife was to play the leading part in the new play.

While his two children slept on top of a double-tiered bunk he and his wife urged me to tell them about the English theatre, in particular about Shakespeare. It would be wonderful, they said, to perform in Shakespeare's plays, but they did not yet understand how to act them. *Romeo and Juliet* had been produced recently in Peking, but it would be a long time before any of

the provincial groups would dare to attempt such an under-
taking.

It seemed they would have listened to my views on Shakespeare
all night, but that was not the purpose of my visit. Eventually I
turned the subject to their own work.

They had both been at the Institute since 1954, where they were
paid comparatively high salaries, the wife earning 150 *yuan* a
month and the husband 120. They paid five *yuan* a month for
their room and ten *yuan* for their food—'and that is very good
food'. They worked approximately an eight-hour day: 'When we
are not performing we rehearse; when there is no rehearsal, we
practise.' In the afternoons they relaxed or, if they felt inclined,
could take lessons in Chinese ('Some of our older actors have
difficulty in studying their parts because they are only just able to
read'). A nursery was also provided for children up to the age of
seven and soon the Institute was to have its own senior secondary
school.

'How are actors recruited?' I asked.

'They come from many sources,' said Tsao, the husband.
'Many came from the old revolutionary base at Yenan, but there
are a large number also from the former Kuomintang area, including workers, peasants and ex-army men.

'Most of our younger actors come straight from the universities or academies and are selected by examination. The first
requirement nowadays is that they should be literate as well as
talented.'

'What are the subjects of the examination?'

'They are tested in acting, dramatic appreciation, singing,
dancing and Current Events.'

He threw in the last familiar item as unconcernedly as if he had
been mentioning Verse Speaking or Skill in Deportment.

'What do you mean by Current Events?' I asked bluntly.

'In general it means world events as published in the newspapers.'

'Supposing,' I said, 'that a candidate was deficient in Current
Events—or spent so much time on dramatic appreciation that

L

he had little opportunity to study the newspapers—would that debar him from entry if he was satisfactory in other respects?'

Tsao saw my point at once, so did his wife, but they both found it vastly amusing.

'The acting, of course, is the main thing,' he said.

'And in the case of a young actor with religious beliefs or with unorthodox political views—would he also be acceptable?'

'If the acting is good,' said Tsao, still laughing as though I had cracked a particularly potent joke, 'the candidate's chances will be good. He will be treated on the basis of the Constitution, which provides for freedom of religious thought. In our present Company, for instance, we have a number of Christians, Buddhists and Moslems, so you can see there is no religious discrimination.'

Which is not to say, I thought, that there is none of a political kind, but there was no point in pushing the matter further. The likeable Tsao was too wily or too naif to put a finger out of place.

Short, chubby and smiling, the Director suddenly appeared with lavish apologies for the necessity of having to rehearse while his guest was waiting. He led me down to the white-walled, blue-curtained reception room, where we were joined by the most sombre and striking figure I was to encounter across the length and breadth of China.

Dressed completely in black, with a thick black overcoat, black astrakhan collar, cropped black hair and magnificent black beard, Tien Yang looked unmistakably what he was, the leading actor in the Company—indeed, he might well have been the leading actor in the world. His black eyes were deep-set in a face which bore the marks and furrows of much suffering. In profile he looked like an Asiatic relation of the late John Barrymore, or as Barrymore himself might well have appeared had he ever been cast as Rasputin. You hardly needed telling that he had fought with the early revolutionaries; he looked like the father and patriarch of all revolutions.

He had acted, he said, in some of the early dialogue plays.

'Life was hard for the actor in those days. You lived on the run and depended on strangers to give you food and shelter. But the plays we performed expressed the soul of our people. The actors were voices and tongues crying out against the injustices of the time.' As a young man he had been whipped and tortured by landlords and government troops. Once, after performing in Ibsen's *A Doll's House*, he had been chained up and seen the leading actor shot before his eyes. Later he had made his way to Yenan and joined one of the communist-sponsored troupes. 'Since that day,' he brooded, 'and every day since then, I have had the joy of serving the people in the work which I chose to do when I was a child.'

'Do you believe,' I ventured timorously, 'that the people should only be shown plays which illustrate their own everyday problems?'

'In a good play,' he said, 'it is impossible not to illustrate the problems of the people.'

'What do you feel about Shakespeare?' I asked. '*Othello*, for instance? Or *Hamlet*? Those are plays universally considered of great psychological quality, but they can hardly be said to express the immediate problems of the people.'

'I would say,' he answered in his grave baritone voice, 'that they illustrate the problems of the English people.'

'Which people? Our Royal Family? Our Army leaders? They certainly have little to do with the problems of the average working man.'

This threw Tien Yang and the Director into a lively argument with each other. It was impossible to know what point of view either was taking but, judging by Tien's fiery exclamations and the Director's rapid, high-pitched rejoinders, there was wide disagreement between them.

It was the Director who eventually replied. Ignoring the problem of Othello, he addressed himself to Hamlet.

'In his case, although he was a royal prince, and would not understand the everyday problems of the working people, the ideas he expresses are those of progressive people in a decadent society. He is in revolt against the tyranny of court and the feudal system of government.'

'But the English worker,' I insisted, 'would not agree. He would see him in a far different light, as a weak-minded, neurotic character so obsessed with self-pity that he is unable to deal with the problems confronting him.'

'That is not how we regard Hamlet. We believe that Shakespeare shows him as a fighter for his country's freedom, as an exponent of nationalism and revolutionary ideas. . . .'

This was too much. Throwing courtesy aside, I cut him short and launched into an elementary history lesson on Scandinavian politics in the thirteenth century and the conditions of the English theatre in the sixteenth. Tien Yang's black eyes flashed disbelievingly; the Director listened with mournful patience; and Little Wang scribbled furiously to keep pace with me. 'As far as the ordinary people were concerned,' I concluded, somewhat arbitrarily, 'they only understood Shakespeare when he was writing down to them—and what he wrote on that level constitutes some of the bawdiest bourgeois thinking of all time. In any case,' I added, 'the respect paid to Shakespeare by the people of his own country can be judged from the fact that nowadays only a few of them ever go to see his plays performed.'

Both Tien and the Director roared with laughter. 'We can learn the answers about Shakespeare from you,' they said, with a discretion that made further argument superfluous, 'but we cannot give them ourselves.'

So we changed the subject, and I got Tien Yang to tell me more about conditions in the old days and the Director to talk about the day-to-day problems of running the Institute, and late into the Manchurian night we sat talking theatre 'shop' without ideological references of any kind.

When at length my Molotova bumped and jolted its way back to the hotel, sometimes zig-zagging round pot-holes in the road, sometimes bouncing over them, I turned to tell Little Wang how admirable the evening had been—but she had nodded off to sleep on the seat beside me. I looked at her with a new respect; she had been working for over sixteen hours without a break, concentrating in two languages at once, and had uttered not a word of complaint.

The following day I was with the acting fraternity again, this time in the Changchun film studio.

It had been built in 1949 and was one of four owned by the State.

The film industry has lagged far behind the theatre in its development, partly because the Chinese have not yet mastered the 'techniques', but mainly because they have to pay ceiling prices for importing camera equipment and celluloid from Japan. The budget for a feature film must not exceed £15,000 and the whole process of production, 'including the time the actors spend in studying life on farms and factories', must be completed within a six-months' period.

In its short existence the Changchun studio had produced fifty-two feature films, among them the modern Chinese classics, *The White-Haired Girl* and *Chinese Women*, but it specialised mainly in dubbing foreign films into Chinese and Chinese films into the languages of the national minorities. At the time of my visit the dubbing department was busy on a series of French films which were shortly to be launched on a nation-wide basis, and three feature films were in production: a local opera; a children's film (showing how a rural branch of the Young Pioneers unearthed a gang of counter-revolutionaries); and a dialectical piece on marriage problems among co-operative members.

Compared with conditions in the Cultural Institute the actors lived in luxury. The studio had a permanent company of two hundred, housed in newly built flats, living on a salary scale of up to 350 *yuan* a month. Among the younger actors this unusual well-being was reflected in smartly-cut suits and a general suavity of appearance. They discussed their work with enthusiasm, but I missed the passionate simplicity of the actors at the Institute: playing before the camera had perhaps made them a shade sophisticated; the actresses even wore make-up outside the studio.

It would have been difficult to imagine a more perfect specimen of classical Chinese beauty than Wu Chi-yen, the heroine of the co-operative film. Her finely slanted features, silken complexion and heavy-lidded eyes would have compelled attention anywhere had she embellished her sinuous figure with nothing more exotic than a padded boiler-suit. I was told—and could well believe it— that she was one of the most popular of the younger actresses.

'If you were in English films,' I told her, intending to flatter, Chinese-fashion, 'you would be the dream-girl of all our young men. Your picture would be pinned up in their coffee bars and clubrooms. How would you fancy that?'

She did not fancy it in the least.

'I should consider such a thing very undesirable, both from my own point of view and that of the public. I believe the duty of the actor is to serve the people, not to be adulated by them.'

'Surely,' I suggested, 'the one must follow the other.'

'It is true that the people should always take an interest in their actors. Tien Hua, for instance, who played the White-Haired Girl, receives many letters from the people. Some praise her performance, but many are very critical and suggest how she could improve it.'

'Does she take them seriously?'

'She knows that people only criticise from a desire to help her. It would be wrong for her to ignore them.'

When I told her of the kind of publicity given to English actresses in theatre-gossip columns and fan magazines she thought I was joking.

'Do you mean that your journalists are paid for writing such things?'

I passed the matter off as just one of our national peculiarities: 'We always like to know how the other half lives. Don't you yourself find that people are interested in your private life?'

'On the contrary, they feel that acting is an exhausting occupation. They would never think of intruding upon my leisure.'

For no reason that I can remember we found ourselves talking about the moral standards of the profession; and suddenly, as if recalling the lines of a drearily familiar speech, this radiant and exquisitely beautiful girl treated me to a dissertation on the mechanics of re-education in the primly impersonal tone of an instructor in one of the Cadre training schools.

'The general public' (I think the phrase is one of my own transposition: 'the People' was the epithet invariably used and would have covered even this multitude of sins)—'the general public consider that actors should have even higher standards than the rest of the community. They are regarded as the *engineers* of morals. They play parts which are moral and instructive, and they would be denounced by the people if they behaved immorally in their own lives.'

'Would you say that all your actors conform to this standard?'

'There have been only a few cases of actors failing in this respect, and they have been strongly opposed by the people.'

'With what results?'

'The actor is taken out of his role and re-educated.'

'What does that entail?'

'His immoral actions are analysed for him, both by the Director and the rest of the company. Their aim is not only to show him why and where he has committed wrong, but also to help him to understand the deep roots of his behaviour. For example, if he has committed adultery, his whole relationship with his wife would be examined, and such factors as whether the marriage was arranged by their parents or made by their own choice would have to be considered.'

'And then?'

'If the re-education process is successful he is restored to his part.'

'Supposing it proves otherwise?'

'He would be allowed to play only minor roles, and in very bad cases he would not be allowed to act at all.'

Later I broached this subject with Vice-Director Chou Shan. He was in charge of the studio's production programme, but was also responsible for re-education—a chief executive with a roving commission in Marxist psychiatry.

A soft-voiced, sympathetic little man, he was greatly disturbed when I told him that English actors by and large took a more lenient view of their colleagues' weaknesses.

'But surely, if they behave immorally their fellow actors will want them to cure themselves.'

'Privately perhaps they might, but they would not tolerate any system of public re-education.'

'But what of the people? Surely they will condemn these actors and refuse to watch them perform?'

Patiently I tried to explain that the people would not be unduly disturbed by what the actors did off-stage if they gave good value on. 'Only recently,' I said, while he listened aghast, 'one of our leading actors behaved so immorally that he was punished by the State, but the people still applauded his performance when he returned to the stage.'

'It is a common saying,' he reflected at length, 'that our actors have much to learn from the English. But the things you have told me are not what we wish to learn. Even so, we have a great desire to see your actors, so please tell them we shall forgive all immorality if they come to visit us. Please convey to them our warm feelings of friendship and respect. And that,' he added, playfully pinching my arm, 'is not said for propaganda.'

Over dinner that night Carl reported another aspect of re-education.

He had been taken to an agricultural co-operative to meet a former landlord.

'But,' he said, groping through the jungle of his ultra-basic English, 'landlord not there. I talk instead to wife of landlord. She very glad he no more landlord. Since Liberation he learn to work in field, but she no mind. She smile all time. There sleep ten in one bed—landlord, wife of landlord, son, wife of son, children, landlord daughter, husband of daughter, children of daughter—all sleep in one bed—in bed like table. But since Liberation she no mind. She very glad. All family happy together in one bed. When one turn, all turn. All turn together since Liberation.'

17

'The World is Eventful'

THESE were the strangest and gloomiest days I can ever remember spending.

While we rushed from one smoke-polluted town to another, with the grey Manchurian winter settling in, and were fêted and applauded by communist officials, at the other side of the world Hungary was in revolt and the British and French were attacking Egypt.

It was a period during which the members of this heterogeneous delegation might have been expected to group themselves into hostile political factions, when relations between communist hosts and western guests might have been strained to breaking point. Remarkably, neither of these probabilities occurred.

For two weeks all we knew was what the Chinese newspapers chose to tell us. On Hungary this amounted to practically nothing; on Suez, news items were so swamped beneath editorial denunciations that it was impossible to arrive at a single reliable fact. My notes at this period are scrappy, bizarre, apprehensive and trivial, but they reflect my own confusion and perplexity in a way which a more coherent account, recollected in tranquillity, would not:

1 November

In disgrace with whole delegation after being late down for breakfast and then keeping them waiting ten minutes on the coach for the Anshan Steel Rolling Mill. Am about to apologise but change my mind when Crabb makes angry speech demanding that in future coach should leave on time regardless of late-comers.

Serious-minded delegates subject me to Social Rebuke. I slink abjectly to back of coach; but Vladimir suddenly pops up and pulls me down beside him with bear-like hug.

'Our delegation very impatient this morning,' he chuckles. 'But what need to hurry? We only go to see machines that make machines . . . that make machines . . .'

The delegates return to life as interpreters produce morning papers. What *is* going on over Suez? It seems U.S.A. and U.K. have ordered nationals to quit. Difficult to make it out in babble of tongues all round.

No news from Hungary. Vladimir says, 'Paper reports all is quiet.' Could mean anything: they only got round to mentioning it two days ago. 'Many changes will have to be made in future,' says Vladimir sombrely. 'Many things were bad in policy of Hungary.' I wonder how much he knows but am reluctant to ask.

We get involved in discussion of English political system. He is fascinated by my account of debate on capital punishment but completely misinterprets my viewpoint.

'Hanging very bad,' he pronounces. 'Very bad system. Why not try shooting, as in my country. Much simpler system for everyone!'

I try to explain Christian attitude. Am greatly surprised when he tells me he once read the Bible. 'I think it is very great book,' he says. 'Perhaps it is wisest book in world.'

2 *November*

Usual morning babel as the papers arrive.

Try to get some sense out of Pan, but he's mentally embedded in an endless editorial calling for solidarity against colonial aggression.

His voice is drowned by Abdul, the French interpreter, who reads everything in staccato barks, like a series of parade ground commands. I give up altogether until Ricardo rushes in wild with excitement. His English is almost as hard to follow as Abdul's French and he accompanies every utterance with a furious waving of arms which serves to increase the confusion, but things

are undoubtedly beginning to happen. If only one could sort out
what!

'Soviet troops—they move from Budapest! Students—intellectuals—workers—all have meeting with government! Rumania
—Bulgaria—Czechoslovakia—Russia make declaration about all
communist peoples. And in your country—England—France—
warn Egypt! Israel troops cross frontier—your government give
Nasser twelve hours to decide. Your troops—French troops—
all ready for war!'

What does it add up to? Cannot believe in ultimatum. Curse
the Chinese Press! Curse the interpreters for trotting out all this
drivel about solidarity and imperialist aggression when all one
wants to know is a single hard fact! Everyone sits round arguing
and nobody knows a thing. Tripp dismisses the Israeli attack as
another frontier skirmish. His guess seems as good as any, but
where does the ultimatum come in? Ricardo prances about
ecstatic at the prospect of war. 'Are you in the British Reserve?'
he asks, patting me gleefully on the back.

3 November

Down at 5.30 for early train to Tientsin. Extraordinary breakfast of Chinese caviare, hors d'œuvre, and sausage-meats while
amiable officials buzz round pouring out Shenyang beer. Conclude meal with pancakes.

Chilly farewells on bleak dawn platform, like going back off
wartime leave. Goodbye to Manchuria. Goodbye, I think, forever.

The papers come on board at first stop. Chaos breaks out.
Abdul barks away in one corner while Ricardo shrieks with
excitement and delegates scamper from one group to another.
The English-speaking crowd swarm round Pan, but he refuses to
be hurried. He ploughs his way through statements from half a
dozen Asian leaders: 'You see, it is like this: The Prime Minister
of Indonesia says . . .' 'The President of Mongolia declares . . .'

It seems that all the governments of Asia are blowing their
heads off, but what precisely has happened? Pan turns the page

and plods on unperturbedly through declarations from Pakistan, Burma, Syria, from the People's Republics and God knows where. Angry speeches have been made by the leader of the All-China Women's Federation, the All-China Federation of Trade Unions, the All-China of this and the Federation of that. 'They call for a halt to the filthy war! The people have demonstrated in Tien An Men in protest against the fascist aggression.'

At last he comes to the point. 'British troops are on their way to Egypt. British planes have dropped bombs along the Canal zone.'

There is a lot more about the bombing of civilian cities, bombs on Cairo, the shelling of hospitals, but this is from Cairo Radio; the other is from London. Pan closes the newspaper with a smile and squeezes my arm. 'The world is eventful,' he says. 'Too —— eventful!' I think, wondering if everyone at home has gone completely mad. Tripp arrives, busily explaining to the Arab delegates what seems to defy all explanation and I, who for weeks have been trying to convince the unbelieving Pan that the British government represents the British people in a way that *his* does not represent the Chinese people, now have to listen to him murmuring consolingly, 'We do not blame your people because we know it is the government who have made this war and not the people.'

Abou, the Sudanese, expounds at length the Arab viewpoint on Israel, and Baghdadi analyses the problem for Muriel's benefit. Vladimir prophesies world war and Ricardo rushes round gesticulating about heaven knows what. Only Pablo seems unconcerned and sits in a corner humming cheerfully to himself; perhaps he doesn't even know what the fuss is about.

The tempo of the discussion changes; passion and argument give place to small talk; there is really nothing to say. Baghdadi and Muriel talk, of all things, about British films. From Baghdadi's cultured French I cull one astonishing statement: '*Nous aimons beaucoup les films d'Arthur Rank parce que toujours il y a une pensée.*'

Abou joins me and renews the debate. He has always believed

in the British system. In Sudan there is a great feeling for Britain and admiration of our institutions. 'When you ruled us we resented you, but now you send us your technicians and teachers and we respect them because they come as equals. But now'—he waves his hand helplessly—'you have lost everything you have gained. You are not fighting for Israel but for the Canal—but that is only one mistake. You are pushing the Arabs into the communist camp. Islam has no love for Marx, but now you have left no choice.'

I turn to Pan, who sits deep in thought, and ask what he thinks of the situation.

'I think,' he says slowly, 'of what you told me the other day about America being afraid of aggression by China and Russia, and now I ask myself, "What are YOU doing in Egypt?"'

At the far end of the carriage the kitchen staff play gramophone records. The voices of the Chinese singers wail and screech monotonously above the multilingual mutterings of the delegates. Abou, Baghdadi, Crabb and the Swedish priest settle down to a game of bridge. Ricardo relaxes for a while with Muriel. Bernini, Tamas and the East German are in earnest conversation. Carl brings out his typewriter and starts a report for his paper on Manchurian industry. Pablo still sits in his corner humming to himself.

We put in to some nameless station. Ricardo shoots out of the carriage and returns with news that the Hungarian Army has gone over to the rebels. Tamas says it is impossible. Who could have given him such news? Vladimir shrugs his shoulders and says nothing. Ricardo is in love with bloodshed, determined there shall be shooting all the time, even if it's only in his imagination.

Bluntly I ask Vladimir to explain the present Russian policy.

'We have made very bad mistakes in past,' he admits. 'We are paying for them now. Difference is that now we begin to see these mistakes. Not so under Stalin.' He freely admits the purges —'These things were known to many people for long time and many protested, but all were shot. Not one hundred, or two hundred, but maybe ten million were killed by Beria. Without these mistakes trouble in Hungary would never have begun. Now who can say what will happen? Kruschev is very brave man. He risked his life at twentieth congress, for he had many enemies, and many more opposed to new policy. But after Hungary he will have great struggle to defend new policy.'

I think this subject is as painful to him as Suez is to me, whether through guilt or anxiety I wouldn't know. One thing is certain: he has no more idea what is happening in Hungary now than I have.

Tamas hears me criticising the British Communist Party. What he thinks about the situation I haven't dared ask and he has consistently avoided it. His face is an amiable mask: courteous, unobtrusive, he seems more interested in the welfare of the delegates than in the turmoil in Hungary, yet Vladimir tells me his wife and children are in Budapest and he has had no word of them, although he has been every day on the telephone to Prague.

He asks what are my impressions of China—in a way which puts me immediately on guard. Here it is—unless I am mistaken —here we come to the basic purpose of the delegation. There is something in the phrasing of the question, in the tone, which suggests, 'Surely you didn't think it was for fun. We've been waiting to catch you, and all the time you were playing into our hands by making friends with the Russian.'

I give the simple stock response which every anti-communist in China gives: admiration for the material progress but no sympathy with the illiberal methods.

He asks if I have considered the basic conceptions of the idealistic and materialistic philosophies: 'If you admit this fact, surely you must accept that. . . . It's a question of whether you believe that you exist to think or that you think to exist.'

I confess that I am old-fashioned and lazy and not very good at thinking about anything, but I believe in the kind of democracy I was brought up in and which for five years I fought for and which Englishmen have died for since the Magna Carta, and I suggest there are many facts you have to admit and accept if you believe in the right of people to live their own lives, and maybe if I got down to it I could produce a reasoned argument on the basic conceptions, and I have always picked holes in my own society, and shall go on picking them even if the majority is against me, but at least nobody puts me in prison for doing so or compels me to accept what I don't believe in.

Tamas is undeterred and embarks upon further basic exposition, but Vladimir stops him abruptly by announcing he must write a letter to his wife and he cannot concentrate with all this discussion going on.

Arrive at Tientsin—the gateway to Peking—in early evening. Usual barrage of bouquets and beaming faces. They're howling for British blood in *The People's Daily*, but nothing disturbs the welcoming smiles of Peace and Friendship. The girls seem especially pretty—most of them in blouses and slacks, some even with make-up.

We're whisked smartly off to the reception, but not before Ricardo has got news that Canada has condemned British policy.

A new variation on official speeches: the German communist is President of the day but there's no German interpreter so the speech of thanks is translated first into Russian by Tamas, then into Chinese by the Russian interpreter, then by the other interpreters into English, French and Spanish.

Usual brilliance of entertainment with jugglers, acrobats, trick cyclists, singers and weight-lifters laid on, followed by the Dancing, with the orchestra grinding out their own version of *The Merry Widow*. I dance for some time with a girl from the Tractor and Automobile College—timid but very pretty. Then the Singing: for some incredible reason Tripp, Muriel, Carl and myself contribute *Tipperary* as the English offering—and Vladimir joins in. He says he was taught the song by his English teacher.

I notice that one of the jollier Chinese dances is to a tune which time and again the welcoming youth have sung on our arrival along the route. Pan says it is the national song of all young people: 'Like a national anthem of youth. It is the song of the students of the May 4th, 1919 Movement, in the great rising against fascist oppression.' He translates it with fiery relish.

'Unity is STRENGTH—
Unity is STRENGTH—
This STRENGTH is like IRON—
This STRENGTH is like STEEL.
It is even stronger than IRON—
It is even MORE powerful than STEEL.
It directs its FIRE against FASCISM—
LET all unDEMOcratic systems PERISH—
LET us SPREAD our FAR-REACHING radiance—
Let us MARCH forward to the SUN, to FREEDOM, and to a NEW CHINA!'

I quibble over the use of 'fascist' in the 1919 context, but he declares categorically that it is a word to describe 'all who are against the people'. He pinches my arm and informs me that I have a very beautiful face. 'Not the face of a fascist but of a big lovely Englishman.' Further compliments are cut short by the ending of the party and the rapid exit of all the girls, discreetly watched off the premises by smiling League officials.

4 November

We while away the morning in the People's Cultural Palace. Carl comments: 'I cannot understand the working of this Palace. You cannot concentrate your culture.'

Vladimir complains: 'I want to walk round streets to see life of people but we must go to *another* Palace.'

All seems quiet in Tientsin. Have had no news this morning—even Ricardo can find out nothing, but there is talk of big demonstrations this afternoon. For first time feel apprehensive about personal position. Tripp wants to ring Legation, but I advise him to wait till we have tested attitude of officials.

Two new delegates arrive at lunchtime, from Malaya and Ceylon. Don't know what they represent or why they've only just shown up.

There's obviously something in the wind. Tamas goes into a

huddle with the officials and the interpreters are earnestly being briefed about something or other.

Purpose of the preamble is explained when Little Wang tells us we are invited to attend the big demonstration this afternoon.

Immediate reaction is to get up and tell them to go to hell. We've come to see China, not to demonstrate about anything.

Second reaction: journalistic curiosity; demonstration would make good story. Go and see what happens.

Third reaction: stay away from propaganda trap. Protest against exploitation of delegates.

In the event I make short speech reminding delegates that views on Egypt are one thing but purpose of delegation another. 'If we're going to start demonstrating about Egypt we should do the same thing about Hungary. Let's stick to the job we came to do, and let the Chinese do the demonstrating.'

General hubbub while Tamas confers again with Chinese. At length he announces that invitation was only given because Chinese felt some of delegates would wish to show friendly feelings for Egypt. 'It is entirely a matter of choice.'

'All the Arab members wish to go,' says Abou. 'But it must be made clear that we represent our own countries only, not the delegation. It would be wrong for the newspapers to report that our delegation was present if we go as individuals.'

Further conference between Tamas and Chinese: 'That is perfectly all right,' says Tamas. 'Our friends have promised nothing will appear in newspapers about presence of delegates.'

'Where is the freedom of the Press?' asks Carl derisively; but the matter is settled. Off go the Arabs and the Asians, the communist fraternity, including the Frenchman, and the ebullient Ricardo, rubbing his hands in anticipation. Back in the hotel stay the English, the Australian, the Scandinavians and the South Americans.

The afternoon is rent asunder with high-pitched tirades and tremendous bursts of cheering relayed from the People's Stadium by loudspeakers in every main street. At length we leave the hotel and walk through the streets to the Palace of Sport for

M

Clerical and Administrative Cadres. We pass by the Stadium. High above the wall dense crowds are jammed in the stands waving and clapping; but outside, nobody seems especially interested. The crowds standing round the gates cheer and shout at the appropriate moments but they grin and make way as we approach.

We arrive at the Palace of Sport, which was formerly a club for British business men, to find Vladimir and Ricardo already there. 'Very dull demonstration,' says Vladimir. 'Everyone say same thing but nobody say anything concrete.'

'Very disappointing,' says Ricardo. 'Worse than fascist meeting. There are leaders in all stands who start to cheer and everybody shout when they shout. These are not true demonstrators but people who have come to football game. I found it very boring.'

The other delegates return, equally disappointed.

'It will go on for a long time yet,' says Abou, 'but we have heard it all. Everybody uses the same words arranged in a different way.'

We go down to the table-tennis room—for the first time I manage to take a game off Tamas. He is an excellent loser. If he had been brought up on cricket, perhaps he wouldn't have fallen for the 'basic conceptions'.

Play several games with young Chinese and am intrigued by their style. They are puzzled by my backhand. They never use it themselves and never seem to spin the ball. They play very close to the table, very fast, and rely upon speed and forehand smashes—however fine the angle, they still manage to smash the ball back over the net.

Walking back to the hotel we run into the crowds coming out of the Stadium. Maybe the Party members treat the demonstration seriously, but these people don't seem to. They wave and grin merrily as we pass. I get the impression they regard the whole thing as yet another carnival laid on to relieve the tedium of the endless production drive.

The moment I have been dreading: Galal and Shakir are wait-

ing at the hotel. They came up from Peking specially to speak in
the demonstration. Now they say very little, but keep to themselves, looking overwrought and miserable. I want to talk to
them, but don't know how to begin—what *do* you say to men
you have been friendly with, when six thousand miles away your
country has just attacked theirs?

A gloom settles upon the whole delegation. Is the arrival of the
Egyptians going to wreck it completely? Everyone is waiting to
see what they will do.

I decide to make the first move. I go over and tell them we
have all been shocked at what has happened; we still do not
understand it.

Galal says they don't understand it themselves. The last news
they had was that bombs had been dropped on civilian towns and
a hospital had been hit. He is grateful that I have come to speak
to him, but sinks into utter dejection and is too depressed to say
anything more.

Shakir says he doesn't wish to talk about it—but he can't help
himself. 'We know there was the problem of the Canal, but why
do you do this to us? Any time during the War we could have
ruined your country by sabotaging the Canal, but we never did.
Maybe now we take Canal from you too soon, but that is no
reason for killing our people.'

I say nothing, but let him continue. He wants only to get back
to Egypt, but he has no idea when there will be a plane. To go
via Moscow would take too long; Hong Kong is impossible;
their only hope is to get to Delhi and then fly on to Khartoum.

Ricardo rushes in wildly having picked up the latest reports
from Cairo and Prague. The air is electrified with rumours: there
is hanging and burning in the streets of Budapest; Nagy has
appealed for American aid; 'fascists' are crossing the Hungarian
border; the gaols have been thrown open; Mindzenty has been
released; fighting has spread throughout the provinces; and in
Egypt forty British planes have been shot down; Nutting has
resigned from the government; the trades unions have called for a
general strike.

Ricardo is surrounded by delegates with everyone jabbering and arguing at once. The Egyptians go gloomily to their room, followed by the silent Tamas. I reflect that in two days we shall be in Shanghai: there perhaps we shall catch up with the news.

'I think we have heard all news for tonight,' says Carl. 'I wish for you tomorrow new Prime Minister.'

5 November

Off early to lively chorus of 'Unity is Strength' from cheerful dawn gathering on platform.

General depression as delegates contemplate long journey ahead without access even to Chinese news.

I settle down to study Russian publication on *The Consequences of the Cult of Personality*. Bought it weeks ago along with manuals on the Chinese Eighth National Congress and the Use of the Intellectuals, but so far have had no chance to open any of them.

Muriel passes by and asks what it's all about. I tell her mainly about Stalin.

'Oh, really,' she says. 'Was he against personality, then?'

I find it increasingly laborious to read and ask Vladimir's opinion on some of the jargon: 'The achievements of the glorious collective farm workers,' 'the heroic endeavours of the peasants,' etc.

'Oh yes!' he declares. 'You have very good taste. This is style of serious political person, not of real writer.'

He is greatly puzzled when I ask what he knows about the Burgess–Maclean case.

'I have heard nothing of this,' he says. 'I will ask journalist friends when I am back in Moscow.'

He insists I spell the names exactly and then copies them carefully in his notebook. I throw in Fuchs, Pontecorvo and Nunn May, but they mean nothing to him, so he adds them to his list. I warn him to take care or he will be in trouble with the security police.

We discuss the H-bomb. 'Last week,' he says, 'Bulganin wrote yet another letter to Eisenhower about banning of bomb. It is said in Moscow that Bulganin has no time for other matters because he is always writing to Eisenhower about bomb. What is reason why America refuses to ban bomb? We will agree to ban. Why not they?'

I explain at some length the western viewpoint on safeguards but he is not impressed.

'Bomb comes first!' he exclaims. 'Then we can talk about details.' Nothing will budge him on this.

Tripp collars me after lunch. 'I'm very worried about this Russian,' he whispers. 'I've just discovered he'll be writing a report on our trip for *Pravda*. I think we ought to be careful what we say, because he's bound to make use of it.'

I assure him that I will be extremely discreet and go back to Vladimir's cabin. He hugs me delightedly, delves into his trunk and produces a bottle of vodka.

'Today is very special day,' he declares. 'It is birthday of my marriage. I am very glad to remember my wife in company of depraved bourgeois Englishman.'

We have left Manchuria far behind. The landscape has changed to rich farmland. The sky is azure; the fields brown and warm in the harvest sun. In the distance stand the mud houses and lonely villages. We are in ancient China, timeless, immemorial.

At Pakou the train is shunted on to a ferry and we cross the Yangtze Kiang. Farther down the river, they say, between Wuchang and Hanyang, they are building the first Yangtze bridge, but we go smoothly, without fuss, the train divided into four sections, on the old-fashioned ferry. The crossing takes twenty minutes. The coaches are clanked together again and we hardly glimpse the river at all.

At Nanking the interpreters and Ricardo go off to get newspapers. I parade the platform with Vladimir and watch Chinese workmen buying cooked chickens and bowls of steaming vegetables from the railway stall.

As we go back on board Little Wang beckons Tamas aside.

'There is good news from Hungary.' She sees that I have heard and drops her voice to a whisper.

Good news indeed! Nagy has been pushed out and Kadar has called the Russians back. Budapest is calm. Order has been restored. 'News is very good,' says Vladimir. 'But troops is not so good.'

The People's Daily congratulates the Hungarians on having rejected the fascists and counter-revolutionaries. The socialist democracy has once again been made secure!

A new gloom settles on the western delegates, which deepens with the news from Suez: Britain defeated in the United Nations by sixty-two votes to five; America has voted with Russia; Cairo reports sixty British planes have been shot down—London admits the loss of one.

Sunday seems to have been the busiest day in China's history. Every town in the country has been demonstrating. The Federations have been yelling their heads off. Half a million people have demonstrated in Peking. The Egyptian Ambassador has been bouncing from one solidarity meeting to another. His wife has appealed to the women of the world. Thousands of volunteers have offered to go to Egypt. Speeches . . . speeches . . . everyone is making speeches. . . . *But what are they doing in England?*

After a wearisome hour Pan announces that protest meetings have been held in London. 'All Britain, except a few fascist Tories, are against the aggression. The protest movement is now assuming unprecedented dimensions. Mass meetings were held yesterday in London, Birmingham, Nottingham, Brighton, and many other cities.'

There's comfort yet. Sometime maybe we shall find out what happened in the first place.

I now share my sleeping-cabin with the Malayan and Sinhalese. Malaya is a big, muscular smiling man of about forty, a school inspector in Singapore, who has come on the delegation without letting his government know: 'They would never give permission for such a visit, so I think it best not to tell them.'

This evening he offended Shakir by an unfortunate wisecrack after hearing that an Egyptian prison had been bombed. 'Freedom-loving British have liberated the prisoners too,' he said.

Ceylon tried to heal the breach by assuring Shakir that he was 'a wild uncivilised man, not long out of the jungle'.

Ceylon is lean and wiry, a devout Buddhist, and proud of the fact that Ceylon has only three communist M.P.s. 'No communism for us,' he declares. 'Ceylon is a religious country, with its own culture and traditions. There is no place for Marx.'

He badly misses his wife and is distressed to hear of general puritanism of Chinese women. The evening finishes on a frustrated, bawdy note.

6 November

Another perfect day. Endless paddy-fields, mule-carts, peasants; a world at peace, like traditional picture of Chinese landscape.

To Pan I have now become 'interesting big Englishman with penetrating views'. I try to explain to him the western meaning of democracy and why the satellites are rising, that the 'mistakes' *The People's Daily* refers to were crimes against humanity, but he smiles tolerantly and tells me my opinions are 'incorrect'. I ask if he knows the early history of the so-called Socialist Democracies, mention names and events he has never heard of, but he refuses to be shaken. 'Very interesting views,' he says, 'but not at all objective.'

Nothing can hold Ricardo down. He has spent most of morning attacking the French communist and now he turns on Vladimir. His father has a German friend who spent twelve years in a Siberian jail. 'This was terrible punishment of innocent man,' he cries. 'Why did your government do this to him?'

Vladimir is stung. He is sure that this must have been during the Beria regime for there have been many changes in Siberia since, but he reminds Ricardo that the German probably suffered less than many Russians did in German prison camps.

The Spaniard admits that the man was not tortured, which pleases Vladimir because Russian newspapers had recently denied the use of torture in these prisons. Ricardo protests that the foul conditions represented a permanent torture, but Vladimir will not give way.

'Maybe this German was fascist,' he retorts. 'There were many such in Siberia.'

'That is not the point,' cries Ricardo.

'That is whole point,' growls Vladimir.

Opposite us the Egyptians sit silent and alone. In the corner Pablo stretches his long body across the seat, dozing gently. Tamas sits brooding by himself (Bernini has flown off to Korea for celebrations of the Russian Revolution). The sparkle has gone from his eyes; he looks washed out. He is probably the loneliest person here. I cross over and ask what was the last news he had from home.

He admits he has heard nothing since the start of the rising. I ask point-blank what he believes was the real cause of it.

'I am like you,' he says. 'I have only a few lines from which to make an analysis. When I left home there was no doubt the workers were dissatisfied. The government had made bad mistakes and everything was coming to the boil. But I did not expect there would be fighting. There are probably many factors we don't yet know about, but I have already heard from Prague that many of my friends in the Federation have been killed. As far as that goes,' he smiles wearily, 'I could give you an analysis, but it would be from a Marxist viewpoint. I don't suppose it would interest you.'

'I hope you will have news soon about your family,' I say.

'The Hungarian Army Ensemble is in Peking and have been told already that their families are safe, but I am sure this is only to help their morale. I shall believe nothing until I receive a special telegram from my friend. I have asked him to tell me three things: about my family, about himself, and whether the Czech border is still open. Unless I receive this information exactly I shall believe nothing.'

Vladimir is looking forward to Shanghai. 'I have heard it is place where before Liberation were many prostitutes, but now not one. But maybe kind Chinese hosts keep specially for delegations one of old prostitutes—now sixty years old maybe. You and me share fifty per cent—thirty years you, thirty years me.'

He had never actually seen a prostitute until last year, when he went abroad for the first time, to Venice. 'It was great shock to pure Russian boy. In my country is thought very bad business. Not so in yours, perhaps.' On his trip he also visited the Casino. 'It was very strange experience for me. We have no such gambling in my country. Very interesting to serious young communist to see bourgeois pleasures. But all people at Casino so serious— especially English people. All try to work out figures, but figures never seem good. It seems to me it is strange sort of holiday for such people.'

He has also heard that before the Liberation there were many bars along the Shanghai water-front but now there are none. I assure him that if he ever visits an English harbour he will find things better arranged. 'It seems to me there are some very interesting things in your depraved country,' he says.

The Shanghai reception is the wildest yet. The welcoming party stampede down the platform and almost drag us from the train. The farther south you go the prettier the girls become. Vladimir whoops and shrieks as he is snatched up by half a dozen beaming lovelies. We are drowned in bouquets and escorted out of the station like a victorious army to the chorus of the inevitable 'Unity is Strength'.

Where they all come from nobody knows. Where they disappear to nobody asks.

The official reception outshines the one in Peking. I am allotted two film directors, two distinguished actors and Tien Hua— The White-Haired Girl—who also played Juliet earlier this year in Peking. Conversation is mostly about the theatre, but is punctuated by hugs and shouts from Vladimir, who wants me to join him in celebrating the anniversary of the Russian Revolution. The hosts have provided their own brand of vodka but he dismisses it as 'vodka for children' and drains large quantities of the local grape wine. 'Wine is only half strength,' he cries, 'so we must drink double amount!'

At the end of the dinner the three Y.M.C.A. men arrive with Shen, who has accompanied them on the special tour. They're followed by Bernini, just back from Korea. He seems highly excited—the first time I have seen him come to life. When I ask him the latest news from Hungary he clutches me vigorously and exclaims, '*C'était formidable. . . formidable . . . mais maintenant tout est fini.*'

Galal is President of the day and makes a short speech of thanks in Arabic which is translated into Chinese by a local interpreter. It arouses great enthusiasm from the hosts, presumably because he's Egyptian.

Tripp, however, thinks otherwise; and so doing precipitates the first real crisis on the delegation.

Back at the hotel he asks Abou why the speech was not translated into English, and Abou, knowing his Tripp, replies flippantly, 'Because he condemned the British and French invasion. He said that Egypt was fighting three hostile powers but would destroy them all.'

Unfortunately Tripp doesn't know his Abou. He buzzes busily around the western delegates demanding they take action. I suggest that even if Galal did say anything out of place we're not in a very strong position to complain. But Tripp's blood is up. Soon he rouses the militant Crabb into asking Galal exactly what he did say; but Crabb, with his fine Australian forthrightness, goes into action like a battering-ram. First he throws the statement in Galal's face and then demands if those were the words he actually used.

I didn't see this incident myself, but it is reported to me by Muriel, much distressed. She says Galal promptly turned his back on the Australian and went straight to his room without a word.

I charge up after him and find him sunk in his chair, almost in tears. He looks up but says nothing. I try to explain that the misunderstanding began with Abou's unfortunate joke.

'Never mind about joke,' he groans. 'Do you think I could say such a thing? Do you think I want to break up whole delegation? I have not talked about Suez to anybody on delegation. As delegate I leave Suez behind me. Why should I start trouble about Suez now?'

Shakir storms into the room. 'What do they think we are?' he cries. 'Don't they think we know how to behave? Why don't they leave us alone? We have our own problems to think about. We have no time for new problems here!'

Vainly I try to calm him down: nobody thinks they are causing trouble; we are glad they are on the delegation; we admire the way they have conducted themselves; the Australian is only a boy; they should not take him seriously.

'But we are *not* boys,' roars Shakir, pounding the table. 'But next time—men or boys who insult us—we get out of the delegation and go to another hotel.'

Galal stirs out of his chair and urges Shakir to be quiet. 'Let us forget this Australian fool, and talk together like friends.'

Shakir will forget nothing. His anger has only just begun to uncoil. All the restrained passion of the last week breaks forth in a torrent of indignant rhetoric.

'You and I have been good friends till now and we stay friends. Today, tomorrow maybe, and the next day. But one day I shall kill you if I have to and one day you will kill me. And whose fault is that, my friend? Can you tell that? We have never had war this century, but we shall face it if we must. One year from now maybe you remember me over my grave.'

I give up protesting and let him talk on. Galal shakes his head despairingly. I had this coming to me, I suppose. I accepted this alien relationship, and chose to prolong it, knowing it could explode in my face; but in the same position I would probably do the same thing again. You can't go against your nature and mine works intuitively, not by logic.

'Do you think . . . do you think,' Shakir thrusts his face tigerishly into mine, 'do you think we *want* communism in my country? That we don't prefer the western way of life? My friend, we know what communism means. But we take help from those who give it. Remember the words of your hero Churchill? "We will ally with the devil himself if he will help us to victory." Why? *Why* do you fight with us? What is the Canal worth to you? Sixteen million pounds a year? Twenty million? A hundred and fifty by the time the Agreement ends? Is that worth a war? What have you lost already, my friend, in planes and material? How much has it cost your country? What will it cost before you are finished with us? Is it worth it, my friend? What is the reason behind what you do? Something is hidden. There is something to be explained. But I tell you this, my friend. You have lost already the Middle East. Not only for now, but forever. We shall never forget. The Arabs will never forget—not this generation, nor the next, nor the next.'

At last Galal stems the onslaught. 'No good to talk. He knows no better than you. It is not only fault of Britain. All troubles began with America and Aswan dam. If we had Aswan dam there would be no blood over Canal. No communism. No bombs on Suez.'

Shakir has spent his fire. Galal thanks me for coming to see him. I ease my way out.

I find a furious Muriel in the corridor. 'I've been giving Tripp a piece of my mind,' she says; and by heaven she has. An abject Tripp creeps up and apologises for causing trouble. He's obviously ashamed of himself. He's offended his own sense of decency, and now I feel sorry for him. He goes off to see the Egyptians.

At last I have discovered the real Muriel. My heart suddenly warms towards her and I ask her to my room for tea.

7 November

Generally dismal breakfast on tenth-floor sun-lounge of swish ex-Sassoon Hotel, formerly Cathay Mansions. Sumptuous décor of imperialist decadence carefully preserved by State; carpets, furnishings, upholstery, splendidly maintained, lock, stock and barrel for comfort of foreign delegates.

Sunlight illuminates dining-room, but all is gloom within. Scandinavians especially depressed, partly over Hungary, more over Suez. They shake their heads sorrowfully and cannot believe it has happened. They are embarrassed for us and we are grateful to them. I never thought I should ever feel ashamed of being British.

Vladimir comes in with old copies of *Pravda* and passes them over without comment. Front page has gruesome pictures from Budapest: security chief hanged by the feet, blood-spattered, beaten to death; another lying on ground with bayonet through mouth and picture of Lenin stuck across chest.

'Very unusual for *Pravda* to show such pictures,' he says.

'There are no rules in a revolution,' I say.

On the back page there is a picture of Port Said after bombing, a smoking landscape of war, reprinted from the *Manchester Guardian*. I think we understand each other. He offers no argument for Budapest and I none for Suez.

I push the paper away as Galal comes gloomily in. I ask if he has had any more news.

'I do not want news.' He slumps into his chair, taciturn, morose. 'In war is never good news. Today you kill four hundred our men. Tomorrow we kill yours. News only makes me sad, so I do not want to know.'

But I do, so I set off early for the Consulate.

It is vast, rambling building, but seems almost deserted. Go through routine of stating purpose of visit on official card and move from one empty reception-room to another: seems rather pointless when there's no-one about but the servants.

Consul polite and ponderous, but doesn't seem to know what's going on and doesn't grasp the fact I want to find out whole sequence of events of last two weeks. He's only been here three months; came from Africa and hasn't quite settled down. Says he had visit from mass demonstration on Sunday with banners and petitions; they marched up to main doors but behaved in orderly manner. They were not so orderly in Peking, apparently. Over five hundred thousand demonstrated in Tien An Men, then swarmed round the Legation and plastered slogans all over the walls.

The Egyptian ambassador claims to have received letters from two hundred and fifty thousand volunteers. He doesn't say how he's going to get them to Egypt.

Consul gives no opinion on how the situation began and sounds as if he doesn't have one. I slope off with copies of the *South China Morning Post*, and read and despair.

Eden describes it as 'police action'—so how can we throw stones at the Russians? Impossible to get at facts but basic fact is that we fired first. Israel looks like a put-up job. What have they done to you, England, my England? Now I've got to go on playing the good Englishman abroad, defending the lunatic government while all Asia shrieks in contempt.

Local version of *The People's Daily* says all is now quiet in Budapest. 'Hail the heroic Soviet Army. Hail the soldiers who have unselfishly shed their blood to save the cause of Socialism!' God help the Hungarians! *We* certainly haven't.

Return to hotel utterly sick with lunatic world. Fools who govern it, maniacs who hold our lives in their hands. What a century! Fifty years of high-powered lunacy and mass murder; the war to end all wars; the war to save democracy; the war to end everything getting nicely under way. The era of the invention of bombs: fire-bombs, atomic bombs, napalm bombs, H-bombs, nitrogen bombs; 'police action' in Egypt, Algiers, Cyprus, Greece, Korea; 'the defence of Socialism' in Hungary; 'Peace and Friendship' in eastern Europe. Where do we go from here?

Tamas has news at last: the telegram he wanted. Wife and children in Prague; friend is safe; Czech border is open. But he admits he has no idea of real position. He talks of 'fascist elements' taking advantage of initial rising and prisons being thrown open —'I mean the criminal as well as the political,' he adds without thinking.

News sounds better over lunch. There is talk of cease-fire in Egypt. Not definite, but seems under way. But Shakir will have none of it. He wants to play the hero. 'What *is* this United Nations? What should they do in my country?'

'They will save Egyptian blood,' I say.

'We have not asked to be saved. What is our blood if we remain free?'

But Galal has smiled for the first time in days.

18

A Way of Life

FROM the uppermost window of the Sino-Soviet Friendship House, the most colossal structure in all China, I looked through the night at the remains of the greatest maritime city in the east with an acute sense of nostalgia. Here were the recognisable symbols of European civilisation: the great banks and commercial palaces, the towering hotels, the wharves and warehouses where the ships of every major port in the world had once plied their trade. Here was the dockside that for almost a century had been a byword among British seamen—the happy haven of the hard-drinking mariner, the garden of paradise for the randy-minded crew, the water-front that opened its welcoming arms to provide the cheapest good time on the Seven Seas.

The symbols were still there—the gay lights glittered along the Bund, dense waves of humanity surged through the streets, the splendid edifices of the Matheson and Sassoon dynasties bulked large in the sky—but the substance was gone; the old Concessions were buried in the limbo of history; the International Settlement was one with Nineveh and Tyre.

In the shadows of the river a convoy of sampans glided towards the shore with their cargoes of rice, flour, vegetables and fruit, but they glided alone. From the harbour sheds the *Wei-ho*, *Wei-ho* of the labourers lapped the night air: but they were hauling buckets of bricks to build new tenements, not cargo from ships' holds. True, thirty ships had been in during the past month and slowly, they said, life was returning to the docks, but, for all that, the river looked dark and desolate, entombing the empty wharves, and the water-front was a rippling avenue of ghosts.

Shanghai was being expanded as an industrial city, devoted mainly at present to textiles and electrical equipment, but soon it would be producing heavy machinery and rolled steel. 'Gone forever,' proclaimed the Mayor, 'are the days when the workers had to share one pair of trousers between several people. Now the men can afford to buy suits for both winter and summer and the women can buy bright print dresses. Many can even afford to imitate city wear.'

Gone forever were many more grisly memories: corpses rotting nightly in the streets; fortunes piled up from opium; children lured or bullied into the brothels; the rampant scourge of tuberculosis; the disdainful prohibition outside a European Racing Club: 'Chinese and dogs not allowed.' Without doubt the communists had treated the commercial magnates abominably: had forced them out of business by the rent and repairs racket; accomplished the take-over by rigging the prices of property at their own estimate of its 'deterioration'; cut supplies of raw materials and brought in trade-union restrictions to a point which spelt ruin for those who refused to get out—but equally, without doubt, whatever they had done to the Europeans, they were making Shanghai into a city fit for their own people to inhabit.

It is here that the paradox of capitalism in a communist society has found its most potent expression—a fact which they reiterate with delight on every convenient occasion. 'There are now eighty-three thousand shops and factories working harmoniously under joint State–private enterprise management,' declared the Mayor—and you readily took his word for it. If, however, you were in doubt, you could tour the factories where the old-time capitalists are honourably installed as Directors or Technical Supervisors, drawing their modest State salaries and a steady five per cent on their investments.

In this city at least the capitalist class, far from being extinct, rears its well-groomed head at every reception, and to leave Shanghai without having shaken hands with a millionaire is not to have been there at all. There are still sixty or more in residence and they are preserved and paraded at receptions like prize ex-

hibits, holding court to visiting delegations and elaborating with
exquisite conviction upon the virtues of the new dispensation
compared with the vices of the old. There was no way of finding
out what they really thought and I saw nothing to be gained from
asking them. They were *alive*; that was the operative point—not
because the State is enamoured of them, but because it needs their
skill and experience as well as their foreign holdings; and the
Chinese communists, being quicker to learn from their mistakes
than any other political party in the world, have rapidly realised
they will gain more by buying them out decently than by continuing to harass them as bourgeois reactionaries.

Even so, the survival of bourgeois ideas is still their dominant
fear; for although the social and economic landscape has been
transformed—wages have increased by forty per cent in five years,
goods are cheap and plentiful in the shops, slums are being
demolished—the communists know too well that a century of
exposure to western influence cannot be cancelled out overnight.
It is inconceivable that the present regime will be effectively
challenged anywhere in China for some time to come, but if it
should be challenged at all they know it will come from here:
Shanghai was never a chip off the old China block but a polyglot
city with a mind and character of its own; so that although
ostensibly the nationalist purge ended three years ago—the
People's Courts no longer pass daily sentence on members of
'the traitorous clique'; the sinister red vans are no longer seen en
route to the execution grounds—the Security Police continue to
search relentlessly for nests of 'saboteurs' and 'counter-revolutionary elements'. Security checks, both on Chinese and
foreigners, are stricter than elsewhere in China, and the quaint
old-world courtesy of the police in Peking is replaced here by a
hard-boiled purposefulness which would do great credit to the
stronger armed gentry of the New York Homicide Squad.

The outstanding success of the new regime in what was
generally regarded as the Number One cesspool of the east has
been the elimination of vice—an achievement about which no

N

visitor—and no Londoner, certainly—can reasonably complain: the communists have accomplished within the span of eight years what the Christian countries of Europe have failed to bring about in two thousand.

Believing this to be of more than ideological significance, I took some pains to find out what methods had been used—to discover, as I should have known, that they were of sound ideological origin.

'Our first task,' said Chun Tse-tsung, head of the Civil Law Bureau, 'was to mobilise public opinion, not against the prostitutes themselves, but against the desire of the people to consort with them. Only when this campaign had been launched could we proceed to the next step, which was to close down the brothels, and then embark upon the programme of re-education through productive labour.'

There were, he explained, after expatiating at length upon the multifarious iniquities of the Kuomintang, eight hundred legally licensed brothels and perhaps four or five times that number unlicensed. Between 1949 and 1951, by mobilising public opinion, the majority of the women in them were persuaded to find other employment as well as to undergo treatment for venereal disease. By the end of 1951, of the licensed houses, only seventy-two remained. These were then forcibly closed down.

'When we started our campaign we found many of these women in an advanced state of syphilis, and many had been destroyed in other ways. These had to be removed to special homes where they will spend the rest of their lives.

'They are not, of course, regarded as criminals. They were driven to practise through their miserable economic plight and fell into the clutches of the brothel owners and gang bosses. Many of these men had criminal records, and were consequently dealt with by the Public Security Bureau' (which is to say, they were shot), 'but those with better records, who showed repentance for their crimes, were accepted for treatment at Reception.'

Reception, which I had no time to investigate, appeared to be a system of corrective training run along the lines of the Peking prison.

'Our aim is to give the prostitute a feeling of security, but because of her lazy nature it is often difficult to persuade her of the necessity for labour training, and in such cases training is necessarily prolonged. Most of these women come from the labouring or peasant classes, with the result that their ideological consciousness is of a very low level. Thus, we first have to make them realise the low nature of their position and the degradation of their work. Naturally, when they first arrive at Reception, they are frightened, for they believe they are going to be punished. These doubts and suspicions have to be dispelled before we can go on to their ideological education, but once we have done this we can then proceed to teach them social discipline, the need for patriotism, an understanding of Current Events and production achievements, and so forth. Alongside this, we also give them literacy classes. Many have learnt to read up to two and three thousand characters, and most of them can now read the newspapers without difficulty.' (One frequently had the impression that the whole of education was directed to achieving the latter end.)

'Labour-training, of course, varies according to health conditions. Some work on textiles in the weaving-sheds, but many are fit only to do light handiwork. After they have been trained in this, they are given payment—in the form of a prize of three to five *yuan* at first—but later they may be paid from twenty to forty *yuan* a month, according to the work they have done. When they have completed the reform period they are given jobs according to their techniques or, if their homes are in the country, they are sent back to take part in the agricultural programme. If, on the other hand, they have neither homes nor techniques, they are sent to work on farms run by Reception.'

This then was the secret of the greatest social clean-up in history. No fancy psychiatric nonsense about early environment, parental influences, latent emotional disorders; no invoking of the oversized libido; no passing the buck on to the male customer. Mobilise the people first, lay on the Reception, get cracking with

the Current Events and the three Rs, and finish the treatment
with a stiff dose of techniques and agriculture. Not a programme
to everyone's taste, you might say, but then neither was the
spectacle of wholesale prostitution.

'In general these women are grateful to the government for
changing their way of life, but we cannot claim to have abolished
prostitution altogether,' said Chun, with exaggerated modesty.
'There are still cases of women who practise privately, but these
are very rare and, owing to our policy of mobilising the masses,
they are invariably reported to us. The Street Committees work
in close co-operation with Social Security and it would be
difficult for any woman to practise for very long without the
Street Committee hearing of it.'

That was the straightest piece of talking from any official I had
heard to date. It was followed by an equally candid exposition
from Ho Chi-wu, the grim-jawed chief of Social Security.

'In method and content we have used the same basic approach
in the treatment of opium addicts, petty thieves, beggars,
gamblers and vagrants. Their labour-training consists of road-
work, railway building, and machinery construction, and in the
course of this programme many acquire high-level techniques and
finish their period of reform as skilled workers. But,' he confessed,
'we have still not conquered this problem completely, although
statistics for these crimes are five per cent down on last year's.'

I put it to him that juvenile delinquency was generally a more
serious social problem than gambling and vagrancy: how had
Shanghai fared in this respect since the Liberation?

He maintained that most cases of this kind could be attributed
to early upbringing under the Kuomintang but, when pressed,
admitted that children 'deficient in ideological understanding'
still tended to gang together in the streets or cause trouble in the
tea houses. Within the past two months there had been an out-
break of this kind, but the police had swooped promptly and the
offenders had been dispatched forthwith for a two-year spell of
're-education through labour-training'. He emphasised that this
was an occurrence so rare as to be scarcely worth mentioning, but

checking on it later, I discovered that it was not quite so rare as he suggested. As with the *stilyagi* in Moscow, Shanghai had recently produced its own version of the Teddy boy, teenagers in search of excitement, for whom 'productive work in the cause of national construction' was a far less attractive prospect than making a nuisance of themselves in the streets. It was true that as soon as they revealed their intentions they were hustled off at the double without reference to their upbringing before or after the Liberation, but the significant thing was that they had appeared at all.

On the other hand, it was not surprising. For the greater part of the day the majority of children were necessarily left to their own devices. Their parents were out at work and they themselves attended school in shifts. 'In addition,' admitted Ho, 'in many families the economic needs have not yet been fully met in the production programme. So that many pedlars and street vendors work late to make more money, with the result that they rarely see their children at all. Add to this the fact that many of our six million population still live in pre-Liberation slums, where conditions encourage them to spend most of their time in the streets—and you will see that this problem has no easy solution.'

I appreciated more clearly the depth of this understatement a day or two later. Leaving the delegation to tour a new housing estate I made my way with a local interpreter to Fan Kua-lun, in the northern part of the city, one of the five remaining slum areas. As slums go, it ranked high on the list of appalling human habitations, making the Gorbals seem like a garden city; it could be compared favourably, perhaps, with the native shanties of Johannesburg or the compounds of Portuguese East Africa, but the demarcation line would have been hard to find. It consisted simply of an area of small, densely-packed mud and straw hovels, patched-up, damp, rotting, where swarming families of human beings somehow contrived to exist in conditions that would have disheartened many self-respecting animals.

Before the war, they said, this had been the site of a textile factory, but it had been destroyed by Japanese bombs. The houses had been put up by 'Kuomintang landlords' in 1940, but they had not troubled to fill in the bomb craters, which rapidly became stagnant pools, infested with flies and mosquitoes. Cholera, smallpox and tuberculosis had been rife. 'In those days', they said, 'we had a local saying: "Every day we see somebody die; every day we pass another coffin". But there were never enough coffins and often the dead bodies had to be left lying in the alleys until the undertaker could find time to collect them.'

Now the pools have been cleared, the alleys cobble-stoned, a sewerage system installed. The Street Committees have carried through an intensive campaign of instruction in sanitation and hygiene; the inhabitants work on a rota basis in keeping the alleys clean, and every week living-quarters are inspected by members of the Committee. 'So far no tenants have refused to co-operate,' they said. 'But some do better, some worse. Many homes are still very dirty, and though we have won the main battle we still have serious problems of ill-health—generally with families who have failed to carry out our hygiene instructions.'

In places the ground was still soft and muddy and the stench lingered, dank and fœtid, in the air. Since I had lightheartedly left England without the usual inoculations I had no wish to hang around. But there was one thing more to do. Having seen the outside of the houses, I also wanted to look inside.

A gaunt hag of a woman sat washing her feet in a wooden bowl outside her doorway and I asked if I could go in. She paddled out of the bowl and beckoned me after her, her face dented and crumpled like a cracked walnut. She said nothing, but stooped against the mud wall waiting for me to speak.

The house was not more than eight feet square and ten feet high. The concrete floor was cracked and covered with a great patch of damp. On the wooden bed which stood about a foot from the ground and served also as a dining-table, a young baby was fast asleep (it seemed impossible to enter any house in China without finding a scene of similar domestic felicity). Beside it, indicated the old woman, she herself slept, and on a wooden plank three feet above slept the baby's father and mother.

The roof of the house had been blown off during a typhoon earlier in the year and had been replaced, but rain still came through and the walls were yellow with damp. There were no windows, so that you could only make out darkly the shapes of cupboard, oil-stove, lamp, cans, utensils and sanitary bucket stacked together in one corner. This was the home of four people; there were no goldfish bowls, no chrysanthemums, no pictures of Chinese opera, no photographs of Chairman Mao, no slogans about 'techniques'.

'I hope soon,' said the old woman, 'to have a brick home on one of the new estates. I hope you will come to visit me then.'

Back at the Cathay Hotel the interpreter asked me why I had gone into that particular home.

'Because the woman looked such a skeleton,' I said. 'I felt I would see conditions at their worst.'

'I can assure you that you have. But please remember if you write about this meeting that we are working to wipe out the slums completely. It will take another seven years because we have a million people to re-house. And if you will permit me to say so'—he pointed to the luxurious carpets and plush furniture inherited, like the hotel itself, from the Sassoon era—'the men who occupied these rooms before the Liberation did very little to help.'

19

The Mirror Up to Nature

B Y this time my curiosity had begun to flag, my critical sense
had been blunted. I had come too far too quickly, with no
pause for reflection, no time to assess the significance of
what was going on; my attempts to probe and pry beneath the
harmonious exterior which everywhere the Chinese presented had
revealed nothing beyond what they themselves wished to be
known. Every western visitor, I believe, whether journalist,
politician, business man or bishop, arrives sooner or later at the
same exhausted impasse. He can batter his head forever against the
ideological bulwarks, can attack the illiberalism of the regime,
condemn the counter-revolutionary witch-hunt, protest against
the arbitrary imprisonment of artists and intellectuals—but he will
gain nothing from his efforts except the frustrating satisfaction of
having made them.

By now I was ready to take much of what the officials told me
on trust. If they said that ninety per cent of the peasant population
of Shanghai had voluntarily formed themselves into co-operatives
I had no doubt they were speaking the truth; if they claimed that
religious worship was freely permitted in the city's two hundred
Buddhist temples, eighty Christian churches and fourteen Moslem
mosques, and that many of these buildings had been restored and
repaired by the State, I did not question their word; if they stated
that one million two hundred and ten thousand square metres of
land had been used for re-housing since the Liberation, I could
readily believe it was so. If they had given me the production
figures of every factory in the city I should have had complete con-
fidence in their authenticity. But I had no wish to gaze at any of

the physical phenomena which the figures reflected. They had, as they intended, convinced me already of their material achievement and of the ghastly conditions they had replaced. I had no doubt either that when they spoke of caring for 'the interests of the people' they meant what they said, and that comrades blinded by 'doctrinaire thinking' or arrogantly insensitive to 'concrete local conditions' would be rapidly put in their places in a way which would have shattered the ranks of their European brethren; but, given all the Peace and Friendship in the world, on the subject of Marx–Leninism and some of the methods deriving from it we should continue, as they themselves respectfully agreed, to go on disagreeing.

So for a few days in Shanghai I decided to sit back and relax. I would neither make it my business to hawk round the democratic torch nor allow myself to be inveigled into visiting a collective farm simply because it was collective or a State–private enterprise mill because it happened to be under new and unusual management. I just wanted to mix with the kind of people I should have mixed with in any other city; and when I expressed this inclination to my hosts, with spontaneous and endearing courtesy they hastened to satisfy it.

At once I found myself in the very position from which I had intended to withdraw.

I betook myself one afternoon outside the city, beyond the sprawling new estates and technical institutes, the cabbage-fields and collective farms, to Futan University.

This was originally a Catholic establishment supported both by the Chinese and French, but it was now run as a comprehensive university with English instead of French—or Russian— as the main foreign language. New dormitories and lecture blocks were going up all round, but the central building retained its original character; and on the lawns in front of it, where students loitered casually arm in arm, the only visible sign of the new order was an enormous red banner proclaiming: 'Solidarity with the Glorious Soviet Republic on the Thirty-Ninth Anniversary of the October Revolution'.

I had gone without an interpreter and wandered about at leisure with senior students of the English faculty. It was an afternoon when I felt utterly relaxed, cheered by their enthusiasm and warmed by their friendly curiosity. We talked about the books they were studying—*Oliver Twist, Jane Eyre, Wuthering Heights, The Vicar of Wakefield*—and others of more recent vintage which I thought they should study; discussed the B.B.C., which many of them listened to; the English theatre, English games, English customs; and it was they, not I, who suddenly digressed on to the subject of Marx–Leninism.

'Is there a compulsory political course in English universities?' one of them asked, and when I replied that there was not, they debated the matter among themselves and then expressed these views:

'*It is unpopular with the English faculty here. . . .*'

'*It is popular with a minority, but we are opposed to it.*'

'*You cannot force people into believing a thing simply by making them learn it.*'

'*We are not opposed to communism, but only to the compulsory teaching.*'

'*We believe communist control is good for the country, but bad for the university. But we have made great progress since the policy of The Hundred Flowers and are allowed to express our views openly. We have been able to criticise the political teaching in our debates and discussions.*'

'*Criticism is not enough; we are opposed to the teaching itself.*'

At this point, I suppose, I should have sought to elicit further disclosures. But whether for fear of embarrassing them or through sheer mental indolence on a restful afternoon, I listened to the only expression of political heresy I was to hear anywhere in the People's Republic and did nothing whatever about it. Whether their remarks had any real significance I could not tell, but in a few moments they changed the subject rapidly as we were joined by a group of eager-eyed students from the Department of Journalism.

There was no doubting their views on Political Education. They were, without exception, delightful young men, vivacious, enthusiastic, bubbling with good humour; and they were also embryonic editors who would never be able to express a single original thought, apprentices to the deadliest form of hackwork devised by man. Their knowledge of Marx–Leninism not only had to be 'correct'; it had to be capable of accepting without a murmur that what was 'correct' one day might be equally 'incorrect' the next.

The one English newspaper they read was the *Daily Worker*; it gave them a chance, they said, to know what the People of England were thinking. They were astounded when I told them what most English people thought about the *Daily Worker*. They also had access to the *Manchester Guardian* and *The Times*, but the available copies were out of date. Recent copies of the *Worker*, however, alongside its American counterpart, were handily placed in each of the reading-rooms.

The availability of these was depressing enough, but even more so was the vast physical evidence of Soviet penetration on the intellectual front. Libraries and lecture-rooms were stacked with recent Soviet literature; the bulk of the text-books were of Soviet origin; Soviet magazines and technical journals were piled on the tables, and those not from the Soviet were almost without exception satellite hybrids.

In the evening the students took me to their English Social. It was a bi-weekly event, in which they gathered at their tutor's flat to hold idiomatic conversation and play what their tutor assured them were 'English party games'. The latter bore as much relationship to English life today as Dotheboys Hall to a modern grammar school—but that was not the point. It was an evening of unequivocal pleasure in which the delight of the students at having a live Englishman in their midst was inhibited only by their inability adequately to express it. One can too easily be cynical about such occasions, but to these young people at least it was abundantly obvious that Peace and Friendship meant rather more than a worn-out Party slogan.

In the old brothel area of Fu Chou Road was the Great World.

Formerly, they said, although ostensibly a place of entertainment and refreshment it had functioned as an emporium of vice, notorious even in the east. Gang bosses ruled it; gambling, prostitution, opium were its stock in trade. It catered for every taste in the catalogue and attracted the scum of the China Seas.

It must have been a remarkable establishment then. It was even more so now.

You entered into a shadowy courtyard. Around it ranged a series of gaunt buildings with jutting galleries and grilled windows, connected together by gaslit arcades and stone staircases. In the yard itself a smiling, black-jacketed motor-cyclist rode the Wall of Death in a series of hazardous figure-eights, first by himself, then dragging a toy cannon behind him, then with two children sitting pillion-fashion, a boy in front and a girl behind— and a flamboyant wave of his hand to the audience each time he reached the upper rim of the pit and began the thirty-foot dive to the bottom. The rickety bamboo enclosure swayed and shuddered to the roar of the machine; in the upper stand the spectators pressed closer together, the back rows leaning precariously over the front; I, for one, was glad to get down to earth again; if the Wall did not frighten the rider, it certainly scared me.

But this was a diversion from the real business in hand, a shock absorber to the tumultuous medley of noise coming from all around. Within the Great World proper the most fantastic form of mass entertainment known to man was in full blast. To be exact, on one or other floor of the various buildings, to the clashing of gongs and cymbals, the beating of drums, the strident crescendoes of brass and the amplified screechings of the singers, five different kinds of opera were being presented at one and the same time, together with a puppet show, a display of juggling and acrobatics and a Soviet film commemorating the October Revolution. Item by item, any one of these performances might reasonably have been compared with others seen elsewhere, but the total ensemble admitted no comparison with anything else on earth. It was shattering and fabulous, exhausting and exhilarating, appalling and irresistible. It began at twelve midday and went on non-stop till eleven at night. It was attended by twenty thousand people a day; it cost them sevenpence a head to get in, and they came and went as they liked with no such nonsense as booking offices, usherettes or commissionaires to worry about; the theatres even dispensed with the formality of doors.

It was indisputably, if not definitively, a people's theatre. They came in their boiler-suits and shawls, with their babies and baggage, from the morning shift and institute, the literacy class and self-criticism meeting, the barrack-room and building site. They sat on hard benches or leaned against grimy walls; young couples chewed wings of chicken; mothers fed their babies at the breast; old men and young boys cleared their throats with rattling ferocity. Children tagged each other down the aisles, climbed along the benches or stood almost on the feet of the musicians, gaping in solemn fascination at the spectacle on stage; while from the dark recesses of the pit rose the smell of steaming rice and the husky patter of the pedlars with their merchandise of nuts, melons, sesame cakes and sunflower seeds.

Tomorrow no doubt there would be the weary reality of the production drive, the sanitation campaign, the hygiene inspection, the lessons in Current Events. Tonight there was the escape into a world of fantasy and folly sublime: the thundering warlords and incredible emperors, the plaintive princesses and comforting concubines, the dragons and phœnixes, the grotesque masks and gorgeous brocades, the swishing swords and fearsome scimitars.

It would be a stony heart, I thought, that could not rejoice— but such was the case with my interpreter. As an ardent member of the local Youth League, he would, I thought, have taken some pride in the performance.

'The amazing thing is how no-one notices the noise,' I said. 'I suppose you grow up with it and take it all for granted the same as we do silence.'

'On the contrary,' he said, 'it is being greatly overdone. The new operas are far less noisy than these. But it is difficult to change people's tastes at once.'

On one floor a young man in a dinner-jacket was performing an extraordinary feat of juggling with a combination of a golf ball, a football and a large fruit-bowl, to the tortured accompaniment of *Good Night, Sweet Ladies* from the six-piece band. 'These are not Chinese players,' said the interpreter with obvious disdain. 'I don't know where they come from.'

'But the juggler is excellent,' I said. 'I have seen none better.'

'I shouldn't say so. He is not one of the top performers, but only good for popular playing.'

In the theatre below an all-female company from Chekiang were performing a love-story from Shao-Hsing opera, the style of which is subtle and delicate, the vocal inflections expressed in the fingers, the music soft and restful. 'Not so striking as the Peking,' I suggested, 'but perhaps it is more precise.'

'As a rule, yes, but not with this company. They have not the delicacy of the best players.'

We moved on to the puppet show, which was an imitation of the actual Peking opera being played in the theatre next door. The bearded Emperor fought with the benign General for possession of the wailing Princess. Their staves whirled and whistled; their heads twitched; they somersaulted and chased each other round the stage while the drums throbbed louder and the gongs were beaten stronger.

I asked to go backstage to see how it was done.

The performance there outdid the one in front.

In a space no bigger than a theatre dressing-room a company of ten people were at work. In one corner three musicians belaboured between them an assortment of drums, gongs, castanets, cymbals and strings. Opposite them, two female singers sang the choral parts into a microphone. Hanging in one wing was the Company's entire wardrobe; oil-stoves and kitchen utensils were stacked on the floor beneath; while in the centre space, under the imaginary floor of the stage, five young men manipulated the puppets. But— this was the astonishing thing—they were not mere manipulators. Instead of simply pulling the strings, they themselves, holding the dolls above their heads, acted in detail every move, gesture and expression of the character they were manipulating. They danced, shook, trembled, twitched, contorted and sang to themselves through every phase of the performance. They became, in fact, the puppets themselves.

If there is such a thing as surrealist drama, this, I felt, was it. I turned and whispered my admiration to the interpreter.

'It is not a particularly good example,' he replied frigidly. 'We have many similar companies with a more polished technique than these. I would rate this as a third-rate imitation of the real thing.'

He may of course have been right: he explained that he was a purist at heart; but in the Great World that night he sounded more like an arrogant young snob.

20

White Man's Burden

IN the last remaining European club in China the ghosts of the
Settlement and the Concession had gathered for lunch.

Danes, Frenchmen, Belgians, British and German: not
more than forty in all; only survivors of a ruined empire, still
hanging on to the ashes, still clutching the hope of better days
ahead.

There were Eurasians too: embittered, hard-faced men, the
last of the bosses, maestros of the big deal, squeezers who had
been squeezed out, old China Hands who had had their chips,
gamblers of the Yangshupu and the South Wharf who had run
close to the wind and been caught with their sails down. They
spoke of the new regime with settled hate. Their trade had been
killed, their profits filched. They carried the memory of their
losses in glinting eyes like scars that would never heal.

The Europeans were different. The bosses and the empire-
builders had gone: Customs men and curates, sharks and charla-
tans, the race was extinct. These were the managerial left-overs,
salvage men, scrap merchants in real estate, hanging on to what
remained—a solitary floor in the Hong Kong and Shanghai
Bank, a single room in the Chartered, a textile mill, a Sassoon
Hotel, an office block—but they did not complain. They had had
it rough until six months back, and it was not too easy now.
Their movements were watched by the police or spied on by their
servants; their staff reported any indiscretions to the trade-union
meetings; they had no personal relations with the Chinese and no
social life outside the Club and the Consulate; but even so, things
were on the up and up. They were allowed to travel out of

Shanghai without permits; they could get newspapers from Hong Kong only two days out of date; once a month they had film shows at the Consulate; food restrictions were off and they could get all the drink they wanted.

'The order must have gone out,' they said, 'for a general letting up.' Perhaps, after all, the hanging on would prove worthwhile.

True, they had everything to gain and nothing much to lose. They bemoaned the missed opportunities for trade, cursed the Americans and the embargo. They had pleaded with visiting M.P.s to press for an easing of restrictions at home, but nothing had been done. They knew that British cars were coming in on the quiet from Hong Kong, and one of them had been told by Chou En-lai that rolling stock was getting in through the back door via Poland and the trans-Siberian railway.

They spoke in muffled tones, of war, and the rumours of war. Australian Radio had reported that Israel was ready to stop fighting. . . . Somebody had heard on the Los Angeles wavelength that an American task force had sailed for the Mediterranean. . . . The Russians were moving planes behind the Syrian border. . . . Eisenhower had written to Bulganin, Bulganin to Eisenhower. . . . Refugees were streaming over the Austrian frontier. . . . Switzerland had withdrawn from the Olympic Games. . . . They all agreed that the big showdown was on the way; anything might happen. The British government had gone mad, that much was certain; the world had marched on from the gunboat days, they had seen that for themselves; no use showing the flag now; the wogs had come into their own; you couldn't push them around any more.

The Club was the last remaining citadel of the old social order. A photograph of the Queen hung above the mantelpiece and beside it one of George VI, taken early in his reign. A faded scroll surmounted by R.A.F. wings indicated that the Club had been founded by the R.A.F. Association. All that was left was the fifth-floor dining-room, the bar, and the old servant who had been

o

there since the beginning. Nowadays he was paid at the union rate; tipping was forbidden.

The members had gathered especially to observe Armistice Day. Roberts, the manager of the Chartered Bank, was to propose the Remembrance toast. A short, ruddy-faced man, who had been out there thirty-two years, he fingered his glass nervously and confessed that he was worried by the presence of the Germans. 'Never had them here on Armistice Day before,' he whispered. 'I don't know how they'll take it.'

But he had no cause for alarm; he was in such a nervous state that his speech was completely inaudible. We waited, silent and solemn, for the signal to raise our glasses.

In the street below, klaxons blared and pedlars yelled their wares. In the sprawling, sky-scrapered city beyond, the wheels of the production drive ground remorselessly on; counter-revolutionaries were tracked down; Street Committees kept vigilant watch.

The speech petered out. A plane roared overhead—Spitfires down the Mall.

'To absent friends.' Roberts raised his glass.

'To absent friends.'

We drank, slowly and thoughtfully. In clubrooms in Singapore, Chittagong, Bangkok, Bombay, across the scattered debris of an empire, lonely groups of men were standing at about this hour in the same way. It was pathetic, forlorn, unreal; but in that silent room, high above the traffic of Shanghai, a doomed island in a closing sea, the words stabbed along the nerves of my memory with a sharper poignancy than they had ever done before.

A chair scraped.

Roberts coughed abruptly and moved towards the bar. We took our places for lunch.

The English survivors accepted their predicament with a kind of heroic realism. They talked of the past without self-pity and of the present without rancour. They were the last people you would have expected to sympathise with the regime, yet they spoke of its achievements with surprising impartiality.

'I'm no communist, old boy!'—they invariably began with that—as though you could ever imagine they might be, as though you would suspect a priest of atheism, or a judge of petty theft. 'Been here thirty years. Lived through it all. Nobody knows better than me how they've smashed up our business, or what they've done to the Kuomintang crowd, to say nothing of the missionaries and Americans. God knows they've not been much use to me. But you've got to admit it. They've done a wonderful job for themselves. They've transformed the city, old boy. Given it a new face and a life of its own. It's clean and it's good.

''Way back in '37, thirty thousand people died in the streets— in one year alone. Used to see them myself when I drove to the office. They'd flaked out on the pavement at night and were dead of cold in the morning.

'Take a walk down to the Long Bar, old boy. You can't recognise it now. They've turned it into a seaman's home. Looks like a luxury palace compared with the old place.'

Nobody was more impartial than George Gregg—the York-shire-born manager of the textile mill. By a feat of economic acrobatics that came perilously near to calculated suicide he had managed to keep it going under entirely British management— the only enterprise to have done so.

'We just dug our heels in and took everything they flung at us. They've cut our supplies down to two and a half per cent of what we got before but we're still hanging on. We've given way on every labour claim, met every union demand, cluttered the place up with redundant workers—till they can't bleed us any more.'

He had, he reckoned, a welfare and insurance service second to none—he had to if he wished to survive—but even so, even for rigidly doctrinaire tastes, it sounded a shade elaborate.

By way of health and education his factory financed and equipped a clinic, a sanatorium, a special diet room and a menstruation room, staffed by two doctors, six nurses and a chemist. He ran a nursery with beds for a hundred and five children, and a

head nurse, fifteen *amahs* and a dietician in attendance; a kindergarten for another hundred children, and a school for five hundred,
with a staff of twenty-six qualified teachers. On the Recreation
front he provided football and basket-ball grounds, a Workers'
Club with dance-hall, reading-room, billiard-room and bowling
alley attached; and, under the sponsorship of the basic Labour
union, he laid on facilities for evening classes in everything from
amateur theatricals to pre-natal care for pregnant mothers,
together with all requisite games equipment, musical instruments
and uniforms for the band. When it came to insurance, pensions
and maternity benefits, his commitments read like a blueprint for
Utopia.

'You can judge from this,' he said, a trifle sardonically, 'how
the worker is cared for by the State. But there's no getting away
from what they've done—especially for women and children.
How long it will go on I wouldn't like to say. Or how long the
workers can keep going flat out for the better time they've been
promised. Some of my men are saying already, "Better time not
much use after we're dead."

'It's a pernicious system, of course, but it's the most effective
in the world: mass opinion geared to a fantastic network of committees and reports. At one time you could see people popping
little notes about their neighbours into the Security street boxes,
and next day the red vans would be round and away they'd go.
It's not so bad now. We've had no more Wu Fans or San Fans,
and the Kuomintang are out for good, but if production figures
fall suddenly anything might start to happen.

'As I said, I'm no communist, but I must admit this place
needed cleaning up. We did little to help and they did even less
for themselves. In the old days even my own servants had to pay
thirty per cent of their wages to the labour bosses to avoid being
beaten up. In this area alone there were ten thousand prostitutes—
some of the loveliest women in the world—and a white woman
couldn't walk down the street alone for fear of being molested.
I know there are plenty of people at home who moan about how
they've been treated, but they never say how much they'd taken

out of the country—or what they made their money from. There's a man I know in Hong Kong today who made a million out of opium—and he thinks he's been badly done to.

'You've got to hand it to them. Things couldn't have been any worse than they were. Communism was the only thing that could have done them any good.'

This was the appraisal of a cool-headed custodian of British capitalism. I quote him without comment: he had worked in Shanghai for twenty-four years, and it would be safe to say that he had not been brain-washed, indoctrinated or re-educated.

21

And Hangchow Below

THE night before we left Shanghai we said goodbye to Galal, Shakir and Baghdadi. The Syrian had been recalled for mobilisation and they were leaving together on an early morning plane.

We had a farewell party in Galal's room. Nobody was invited: the guests just happened to be there. Galal produced a bottle of cognac from somewhere; Vladimir fished out another bottle of vodka; and Carl contributed some schnapps—'I keep this for special occasion. Occasion now come!' Abou appeared in a majestic Sudanese nightshirt like an emir attired for his harem, and Tamas, Muriel, the Malayan, the Sinhalese and the little Algerian completed the party.

Inevitably the atmosphere was strained, the gaiety a little forced; and the language problem did nothing to help. So we played an absurd game of Abou's invention: it consisted simply of suggesting, on the basis of physical appearance, what job each guest would be best fitted to do if he had his time over again. As a party game it was no more and no less tedious than most, but it took such a singularly bawdy direction that it rapidly served its purpose. Thus the party began. Shakir put on his best firework exhibition of explosive merriment. Baghdadi wooed Muriel with the ardour of last-minute desperation and a wealth of elaborate advice from the Malayan and Sinhalese—and Vladimir and myself exchanged lower-deck songs learnt during the War in our respective navies. Nobody mentioned politics all night.

When the party broke up Galal took me quietly aside and pushed a piece of paper in my hand. 'I give you my address in

Cairo,' he said. 'In better days I hope you come see me.' I assured him that in better days I would, and we simply shook hands and left it at that.

In the morning we were off—for a two-day rest in Hangchow. At least that's what they had said; but the first thing on arrival was the announcement of the Programme.

For once in a while the delegates rebelled. Liu, the young official permanently attached to us, was arbitrarily instructed to get the Programme cancelled. With many apologies and humble prostrations he promised to do his best. In the end we settled for nothing more strenuous than a visit to a silk factory and a workers' sanatorium.

By now Liu and myself had come to an understanding. He took it for granted that it was no use offering me the Programme as such; certain things, as he had explained earlier, such as a visit to Tibet, were impossible, but in every other respect he went to endless lengths to arrange things to my liking. Nobody, in fact, could have worked harder to please. 'How was the Programme today?' he would ask anxiously over dinner. 'What do you prefer for tomorrow?' He addressed himself with the same zeal to the requirements of the other delegates, and for a young man handling his first major assignment he rated an emphatic alpha plus.

He had come to communism the empirical way, but he was no blind adherent to the Book. He accepted criticism more willingly than any other communist I met, and in replying to it never took refuge in jargon. On the question of indoctrination, I wondered sometimes, as I outlined to him the working of the British parliamentary system or the principle of a free Press or the American case on China, if his thinking was not being corrupted a good deal more than mine. He even got to understanding my aversion to comparative statistics; once, while the Director of a textile-mill was reeling off production figures before and after Liberation, he nudged my arm and whispered with a grin, 'No good for you. Propaganda speech only.' He assured me that the purpose of the visit to Hangchow had been to give the delegation a genuine rest in 'pleasant surroundings', but the local officials had naturally wished to show off their production achievements. 'Hangchow is enough in itself,' he declared. 'I know you will not want to see the other achievements.'

It was an understatement of some magnitude. To describe Hangchow as a place of 'pleasant surroundings' is to describe Everest as a fairly high mountain or the South Pole as a somewhat lonely spot. They have a traditional saying (so traditional in fact that it brought forth a deep groan from the young people present when quoted by the official at the Youth League reception): 'Above there is paradise, and below there are Soochow and Hangchow.

It is a town set on the eastern edge of a wonderful blue lake, at the foot of cypress-studded hills. Its history goes back to a thousand years before the birth of Christ. At the foot of the Solitary Hill the tomb of the ancient poet Lin Ho-ching can still be seen and a pavilion of the Sung dynasty marks the spot where he planted his plum trees and kept his pet cranes. The lake itself, fed by nearby springs, is comparatively small—only three miles wide and two miles long—but its tranquil beauty is enhanced by causeways and islands on which, in remote dynasties—before Charlemagne founded the Holy Roman Empire or Alfred created the English nation—the Chinese emperors laid their fish-ponds and flower-beds, built their balustrades and bridges: the Bridge Reflecting the Moon, the Bridge Locking the Current, the Bridge for Watching the Mountain, the Bridge Crossing the Rainbow; here they raised their temples of Purity and Benevolence, of Fidelity and Heroism; and on the outer shores of the lake, stretching deep into the hills, they planted their orchards and groves, their willows and cypress trees, their avenues and parks.

No picture could convey adequately the sublimity of all this, not in tones and colours only, but in the elegance and symmetry, the richness and rightness of the design; here, you felt, man and nature had moved as one: each had interpreted the other aright; and now everything is preserved, repaired, tended with loving care, not for the pleasure of The People only, it seemed, but for its own loveliness also.

At the foot of the Mountain of the Smoke-like Evening Clouds, between the Peak that Flew from Afar and the Cave that Leads to the Sky, a Buddhist temple, originally built about the time that Saul was anointed king of Israel, was being restored by State-paid craftsmen; in front of the Ch'ien Wang Temple, where the park known as Orioles Singing in the Willows had been allowed to run into a wilderness, the ground had been cleared and the willows were growing again; on the slopes beyond, in the last year alone sixty thousand trees had been planted. 'The people are working now,' they said, 'to make Hangchow always like Spring.'

If I was enthralled by all this Vladimir was enraptured, not by the visual beauties alone, but by the preservation of the religious relics. He scampered from grove to glade, taking photographs of Buddhist temples and Taoist shrines, and finally came to a halt, astonished, before an enormous stone carving of the Laughing Buddha in the Lin Yin Temple. Sensual, overblown, magnificently gross, the Laughing Buddha stirred the hedonist in him. 'This is *very* fine religion,' he declared admiringly. 'Chinese very clever people to pick such sensible god.'

The only offensive speck on this otherwise idyllic horizon was the hotel they had recently built for the housing of delegations. On the shore of the West Lake, than which I have tried to convey no lovelier stretch of water can have been gazed upon by human eye, they had erected what was surely the *longest* establishment in China. A single uninterrupted corridor nearly two hundred yards long ran from one end to the other, like an indoors sprinting track; it was, in fact, used as such every meal-time when Vladimir and myself raced from our rooms in the right wing to the distant dining-room in the left—to walk would have taken too long. But they had built it also as though by memory from some strictly functional prototype in the outer recesses of Omsk or the suburbs of Novosibersk; but somewhere along the line memory had played them tricks, for they had added little cornices and cupolas which might have belonged to the Byzantine or the Third Empire or any other period, but which incontestably did not belong to Hangchow. It sat upon the West Shore like a vast and meaningless back-cloth dropped inadvertently in the wrong scene. Looked upon by itself it was a freak; viewed against its surroundings an outrage. It was, they admitted, 'a mistake', but a mistake for which the designers, who may, for all I know, have done it on Soviet advice, might reasonably have been given a stiff dose of re-education through labour-training.

More admirable in design as in purpose, another new building had just been completed high in the Western Mountain, looking down superbly over the lake. This was the Ping Fung San, the third workers' sanatorium to be built in the area. It was to specialise in the treatment of arthritis and rheumatism—which are the major health problems in the south, and the Director was also waiting for the arrival of physiotherapy equipment for the treatment of polio. Light, airy, spaciously planned, splendidly equipped: with its reading-rooms, games-rooms, private cinema —and Hangchow below—the Ping Fung San did the workers proud; the only unfortunate thing—and in a building so essentially designed for human benefit you felt as grieved about this as the Chinese themselves—a large crack had already appeared in the marble floor of the entrance hall.

Even the silk factory would have been difficult to find fault with. It represented a bold attempt to revive a skill which had been dying out, they said, long before the communists took over. Ten local manufacturers had amalgamated under joint State– private enterprise. Their machines were obsolete, their 'techniques' old-fashioned, their working conditions dangerously cramped, but they were producing cloths and tapestries, screens and scroll paintings, cushion covers and brocaded gowns, in the richest traditional style. It seemed somehow very right and proper that this factory, the only one of its kind in China, should be situated in Hangchow.

There was the usual Social Evening before we left—but this one was less usual than most. For the first time the girls responded to the idea that dancing close to their partners might be more pleasurable than holding them at arm's length. If the discovery went to their heads it had an even worse effect upon some of the delegates. The enforced frustrations of weeks clamoured for release. Ricardo got himself obliviously entwined round a dusky beauty from the Geological Institute; the Malayan clutched one of the sanatorium nurses to him as Samson might have held the pillars of Gath; and the stout Abou, mopping a fevered brow, had to retire from the hunt altogether, unable to trust himself further: 'It has made me hot and impulsive,' he gasped. 'I have no control over hot impulses.'

The only delegate who seemed unaffected was Bernini, who continued to hold his partner away from him, nose cocked sideways in the air, as though pushing a trolley-load of stale-smelling food. 'Look at little big shot,' murmured Vladimir. 'Very serious man. All big shots serious. It is their duty to be so—even at carnival dance!'

But the pace was too hot to last.

Nobody had gone into action with keener verve than the convivial Carl. For some time he had manœuvred an alluring young languages student about the room to a quaint little step of his own, designed to reduce movement to the minimum and propinquity to the maximum, when suddenly, at the beginning of a new dance, she drew herself stiffly back. Soon the other girls did the same. The evening went as flat as a wet garden party on the vicarage lawn.

'Very strange thing happen,' said Carl, at the end of the dance. 'At first we hold hands very warm—so! She put head on shoulder—so! Next dance she go with chief of Youth League. She come back—and now she push me away—so—and dance very stiff—so!'

There was present on this occasion a twenty-year-old girl named Wang whose serenely beautiful features had somehow survived the austere aftermath of female emancipation. She wore long pigtails, had gently curving cheeks, and looked at you through dark and trusting eyes as though she were ready to melt and curl into your arms.

She could not, of course, speak English, so there was nothing to do but sit and gaze appreciatively upon her. 'She is very pretty girl,' exclaimed Vladimir, his boyish face aglow. 'Very, *very* pretty!'

She smiled and nodded her head, but she did not understand. It was of great importance that she should; it was something perhaps she had never been told before; so Vladimir urgently summoned an interpreter.

'Please tell her,' he instructed him, 'we think she is very pretty girl. *Very* pretty. Very sweet. Very charming. Very, *very* pretty.'

'Very, *very* pretty,' I echoed. 'She is the prettiest girl in the whole of Hangchow.'

'Oh, no! no!' she cried in the fragile accents of a wonderful singing doll.

'Oh, yes, yes!' I insisted.

'But not so pretty as an English girl.'

'Much prettier than most English girls.'

'Much prettier than *all* Russian girls!' cried Vladimir, chivalrously.

And that being about all we could say, we sat together for some time like a rather pointless comic trio, Vladimir holding her left hand and I her right, repeating at intervals what we had already made abundantly clear, that we thought she was indeed very, *very* pretty.

One of the strangest dances of the evening was a rollicking, thumping affair to a tune vaguely suggestive of an oriental Highland fling. The delegates plunged into it with zest, and none more merrily than Vladimir. 'Chinese have very strange habits,' he explained afterwards. 'This was not tune for dance at all, but tune of Russian revolution!' With a nice relish of the irony, he sang the original words: 'Let's join together in bloody struggle—with swords and smoking guns—and wipe out tyrants of filthy bourgeoisie!—and last line!' he roared—'last line says, "Shoot them all down and HAVE GREAT FUN!"' It seems to me,' he chuckled, 'very strange song for our peaceful delegation!'

At the end of the evening, as President for the day, he distinguished himself by making the shortest speech of the whole tour. First there was a rambling peroration from the League official (translated only into Russian: 'All about Peace and Friendship,' whispered Vladimir. 'Very unnecessary!') to which he replied with simple brevity: 'On behalf of delegation, I say sad goodbye to Hangchow, and especially'—he cast a sidelong glance in the direction of Wang—'especially to all *young* people of Hangchow.'

But at ten-thirty sharp the young people were seen rapidly off the premises. 'Great pity,' remarked Vladimir, as we went up to our rooms, 'that we could not take very pretty girl for little walk in moonlight round pretty lake of Hangchow.'

22

Living in a Vacuum

THE train steamed slowly south through miles of paddy-fields, past yellow farmlands and mud-brick villages, beside ancient burial-mounds and irrigation ditches, while, stretching forever into the distance, gangs of coolies carried and dragged their endless burdens over the plains of eternal China.

We had a long way to go, over twelve hundred miles to tropical Canton, and it would take us forty hours to get there. 'The trains are slow,' said Liu, 'and in that we are very backward. But they are also very safe. In the old days there were many accidents. It was a common thing for the engines to come off the rails. Now they do not exceed thirty miles an hour and our people can travel in safety. Better to arrive slow than not to arrive at all.'

The mood of the delegates had changed: for one thing, Hangchow had done us all good. For another, Galal and Shakir had gone and we could discuss Suez with fewer inhibitions. And for a third, we had accepted the futility of bickering over events which we could in no way control and which we still knew so little about. *The People's Daily* was full of reports from Cairo: 'the aggressive forces of imperialism' were intensifying their attacks, although they had agreed to a cease-fire; a United Nations force was on the way to Egypt, but the aggressors intended to use it for their own purposes; the U.S. forces were exploiting the aggression in order to get control of Egypt for themselves. In Hungary all was alleged to be calm. Chou En-lai had congratulated Kadar on saving the People's Democracy, and the Worker–Peasant Revolutionary Council had refused to allow Hungary's internal affairs to be discussed in the General Assembly. Elsewhere China was pre-occupied with celebrating the ninetieth anniversary of Sun Yat-sen's birthday and the thirty-ninth of the Russian Revolution. Their athletics team had withdrawn from the Olympic Games in protest against the separate entry of the nationalist team; and in a remote corner of the paper it was casually reported that Eisenhower had won the American election. Later, in Peking, I was to piece together from old English newspapers the story of the Hungarian rising, of the tumultuous repercussions throughout the west and in the communist countries themselves; and was to read also of the upheaval in England during the Suez adventure.

But all this was to come. For the time being we chugged slowly south at thirty miles an hour, in a vacuum of ignorance and uncertainty. We played cards and read and talked about other things. Even Ricardo could find nothing to report.

By this time Vladimir and myself took our personal relationship for granted. Now, looked at in retrospect, this seems to me to have been a remarkable thing. Although it might be commonplace for Englishmen of opposite political parties to live on terms of personal friendship with each other, I should have thought a similar rapprochement impossible for a Russian communist—especially at a time like this! The farther we travelled, however, the farther Vladimir moved away from his own kind in every sense but the political—there his loyalties remained with the Tamas–Bernini group as surely as mine with the western. He was visibly shocked by the stories from Hungary—not so much by what the Russian had done as by the summary justice served out by the rebels on the Hungarian communists. 'It is the same with all counter-revolutionaries,' he said. 'They go too far too soon.' He interpreted the rising as a result of 'terrible mistakes of Stalin and Beria'; and, when I showed him an English newspaper with a picture of Stalin's statue being hacked to pieces in a Budapest square, he commented grimly, 'Between you and me, not only in Budapest.' But, though he granted that many workers and peasants had taken part in the revolution, he would not concede that they represented the mass of the people.

I did not blame him for his views. After all, it is difficult to alter the mental habits of a lifetime within a few weeks. He would go back to his beloved Moscow and fall into the familiar ruts of Marxist thinking, but for the time being at least he was accessible to new ideas. I plied him with the newspapers I had brought from Shanghai, and he read them with avid curiosity. I suppose that to him the English reports from Budapest were as distorted as those in *Pravda* were to me, but he was able to read the one, while I could not even attempt the other.

What interested him most, however, was not the political content but the treatment and presentation of news. It was a kind of journalism he had never seen before. He was utterly fascinated by it—particularly when I showed him a copy of the *Daily Express*.

Far from being shocked by the banner headlines denouncing Soviet intervention, he whistled in admiration. 'This is very clever technique. Very, *very* clever paper. Reader cannot fail to be interested. News is presented in very colourful way—very attractive to eye. This is paper of very clever journalist. Maybe bad reactionary outlook but good style of writing. And this photograph' —it was an unflattering profile of the Russian Ambassador in London who had just been cold-shouldered at the Lord Mayor's dinner—'very fine technique. Not nice to show our Ambassador so, but very clever method. Very interesting for me because in our papers technique of reproduction is very poor. In *Pravda* are very few photographs, but all look as if taken with camera in wrong focus.' (This I had seen myself in pictures of the Budapest hangings. The scenes were gruesome enough in all conscience, but the distorted reproduction made them look like grisly rites in hell. I had thought this was the result of deliberate touching up by the Art department, but apparently it was not so.)

Never having seen newspaper advertisements before, he read through them as if they were news stories. He was amazed by the cash-prize competitions, and appalled by stories and photographs with a sexual background. 'Not proper subject for good journalist,' he declared. 'In my country are no such stories.'

His curiosity was as stimulating as it was unexpected. It might be said, of course, that a horse which has been tethered in the stable for years will naturally run riot when the padlock is removed; but equally it might be content to graze in comfort in the nearest pastures. To Vladimir finding out was an occupation in itself. His interest in things English was inexhaustible. He would have made an ideal pupil for a British Council teacher frustrated by local indifference to his work—a brand plucked from the burning, a warm hand held out in an ungrateful city. He did not seek the English viewpoint in order to refute it or knowledge of English manners in order to deride them: it simply delighted him to be familiar with them.

In this respect nothing delighted him more than his discovery of the English vernacular. This was of no relevance to anything else happening in the world or to any aspect of delegation life, but it provided a welcome relief from the gloomy awareness of more fearful things. Somewhere along the way Vladimir had come across that hardy old-fashioned Saxon word which English people today most dread to hear spoken in public. It was a wonderful revelation to him, of almost mystical impact; a moment of truth. 'It has always been my dream to know this word,' he cried and, roaring with delight, rushed to copy it down in his notebook. Having stumbled upon the word, he addressed himself to learning its derivatives and their usages, and thereafter, during the rest of the trip and, indeed, all the way back to Moscow, he introduced them regularly into his conversation with a loud and fiery relish which completely bewildered the Chinese and utterly shattered the English.

This time last year, he recalled, his dimpled cheeks aglow, he had been sailing down the Volga with four of his friends: 'Ate much good fish—drank much vodka—and during night all sat together round fire—and do you know what we do?' . . . I waited expectantly for some romantic evocation of the joys of Marxist comradeship. . . . 'We tell each other—how you say?— all night we tell each other RUDE STORIES!'

Although he had made prolonged efforts to pick up useful Chinese phrases from his interpreter, he admitted himself as

P

defeated by the language as I was. 'It is too complicated,' he said. 'They never say what they mean about anything. Even my interpreter [he came from Mongolia] cannot understand them. They never come to real point, but make everything so diplomatic. For professional diplomats it must be terrible. For us it is impossible!'

He had seen, he said, a 'most amazing sight' in Shanghai, which only emphasised the gulf between even the working people and ourselves. He had been crossing an old market square when he came across a crowd of factory workers playing a lunchtime game. They were sitting cross-legged in a circle around a young man playing a Chinese flute. A girl with a basket under her arm danced slowly round the circle.

'Suddenly music stop and nearest person pick piece of paper from basket. It seems he has to do what paper says. First instruction is to read story from newspaper. All people listen—very interested—then all applaud loud at finish—*very* much applause. Then music start again, and so to next piece of paper. This time instruction says, "Give details of recent production in factory." Again all people listen with great interest and give great applause.'

'And the next instruction?' I asked.

He shrugged his hands. 'It was too much. . . . I went away.' He shook his head despairingly. 'It will be years before we can understand such people.'

I went to my sleeping compartment to find the Malayan and the Sinhalese groaning on their bunks with the pangs of enforced celibacy. Much as they admired the Chinese achievement, they deplored its puritanical ethos.

The Malayan was convinced that the government were trying to alter the sex instinct of the whole population. 'They are like the masters in your English public schools. They know they cannot kill the instinct, so they try to purify it by keeping mind and body constantly at work.'

The Sinhalese stirred fitfully on the bunk above me and swore he would never come back to China until a more tolerant system had been devised, or unless he were able to bring his wife with him.

There was a sudden rumble of gunfire from the nearby hills. We looked out to see searchlights sweeping the sky. They soon found what they wanted—a lone aircraft heading south. Shells exploded all round. For a moment the plane seemed to hover as though uncertain whether to dive or turn back; my heart went out to the pilot—he had no chance. A red flare gashed the mauve sky. The plane plunged down like a blazing stone to illuminate the nearby trees.

Next day *The People's Daily* reported simply: 'The bodies of nine airmen of Chiang Kai-shek's Air Force were found in Siaoshan County. . . .' The claim was denied a day or two later in the Taipei Press.

23

The Different City

THE brown farmlands turned to green and gold, the soil of
the distant foothills to deep scarlet. We chugged slowly on
through fields of rice and sugar-cane, past lotus-blooming
ponds and level swamps where water-buffaloes dragged ancient
ploughs and peasants threshed their rice by hand as they had done
since time immemorial. The abundant sun flooded the country-
side. The fertile Kwantung plain stretched away into the blue
haze of the western mountains like a triumphal harvest procession.

On the approach to the city the railway line swung in to run
parallel to the River Pearl, sluggish and grey with mud. Propped
above its banks, rickety and precarious like a street built on stilts,
but firm against flood and deluge, stood the wooden huts of the
peasants. On the water below floated the sampans and barges, the
suburbs of the river-side people.

They had said Canton was 'different': they did not exaggerate.
The difference dazzled the eyes as soon as we stepped off the train.

The reception party had dressed up to kill. There was not a
boiler-suit to be seen, not a single padded jacket or high-necked
tunic. They rushed down the platform in a blaze of colour like a
holiday-camp crowd gone berserk. The young men looked
startling enough in their vivid shirts and gay silk ties—but the
girls were truly sensational.

It was not merely what they had done to their bodies, although
their frocks were a riot of colour that would have stopped the
show on the busiest Bank Holiday in Blackpool, but they had
smeared and daubed their faces with enough make-up to supply
an American musical for a month or an English touring company

for a year. Their lips were aflame with carmine, their cheeks with crimson—as if, after years of prohibition, they had suddenly broken into a cosmetics factory and gone mad with the spoils. Their gaudy, grinning faces reminded you, at best, of the grotesque heroines of Peking Opera, at worst, of a group of newly recruited harlots out on the spree. For the first time on these occasions nobody broke into 'Unity is Strength', and you felt it would have been perfectly in order to have offered to any one of the welcoming young women a friendly, appreciative kiss.

We arrived too late for lunch, too early for dinner, so we were taken for a 'snack' at a widely-famed tea-house.

I had by this time discovered that Chinese food as cooked in delegation hotels bore little comparison to similar food cooked in the restaurants and tea-houses. The former was the work of men who cooked for a living, the latter of those who lived to cook. The *spécialité* of this *maison* was shrimp and we ate it in fourteen different ways: in rice rissoles, in lotus cakes, in cauliflower dumplings: fried with shreds of chicken, roasted in morsels of duck, and wound round in nameless leaves and weeds and bits and pieces of aqueous vegetation. Only Abou, whose stomach was allergic to fish of any kind, failed to appreciate the occasion.

There were the usual sights to be seen: a vast new park outside the city; an artificial lake; two enormous swimming-pools, and a network of smaller pools for the children; a football ground scooped out of a hill with seating for fifty thousand; and the Sun Yat-sen Memorial Hall, a magnificent circular building, meticulously fashioned in traditional style, capable of seating five thousand, and erected without a single supporting pillar between floor and roof.

Canton is proud of its revolutionary traditions. It was here that the famous seventy-two martyrs were executed, where Sun Yatsen launched his first northern campaign and Mao set up the headquarters of the peasant movement. A new museum preserves the relics of those years of upheaval like a history of modern China in microcosm: the student risings, the secret meetings, the early achievements of the Kuomintang, the double dealings and subterfuges, the mistaken alliances, the tragic missions.

In the National Institute of the Peasant Movement the furniture used by Mao and the early peasant leaders in 1924 had been kept intact. Here Vladimir gazed in astonishment at a notice indicating the chairs on which the Christian members of the movement had sat. 'It is fantastical!' he exclaimed. 'Why, in my country at this time we were crashing down churches and wiping out Christians. There was a popular song of time'—he sang it first in Russian —it sounded like a merry little jig:

'We shall kick out all priests and kick down all churches,
Then we shall climb high in sky and kick out God!

Of course,' he hastened to add, 'that was thirty years ago, not now.'

Canton had also its House of Sino-Soviet Friendship, a vast establishment recently completed at colossal cost but of immeasurable solidarity value. Similar Houses, on an equally grandiose scale, dominate the skyline in most of the other large cities and can be expected to do so, sooner or later, in all of them. They fulfil emphatically the function implied by their name, for they provide a mammoth showroom for displays of Soviet and satellite achievement which most of the populace seem willing and even anxious to queue for hours to see.

That week the Sino-Soviet House was holding something new in the way of exhibitions. China had put her own goods in the window: ostensibly of export commodities, the exhibition contained samples of practically everything produced in the country in the last seven years.

There were the latest show-pieces, of course—diesel locomotives from Darien, jet planes from Harbin, centrifugal pumps, X-ray equipment, Liberation lorries from Changchun—strictly not for sale—and the standard exports: tung oil and tea, bristles and porcelain, textiles and tallows, silks and laces—but there were more than forty thousand other products as well, which represented a performance of some magnitude.

The Foodstuffs department was more in my line than the machines; here the names alone constituted an epicurean lyric: Canton lichees, Tientsin pears, Tsingtao cherries, Fukien loquats, Lian Hsiang chestnuts and Hsingkiang Hami melons; Yunnan ham, braised bamboo shoots and long-tailed anchovies. Some of the meat exhibits evoked less pleasurable sensations: pig's sinews, duck's gizzards and—a great delicacy, they say—bear's paws; but these were cancelled out in the 'Bristles Room' of the Animal By-Products Section next door, where the labels read like a page from a Shakespearean glossary: cock saddles and great bustard tails, mallard scapulas and teal plumages, red heron feathers, short white ospreys, Lady Amhurst headskins and black-eared kites.

There was no doubt the Chinese meant business. Everything had been laid on with a high degree of efficiency and considerable artistic sense. Two whole wings had been set aside for enquiries and orders, with well-appointed post and telegraph offices, elaborate facilities for banking and insurance, and a bureau of advice on customs, inspection and testing. The thought came again: if they can do all this *now* what will they be turning out in twenty and thirty years' time?

'Originally,' said the Director, 'over a hundred British business men had accepted invitations' (it was agreeably surprising to notice that all goods were labelled in Chinese, Russian *and* English), 'but,' he explained delicately, 'there were some difficulties of transport and communications as a result of events in Egypt.'

I did, however, find one Englishman, a Manchester cotton merchant who had just ordered £100,000 worth of textiles, and he confessed himself staggered by the whole turn-out.

'Goodness knows I'm no communist, but I've been over-whelmed—not just by a few home-made trucks and trains, but by the terrific range of goods. It's an astonishing achievement. I came here with the idea that everything was the same as a hundred years ago, but what they've done is beyond belief! And in the Cultural Palaces—I've never seen anything like it! Thousands of young people enjoying themselves in games and dancing—don't tell me that our Teddy boys are an improvement on that! The only odd thing was to see men dancing with men—I can't think that's good for anybody.'

'And what do you think,' I asked, 'about the Peace and Friendship? Do you think they really mean it?'

'Ah,' he said, 'there I am afraid. Now they are told to believe in peace but they could just as easily be made to believe in war—for the sake of peace—and if that should happen it could be the end of the western world. I believe the time will come—within our lifetime—when China could swallow the whole of the British Empire and America too—and do it without indigestion.'

It seemed a remote possibility; but seven years ago that exhibition must have seemed equally remote.

The main stream of the industrial revolution has passed Canton by. Although it can boast a thriving textile industry and a large paper factory, in essence it remains what it has been since the British opened it up last century, 'a land of fruits', an international market-place for oranges, bananas, pineapples and melons—the 'money crops' of the south.

Perhaps because it was the first Chinese city to trade with the west (it still maintains, they say, amicable smuggling relations with Hong Kong), its people have a peculiar sophistication of their own. They do not smile at strangers as readily as most of their countrymen do—are just as likely in fact to pass them with sullen glares; they do not make friends so easily, although when they do, they say, it is for life; they shout and bang and clatter more noisily about their business than most other Chinese, but they seem to chatter less. Perhaps because they have been bred eternally on the river or have had to eke their living from flood-washed land they seem dour even to the point of moroseness.

Facially in fact they do not look Chinese: they tend to have wide jawbones, exceptionally flat noses, eyes set deeply apart and curling negroid lips. They are famous throughout China for their habit of wearing clogs; it is thought to be very funny indeed that they should wear them 'even for receptions'. They are also addicted to their tea-houses, which even the poorer classes are said to patronise at least three times a day. They are colourful, individualistic and utterly enigmatic; even the Chinese of other cities confess to being baffled by them.

The lifeline of the city is the sampan-studded river, and it was the sampans I wanted to visit most.

The officials seemed surprised by my request; apparently it was not usual for visitors to express such a wish. When I went down to the river I quickly saw why.

The sampan is not, as the romantically-minded might imagine, a kind of exotic houseboat or cosy holiday launch. It is a habitation, a place of business and a public conveyance, and its resources are pitifully inadequate to most of the demands made upon them.

Over sixty thousand people, called for some obscure reason 'The Family of the Egg', live in these boats, for the most part in conditions as appalling as any in the Shanghai slums. The average sampan is about as spacious as a small motor-launch, which is to say that it has less overall space than a London council-house kitchen. It has to accommodate families of rarely less than four and often as many as ten people: strapping young boys and gnarled old women, new-born babies and crippled old men—they sleep on the deck and on wooden planks laid across the deck. If lucky, they have a timbered roof above them, but in most cases merely a canvas awning supported on bamboo rods. For most of the year they are dry, but when the rains fall they may remain wet for days on end. In the stern of the boat they carry their goods and chattels: sticks of furniture, kitchen utensils, bags of wheat and rice, sacks of coal and crates of ducks and chickens. Many of the sampans reek abominably of livestock and excrement, but in some incense burnt at little Buddhist shrines in the bows provides an unusual deodorant. The sampan is not merely the river dweller's home—it may also be his temple.

For these people times have always been hard, and in some ways they have improved little since the Liberation. Most of their old work of haulage and transport is now done by steamboats. A few months before my visit a pool of co-operatives had been formed for ferrying and fishing, but it was too early to say what difference it would make. Some said they were making less money than before, some slightly more, but even at the best it amounted to a mere pittance.

The old people and the infirm were feeling the pinch most. They benefited from the new health service, of course, and inoculations kept them free from cholera and tuberculosis, but what was the point of being healthy if you had nothing to look forward to?

For the young folk it was different. It was a good time for them to be growing up; they had a fine future ahead of them. In the old days there had been no schools to attend. Nearly everyone was illiterate—and rather proud of the fact. They had despised schooling and had nothing in common with the folk of the city. Now they were glad to see their children going to primary schools and literacy classes, and some even to secondary schools and colleges. Of course, all this schooling meant that the young men were drifting away from the river to work in the factories and handicraft co-operatives, but it was good to see them doing well for themselves—some were even earning enough to buy luxuries like watches and gold rings, and they could all afford quilts for their beds. In the last year fifteen young people from the river had actually been elected to the local congress.

Oh yes, it was a great time for the young, and there was no doubt it was going to be better. There was even a wonderful scheme for building enough new houses within the next seven years to clear the sampans off the river completely . . . that would be fine for their children and their children's children—nobody lived on the river from choice—but seven years might be too long for some of the older folk to wait. . . . Meantime they would go on picking up what trade they could . . . waiting to hear more about the new houses . . . and watching the big steamboats go by. . . .

Cultural Palaces, spacious parks, schools, department stores, new housing estates; sampans and slums. The forces of the old order and the new rubbed shoulders here in starker propinquity than in any other city I visited.

There was, immediately behind the skyscraper hotel where we were staying, a wonderful market: bustling, colourful, gay, ripe with the smells of southern fruit. It was separated from the main street by a network of narrow alleys and passage-ways. They looked dark, sinister and dangerous, like the setting of a Fu Manchu story.

If it was really true that a foreigner could pass unmolested through any street in China even at night, these alleys, I thought, would be a good testing ground. They demanded to be explored.

Being of a cautious disposition I did not go alone but asked my Sinhalese friend to accompany me, on the protective principle that, should trouble threaten, his Asiatic instincts might anticipate it in time to take appropriate defensive action. On a more concrete principle, I also took an old Burmese dagger—acquired obscurely one night in Chittagong towards the end of the war—and a spiked ring removed from the finger of a French matelot in Beirut in December 1943, on the night the French killed one of our own sailors on the steps of the Savoy Canteen.

The Sinhalese did not stay with me for long.

As we turned off the main road the good ripe smell of the fruit from the market was swallowed up in a stench of such foulness that we both stopped dead in our tracks. It made the odour of the sampans seem like lavender, the smell of the Fan Kua-lun slums like sweet perfume. It almost dispelled my interest in the expedition—but it finished off the Sinhalese altogether. Declaring he would be sick if he went any farther, he put his handkerchief to his nose and quickly made his way back to the street.

Some stubborn streak of curiosity stopped me from following him. I took several deep breaths to get quickly acclimatised, tightened the ring on my finger and pressed cautiously on.

But there was nothing whatever to fear: no footpads, no bandits, no lurking watchers or loiterers of the night. There was instead a community of people quietly gathered in their homes for their evening rest. But the difference between these people and most others was that their homes were ramshackle sheds and stables, and they themselves were living little better than animals.

I had seen the slums by day, but never by night, and seen them generally from the outside, but here I was looking in—not through windows, for there were none—but through great slits in the walls where windows should have been. The sheds were lit by oil lamps, burning low, and perhaps their pallid glow made the interiors seem worse than they were: rotting timber walls and patched-up roofs; families of six and seven, sitting cross-legged, knotted tightly together, eating their meals on the floor; babies fast asleep on wooden planks in dark corners; children bent double against the walls trying to catch enough light to read by; two naked figures in cramped copulation on a carpet of ragged sacks, writhing under the lurid glow of the lamp like doomed souls in the shadows of the Inferno, while their three children slept on the floor at their feet; an aged scarecrow of a man, completely naked, standing to wash himself in a black iron bowl; ducks in wicker cages and hens roosting along the walls; every inch of space occupied either by human bodies or their basic impedimenta—the means of existence only, the bare, primitive equipment of survival.

From within the hovels rose the buzz and murmur of family gossip—the world in the evening, settled to its leisure—while outside, the alley-ways were hushed and deserted; but I had not yet seen the worst.

I turned into a passage so dark and narrow that it was difficult to move down it without bumping into the walls on either side. I sensed rather than saw faces watching me from the narrow openings and once I felt somebody's breath on mine. At that point I was afraid and would have gone faster if I could have seen the way. Eventually I came to a turning and saw with infinite relief the glow of a street lamp at the far end of the alley ahead. As I walked towards it the shapes of the alley-way became clearer; on one side the thin, ochre light of the lamp revealed some half a dozen habitations that could scarcely even be dignified by the name of hovels: they were, to be precise, human kennels.

There seemed to be one man in each—there was no room for more—and these men, I repeat, *men*, were standing, partly because there was no room to sit, partly because they had no lamp to see by; standing, with their heads peering out of the black shadows of their kennels—as though their legs had been chained to the walls inside; standing to eat their evening meal by whatever light they could catch thrown from the lamp in the street.

It was too dark to make out their faces and I did not try too hard. I had a macabre impression of black eyes staring from sunken sockets in gaunt, bearded heads and—imagination, perhaps—when they were aware of my scrutiny a sense of glowering hostility and hate. I moved hurriedly on and was glad to get back to the street.

Why these men still lived like this nobody knew, or if they knew they would not tell. 'Many things are still very backward,' was all the Cantonese would say. 'We cannot put everything right at once.' Even Shen, who always spoke to the point and had himself grown up in Canton, could not, or would not, explain it. 'At least you came back alive,' was his only comment. 'That might not have been possible before.'

The next afternoon, Shen took me on a tour of the oldest part of the city.

He was an excellent guide, unobtrusive, making no attempt to force things upon me, supplying information when he saw something of special interest, and willing to branch off from his appointed route down any alley-way I suggested.

We walked through a maze of centuries-old passage-ways and streets, round ancient bazaars and markets, past stalls still selling fine silks and scroll paintings, humming birds, intricate wood carvings and curios in ivory and jade. We looked in at workshops open to the street where men and women were busy weaving and spinning, shaping bowls and jugs and moulds for the oven, blending mysterious herbs, stitching pigskin bags, and mending copper implements on antique lathes.

It was a journey back through time into the orient of one's old imagining: people teemed and bustled through the doorways;

vendors urgently shouted their wares; children clip-clopped about in their clogs with bundles of even smaller children slung across their shoulders—there was all the colour and confusion, the sweat and fervour of the ancient eastern market-places: a way of life as remote from the ideological background as the pedicab from the Rolls-Royce—or so you would have liked to think.

Then I stopped outside a carpenter's workshop. Within there was a scene of remarkable activity. Back to back, elevated on wooden benches, some four or five feet from the ground, two rows of boys and girls, about thirty in number, pedalled furiously away at old-fashioned drilling machines—drilling holes in wooden abacus beads. Some worked in their shirt-sleeves, some in grubby vests, some stripped to the waist. Two boys were taking time off to sleep on a makeshift platform opposite the primitive lavatory in the far corner of the building. Sawdust and shavings were piled on the floor; washing hung from the grimy walls. As they pedalled away to the grinding whirr of the machines, sweat glistening on their backs in the light of the single electric lamp, they looked for all the world like a squad of Dickensian waifs, born out of time and place, orphans of the totalitarian storm. But the illusion was short-lived: when they saw me walking in, without waiting for the supervisor's permission, they switched off their machines, scrambled down from their benches and practically fell over themselves in the rush to be sociable. They were children of Dekker rather than Dickens, of Eyre's shop rather than Fagin's kitchen; if it had been a holiday they could not have looked more carefree.

Their ages varied between fifteen and nineteen and they were serving an eleven months' apprenticeship. They worked an eight-hour shift and were paid between fifteen and thirty *yuan* a month, of which they paid back twelve *yuan* for food. When they qualified they would hope to join a co-operative where they would start on fifty *yuan* a month and eventually go on to piece rates. Were they happy about their prospects? They could not have been happier. Drilling abacus beads was nothing to rave about, but when they had learnt the 'advanced techniques' there would always be interesting work for them to do—with the satisfaction of knowing that they were directly serving the people.

They were different from the usual Chinese youths I had met in that they did most of the talking—and were uninhibited in more ways than one: as they crowded round me at the supervisor's bench I had the distinct impression that the boys and girls in the rear rank were seizing the opportunity to practise some Chinese variation of old-fashioned slap and tickle. The occasion was altogether charming, friendly and gay—then suddenly it burst into melodrama.

There were on the wall opposite me two drawings in black and white. They were similar to posters I had already seen on a larger scale, in flaming colours and giant lettering, on the public hoardings, but they had an intimacy which the posters had lacked. The first one showed a fat, bull-faced Englishman and a leering Frenchman machine-gunning a field of women and children beneath the bleeding shadow of the Sphinx; the second depicted a magnificent young Russian giant—a kind of Soviet Superman— wielding an enormous broom to sweep the floor of a cluster of rat-faced counter-revolutionaries—while an evil-looking American hurried after them dangling a bagful of £20,000,000.

Sensing my interest, the apprentices pushed forward the artist responsible, a shock-haired, cheerful-looking lad of about seventeen. I turned to Shen and asked him to translate the inscription on the Egyptian cartoon. He looked extremely perturbed and said he would rather not.

'Don't bother about my feelings,' I insisted. 'The words can't be any more vicious than the drawing itself.'

'All right,' he said. 'But I've warned you that you won't like it.'

'*We condemn the filthy aggression of the imperialists,*' he read. '*Britain and France have invoked the wrath of the Chinese youth. We demand a peaceful solution to the Egyptian problem. We are against the use of force, but we will support to the death the righteous struggle of the Egyptian people.*'

I turned to ask the artist where he had found his inspiration— but suddenly, inexplicably, he had gone, vanished into the streets.

Somebody explained that he had had to go home for an early dinner, but I found that hard to believe, since nobody else seemed to be under the same domestic pressure. It may have been, of course, that he was exceptionally shy and embarrassed by the occasion—or perhaps, even, felt that he had embarrassed the English visitor and ought to get out of the way.

Be that as it may, I thought it highly improbable that 'the Chinese youth' could be invoked to wrath over something they knew so little about or over the affairs of a country so far removed from their own: but I was mistaken.

'How many of you have learnt to read?' I asked.

'Ninety per cent of all the apprentices,' they said.

'Which newspapers?'

'*China Youth* and the Canton edition of *The People's Daily*.'

'And how many,' I put the question with caution, 'feel that Britain and France are in the wrong about Egypt?'

The atmosphere of relaxed good humour and youthful friendliness vanished in a flash.

'Everyone in this workshop does!' they cried heatedly. 'And everyone in this street! And everyone in Canton!'

'So if I go into every workshop I shall find the same feelings—and the same kind of drawings?'

'Everywhere you go. Not only here but with all the young people of China—they all think the same!'

One lad of about sixteen with a broken nose and hard-bitten face pushed his way violently to the front and launched into a fiery tirade against the British aggressors. He had, I felt, been eyeing me suspiciously all along. He snarled and shouted and stamped his feet and did everything except shake his fist in my face, while the rest of his friends angrily urged him on; and in the background Shen and the supervisor looked equally disconsolate about the whole thing.

'All right,' I said, when he appeared to have finished. 'Supposing that the British have done wrong. Don't you think that what the Russians are doing in Hungary is just as bad?'

This time he did shake his fist and all the other young people, so delightful and gay five minutes before, closed in towards me shouting in indignation. For a moment I had a detached impression of the water-front gang moving in upon their victim in the famous Kazan film. There were thirty of them, and even with the faithful Shen at hand I did not feel particularly comfortable. He had by now given up trying to interpret and was anxiously urging the supervisor into action. The broken-nosed boy, quivering with rage, thrust his face closer into mine while the others formed a menacing circle behind him. I braced myself against the wall, ready for action.

But there was no violence—somehow there never was. The supervisor suddenly shot to life, pushed his way to the front, spoke sharply to the ringleader, and ordered everyone to calm down. The tension relaxed. They lowered their fists and in a minute or two were all grinning at me rather sheepishly—except, that is, for the broken-nosed lad, who turned his back on the supervisor and went on muttering angrily to himself.

'It's getting late,' said Shen. 'I think we'd better go.'

It seemed a trifle inappropriate on this occasion to leave behind the usual message of peace and goodwill on behalf of the young people of England, so I simply shook hands with the supervisor and thanked him for having me.

'I would like to make it clear,' he said, 'that they do not regard you as being personally responsible for the aggression in Egypt. They know that you are one of the People and are not to blame for what your government has done.'

'Tell them to remember that every government can make mistakes,' I said. 'Even the Chinese and the Russian.'

I walked back with Shen for some time in silence. 'I hope you were not too upset by what happened,' he said eventually. 'Canton people are sometimes quickly excited. You must remember it is a different city.'

It was different again in the evening.

There was another Social, this time with over a thousand in attendance.

Q

My enjoyment of these over-gregarious occasions had by now
diminished in inverse proportion to the number of people present;
the more there were, the fewer with whom you could achieve a
state of mutual coherence. The young people had looked forward
to the event for weeks and had queued and drawn lots for tickets;
for many it was their first opportunity to meet anyone from
abroad, especially from England, and it was unthinkable to dis-
appoint them. But the business of sitting surrounded by dozens of
beaming and largely incomprehensible admirers, feeding them
with endlessly repetitive titbits about the English way of life
through the medium of a third person—a schoolboy or student
whose command of English was, in the nature of things, tentative
rather than practical—and then being dragged round the floor by
one vivacious girl after another because she felt that that was
what you most desired, made them into an exercise which you
started with mild exasperation and finished in a state of ex-
haustion. I even began to feel a sneaking sympathy for Bernini:
several years of this would make any man look like a dried-up
codfish.

But, again, Canton was a different city. . . . If you showed no
desire to dance, the girls did not suggest you should; if you
seemed reluctant to talk they did not force themselves upon you.
As social evenings went it was admirably relaxed: gay but not
boisterous, friendly but not frenzied. I wandered about casually,
talking to nobody in particular, or sat back quietly listening to
Pablo entertaining the crowd with his Cuban melodies; and then,
unexpectedly the evening blossomed out into something strangely
moving.

Out of the crowd there emerged an unusually animated young
man who introduced himself in a kind of twitching ecstasy. He
pumped my hand vigorously, bounced rapturously up and down
and jumped about as excitedly as if Uncle Mao himself had
popped in on the off chance of seeing his children at play.

He was, he said, 'mad for Shakespeare'. He had heard his tutor
speaking Shakespeare in class, but he had never heard Shakespeare spoken 'properly'. Now his heart was full of joy because

his great dream was about to come true: I could speak the great poetry of Shakespeare to him—any verses would do—in the glorious native tongue of the poet.

The circumstances were not exactly ideal. The orchestra had broken into an ear-splitting version of the polka; the dancers stamped and thumped their feet on the floor; young people milled around us, collecting their partners; but I did my best to oblige.

If he had been excited at the start he seemed on the point of delirium when I had finished, and when he had recovered rushed me off to meet a friend of his, a poet named Lan Li-Sing.

Lan was a student at Sun Yat-sen University, but with his loose-fitting red sweater and fawn-coloured slacks you felt he would have been more at home on some athletic campus in California. It took a little time to convince him that I really wanted to hear some of *his* poetry, but eventually, in a voice scarcely audible above the wailing of the *er hu* and the clashing of the gongs, he recited the piece he had just completed, '*So many days have passed*'. It ran into twelve stanzas and was translated line by line by his friend on some linguistical hit-and-miss principle worked out as he went along; but even this could not obscure the depth and sensibility of the writer's feelings.

The theme of his poem was the separation of a mother from her son, the son being obviously Lan himself. The boy has just left home for the first time to attend university and he asks his mother not to grieve at his going.

He imagines her counting the days to his return, smoothing down his pillow at night, cherishing fond images of his boyhood —their daily life together, his struggles at school, his father's death, the day his sister went away to be married, the mixed feelings of pride and sadness with which she heard that he had been accepted by the university. . . . '*So many days have passed . . . but every night I know that you remember . . .*' and finally, he imagines her thinking of his new life among the students, and, realising that now he is a man, he will give his affection to his comrades as well as to her. . . . '*So many days have passed . . . but do not believe I have forgotten you.*'

Although once or twice I thought I caught a dutiful echo of Youth League patriotism, it did not mar the poem's emotional impact. The young man's feelings broke through the crudities of the translation; he had written from the heart—so much so that when he had finished I felt I had intruded upon a private sorrow. Even his effervescent friend was affected and for a time could think of nothing at all to say.

Lan was unwilling to recite anything more and we fell to talking about the usual things, his work, his plans, the student's life, while the dancers swirled and stamped around us and the musicians hammered the helpless air. Before I left he promised to send me a copy of the poem, properly translated, but I have not received it; and all that is left of my one encounter with a genuine young romantic is this wholly inadequate paraphrase.

After the Social we went for a last look at Canton—Vladimir, Carl, Tamas and myself.

A few grain and ferry-boats were still passing down the river; the sampans, tied together in rows of seven and eight alongside the jetty, swayed and gurgled on the tide; bodies lay crammed and stretched across the decks; chickens huddled together in panniers in the stern, all the household paraphernalia stacked around them; but there was no movement, only a low murmur of conversation and the occasional sound of snoring 'How do such people *live?*' said Vladimir. 'It is impossible!'

In the harbour shadows pedlars hurried by with their bamboo loads of fruit and sesame cakes and hardware. In the streets beyond, children still roamed about, singly or in twos and threes. They clip-clopped past without curiosity, quietly enjoying the fading light of the lamps as long as they could. Here and there a few fruit-stalls were still open—what for, at this time of night, it was impossible to say—perhaps they hardly knew themselves; old women shifted loads and bundles for the night; families squatted round little stools on the pavement or stood at oil-stoves cooking themselves soup or fish or beans; all along the pavement people lay sleeping on straw mattresses, their heads against the shop walls, feet pointing downward to the street—on one mattress three babies, on another an old crone, between them a coolie fast asleep on a tiny stool, his bed for the night; the pavement-sweepers brushed carefully past, trying not to disturb them. 'It is a city of very *pure* people,' said Carl. 'Very different to Copenhagen.'

On the building sites work was still going on. Coolies glided by carrying buckets of bricks and cement under the bamboo yoke, their bodies swaying rhythmically from side to side to help balance the load. Four men dragged a great pine-trunk, about fifty feet long, into the road and hauled it painfully on to their shoulders, then set off, for some unknown destination; '*Wei ho* . . . *wei ho* . . .' gasped the two men at the front. '*Wei* . . . *ho* . . . *wei ho* . . .' came the groaning response from the back. Their faces as they passed us were taut with pain, their backs dripped sweat, and their eyes, tight-drawn, were fixed glassily on the road ahead.

'*Wei ho* . . . *wei ho* . . .' floated the cry from the river . . . from the barges unloading in the harbour . . . from the ferry-boats hauling to the shore. . . . '*Wei ho* . . . *wei ho* . . .' came the murmur from the markets . . . from the coolie gangs on the railway . . . from the labourers digging roads. . . . Canton was a different city, and the old order was taking longer to die here than anywhere else.

'I saw a very strange thing this morning,' said Carl. 'Two old bodies of men—how you say?—two skeletons—on sale in market. People say they have been found in ground under street, but nobody want to buy them.'

'That is very good story for bourgeois journalist,' said Vladimir sardonically. 'Make much money in American magazine: "In Red China people die in streets and dead bodies are sold in market!"'

'Ah, yes,' said Carl, with a nice statistical irony, 'but two bodies together—not one. "Before Liberation, only *one* man die, but after Liberation there is *two*!"'

Even Tamas, who did not normally banter about these things, permitted himself to enjoy the somewhat macabre joke.

The families squatting on the pavement began to pack their stoves and dishes away and lay down their mattresses for the night; in the houses behind, the bodies huddled tighter together on the floors and wooden ledges jutting out of the walls; an old woman shuffled out of an alley to empty a lavatory bucket down the street drain; and gradually the lights down the street and along the harbour side began to go out.

24

Return to Peking

WE flew back to Peking in an old Russian plane. It was badly pressurised and Vladimir complained continually that his ears were troubling him.

We flew from the land of fruits into a frozen city, from summer into winter. The glazed tiles and green roofs of the capital, the Imperial Palaces and Workers' Institutes, were covered in snow. The wind whipped across the airfield biting into our cheeks. People hurried along the streets in thick blue overcoats and fur-peaked hats. The great square in front of Tien An Men was bleak and deserted. Even the children had stayed indoors.

Yet the work of national construction went on. Where a few weeks before a building site had only just been cleared now a new tenement block stood half-completed; piles of rubble had disappeared from waste land, and everywhere scaffolding rose gauntly from the snow.

The atmosphere in the Ch'ien Men hotel had changed with the weather—or with the political situation. Our rooms had not been booked and we were left to hang about for some time. The hotel had been practically empty when we first arrived, but now it was seething with life. There was an Hungarian Army Ensemble, the members of the Moscow Circus, a large East German delegation, a Bulgarian Trade Mission, and scores of grave-faced Japanese who bowed and nodded inscrutably when you bumped into them in the lift.

The service had deteriorated appreciably. The usual packet of cigarettes no longer appeared on the bedroom tray each morning. The laundry service seemed to have packed up completely, and it was a minor feat of perseverance to chivvy a piece of toilet soap out of the servicemen. Most of them were apparently new to the job and had perhaps been bowled over by the sudden army of new arrivals. Correspondingly, transport had become difficult to get and the interpreters were almost reduced to a state of nervous collapse first in trying to cater for everyone's needs and then in pleading forgiveness for having been unable to do so. Significantly, every wireless set had disappeared. One explanation was that they had gone for repairs, another, that hearing the foreign stations would be emotionally disturbing for the Hungarians.

Shen was now my main interpreter. We had got to understand each other well. Earlier I had respected him for his forthrightness and honesty but now I came to like him as a tolerant and good-humoured companion. I had even established a better relationship with Little Wang. She had thawed out in the course of our travels and on numerous occasions had put herself out to please when no official obligations were involved. I felt about her as I did about so many Chinese girls I had met: take out the Marx–Lenin and you would have an admirable woman in the making. I think she regarded me as a peculiar kind of bourgeois joke and therefore in need of special care and protection.

My devoted Pan had left the party in Canton with never a word of farewell. I had not known he was staying behind until the plane was about to take off, when I suddenly noticed him waving goodbye with the party on the tarmac. Somebody said he was going back to Shanghai for a holiday with his mother, but I felt disappointed that he had not told me so. I missed his imperturbable smiles, his curious hugs and squeezes, his sharp pinging voice on the telephone every morning urging me to please HURRY, his insistence upon the 'objective' viewpoint, and his cheerful indifference to his extensive linguistic inadequacies. Our last outing together had been to a theatre in Canton to see Miss Hung Hsien-mien in *The Raid on the School*. Miss Hung had recently returned to the mainland, having fled to Hong Kong nine years before. Her return had been widely publicised as proof of the new artistic freedom, so after the performance I asked her point-blank if she believed that this freedom would apply to plays criticising the government. (She had replied with some subtlety that she thought it would, or rather: 'If ever we felt the People were not represented by the government we should, of course, show plays criticising the government.') *'Very* penetrating question!' exclaimed Pan, when we were outside. 'You have *astonished* her!'

He proceeded to pinch my arm with a bland and knowing smile. 'Very curious Sherlock Holmes Englishman!' he declared. 'Seeking always evidence of crime—*but no evidence to find!*'

With the departure of Pan, much of life's comedy had departed too.

Most of the delegates were anxious to get home as soon as they could, but there were still some things I wanted to do. First was a visit to the Foreign Languages Institute, or, to be exact, to the English Department of it. There being no need for an interpreter I went there one morning by myself.

It had been built well out of the city and, under the damp grey sky and falling snow, the square classroom blocks and asphalt surrounds looked unusually stark and forbidding. The white-washed walls and concrete corridors within were scarcely more cheerful. It was like entering a particularly Spartan public school which had decided to concentrate its traditional resources on the character training of young technologists. Large spittoons stood at suitable vantage points along the corridors; on the staircase, oblivious to anything else, a number of students were privately engaged in oral language exercises; on the notice-board were posted various students' essays: 'A Day at the Agricultural Co-operative'; 'Tractor Driving in the Holidays'; 'A Young Girl Goes to Meet Chairman Mao'.

The English faculty, over four hundred strong, was the largest in the Institute. Within the last six months there had been a great increase in the number of students taking English as a first choice —both here and in the schools and universities. In the light of The Hundred Flowers policy and the need to learn 'advanced techniques' from the west, it was also in great demand in the engineering schools and science colleges. 'Our problem,' said the

Director, 'is not one of a surplus of teachers but of a severe shortage.'

Most of the present pupils had started from scratch. Their four-year course would soon daunt and exhaust the spirit of the average English languages student in a comparable position. Learning English, after all, can be no whit less mentally numbing for a Chinese boy than for an English boy to grapple with Chinese; and, with the limited equipment at their disposal, it remained a mystery to me how these students ever succeeded at all.

They spent eighteen hours a week on 'intensive analysis' in the classroom and eighteen in 'preparation and study', although analysis, said the Director, 'was not the focal point.

'Our main aim is to achieve a practical understanding. Thus, all lessons are conducted in English from a very early stage. Fourth-year students, for instance, should be able to study in detail four novels in a period of six weeks. Of course, our main problem is still to bring the student from the ABC stage up to the top level. Until recently the material has not been very good, but with the new emphasis on The Hundred Flowers we are getting a better quality of student from the secondary schools.'

The range of literature seemed to have been dictated by the books available when the communists took over; it was catholic, if a little bizarre. *Pride and Prejudice, Vanity Fair* and Jack London's *Martin Eden* were the most popular novels and, for specialised tastes, there was *Silas Marner, Babbitt, Our Mutual Friend* and *The Cloister and the Hearth*, with a good ration of Dickens, George Eliot, Galsworthy and various Georgian anthologies. On the language side the course seemed designed to instil a judicious blend of linguistical appreciation and ideological enlightment. I picked up at random some third-year comprehension exercises: one was headed 'Bethune's Interview with Chairman Mao', another, 'How the Soviet People Beat Hitler', and a third, 'Byron and the Cause of National Freedom'. The latter was a model of Marxist interpretation.

On the other hand, the fifth-year research papers had an austere purity which one could but gaze upon with a kind of dumbstruck awe. In addition to translating from the Anglo-Saxon some of the beefier portions of *Beowulf* and several hefty slices of the Chronicle, the students were required to deal with 'The influence of Latin in the English language', 'The nature and extent of the Scandinavian influence in Middle English', and 'The situation of French and the English dialects in Middle English times and the rise of the modern English national language'.

From *Aelfred cyninge on fest Radestone* I went down to a fourth-year class and *The Grapes of Wrath*, with Tom Joad driving west through the Colorado desert. . . . This turned out to be the most remarkable lesson I have ever sat through.

In the bleak, bitterly cold room, a mixed class of fourteen students applied themselves with iron concentration to the idiomatic peculiarities of America's most indigenous epic. They sat hunched grimly over their narrow desks in blue winter kapoks and white plimsolls, with here and there a bright splash of yellow sock or red scarf. The text-books consisted of half a dozen extracts from English and American novels stencilled on to thin sheets of quarto-size paper—a practice adopted in schools and colleges throughout China in lieu of bulk purchasing of new foreign texts.

The teacher himself had been at an American university before the War. A slim, quietly-spoken man of about thirty-five, smartly dressed in a brown check suit and a rust-coloured tie, he was manifestly on top of his job. His manner was friendly but his reactions swift and emphatic and, before the lesson had gone very far, I realised that he knew a good deal more about the English language than I did.

The compilers of the present selection had chosen to inflict on these already heavily overburdened students what, to anyone outside the sociological field, must surely be the grittiest passage in the whole of Steinbeck:

> Along 66 the hamburger stands—Al and Suzy's place—Carl's lunch—Joe's and Minnie's—Will's eats. Board and bat shacks. . . . Near the door three slot machines. . . . And beside them the nickel phonograph piled up with pies. . . .

For some time the students read round the class in flat, plod-ding monotones. The dialogue meant nothing to them—how could it? It broke every grammatical rule they had ever learnt; it spoke of objects they had never seen or heard of and could not possibly have imagined.

'Now,' said the teacher, with patient optimism, 'we will start our analysis. "They set their faces to the west and drove towards it, forcing the clashing engines over the roads." Now, Liu Chung, why did they *force* their engines?'

After a minute or so of painful concentration, Liu Chung ventured: 'Because the engines were in a wretched condition.'

After further strenuous thought: 'Because the cars were old.'

'Right. Now, in this sentence, "Why, sure, be proud to have you. What state you from?" Tsao Liang, how do you interpret, "Sure, be proud to have you?" '

Tsao could not interpret it at all: and nobody else offered to. 'It is not possible to paraphrase such a sentence.'

'But how do we interpret, "be proud"? Does it mean "we *are* proud"? Or "*will be* proud"?'

A slow shaking of heads confessed that nobody knew.

'No! It means *would* be proud. Now I want you to learn the use of "would" which is alien to our language.'

While he clarified his point my eye wandered detachedly round the room. The whitewashed austerity of the walls was broken only by two red-and-gold banners immediately behind me: they were worth a second glance. In large block capitals the first pro-claimed the unusual message: 'BE ACTIVE AND HAPPY!' and the second, like a text removed from a missionary hall, the pious and homely injunction, 'UNITE AND LOVE EACH OTHER!' No mention of productivity, national construction, advanced techniques.

' "And the great question. How's the water?"

' "She doesn't taste so good. . . ." Now why does the writer use *she*?'

Nobody could tell.

'Would *you* use "she", Chien Hsia-tung?'

A slow pause: 'I . . . don't . . . think so.'

'Or *you*, Wu Nu?'

'Does it perhaps mean . . . "it"?'

'Yes, but what is the rule from this?'

There was a moment of tortured silence.

'Well, the general rule, comrades, is what we call in phonetics the loss of plosions. Now, what do we mean by plosions?'

There I confess he had me as well as the students; I hoped he would not feel tempted to seek my opinion.

' "Why, sure, be good to have you." . . . Now what general rule can we deduce from that?'

A shy suggestion from the girl at the back: 'The loss of the auxiliary . . .'

'And, "She doesn't taste so good?" Don't you find something wrong with the use of "good"?'

She appeared not to.

'This reference to genders, now. Can we make a rule for their use with inanimate objects?'

The question was rhetorical. 'I don't think we can. But we find it sometimes used as a term of endearment, peculiar to slang or pattern speech.'

' "Then down from the car the weary people climbed." Now what linguistic fact do we need to take care of there?'

At first, profound uncertainty; then, a hesitant murmur: 'Inversion.'

'Now we will go back and paraphrase the passage from the beginning. I want you to make a frontal attack on the text.'

He clenched his fists together to emphasise the fighting approach required. 'Employ your whole resources—and don't bypass any difficulties!'

The students went tenaciously into battle. I shook the teacher warmly by the hand and, feeling chastened and humbler than before, crept quietly out.

'Although it is a very concentrated course,' said the Director, 'the students have the satisfaction of knowing that there will be opportunities open to them when they are qualified. Teaching is only one of them. For years to come there will be a continuing demand for translators in political and scientific work, while in the literary field the possibilities are immense. There is a great renaissance of interest in foreign literature and many world classics are now being translated for the first time in China. We want many more—and many versions of them so that the best will stand out.'

Noticing with some surprise that there was an old Everyman copy of *Cakes and Ale* in his bookshelf, I asked if Maugham was ever likely to come up for translation.

He replied rather curtly that he was not. 'We don't particularly like Maugham'—somehow I had not supposed they would—'but many of his novels are still available because they were taken over from the old college libraries. We shall, however, be translating a number of Thackeray's works. His novels are very popular here, *Vanity Fair* especially.'

Ever since I arrived in China I had been puzzled by this extraordinary predilection for Thackeray. In Russia perhaps, where the nineteenth-century novel has some affinities with its English counterpart, the taste could be better understood, but in Red China it seemed unfathomably perverse. Here at last, I thought, is the man who will know. But it was not to be. The Director left the mystery veiled in a kind of neutral obscurity. 'We feel on safe ground, linguistically speaking,' he said, 'with the nineteenth century—and with Thackeray in particular because the style of his books is most interesting, as well as their content. You see, one of the good things about studying English in a foreign language is that you don't have to follow the fashion.'

I readily took his word for it; but for the life of me I could still not understand why they should choose to follow Thackeray.

It had been impressed upon me repeatedly that the Chinese were anxious to see British films, but apart from an isolated showing of *Great Expectations* in Shanghai, when people had queued weeks in advance to get tickets, there was not a single British film in the country, nor indeed had any been seen since

1949. Since a French Film Week had just been staged in ten major cities, with an overall attendance of three million, I felt it incumbent upon me to carry the British torch—so one morning I betook myself to the government-controlled Film Bureau which handles all foreign bookings.

'In point of fact,' explained Yang Shao-jen, the Director, 'we established a contact with the Rank Overseas Organisation about a year ago. They have since sent us nine films, but we considered them unsuitable for showing.'

'What did you find wrong with them?' I asked.

'They were altogether too frivolous for the mood of our people. They are not interested in your musical films or your stories of crime or sex. They prefer something more serious and realistic, which touches upon problems they might themselves understand.'

'British films of that kind are always hard to find,' I explained. 'Our people seem to prefer something as far removed from every-day life as possible. But what do you feel about our comedies— would they appeal to Chinese taste?'

'We believe that comedy has a universal appeal. Some of the French films we have had, for instance, were a great success with our audiences, although the idiom and style were alien to our own. In the same way we should like to see some of *your* comic films—but they would have to be of a serious kind, if you under-stand—not comedy for children.'

'Not slapstick?' I suggested.

'If it was sympathetic, yes. But not the destructive kind where the humour comes from the use of violence and brutality.'

I pressed him several times to name the films they had actually received, but by the time the titles had been translated they had become meaningless.

'You must remember, of course,' he said, 'that although your films are technically good, very few cinemas in China showed them even before the Liberation. Even now in Hong Kong many of them would never be shown unless the government had fixed the quota.'

'Do you mean the demand there is for American films?'

'Of course. But they are mostly nonsenses.'

'Would they appeal to your own audiences?'

'By all means they would not. The level of appreciation in China, in the cities especially, has risen greatly in the last few years. Our people would be indignant if we offered them American films.'

I tried to explain that certain American films were very far from 'nonsenses' and that there was a Hollywood school of criticism and self-criticism which would make the efforts of the communist Cadres sound like the mewling and bleating of a kindergarten at play.

He agreed that upon occasion the Americans had been known to produce intelligent films: 'But they would not be popular here. After all, we can see a great many films from many other countries.'

He felt that the British had made little effort to break into the Chinese market. 'We have been in contact with the French for only six months and already we have dubbed more than thirty French films. In your case a year has gone by and we have had hardly any response, except, as I said, with films we would never wish to show.'

It had been reported in the paper that as a result of the recent Film Week, French technicians would now be invited to work in Chinese studios in an advisory capacity. I asked if similar invitations might be extended to the British. He thought that such a development might well occur when 'a more satisfactory contact' had been established.

'And what would be the prospects,' I asked, 'of any English company being allowed to make a film here?'

'Certain countries have already made enquiries in this respect. The difficulties, of course, are great.'

'Technically, or with regard to the script?'

'Both. Our resources, as you know, are backward, and as for the screenplay, I am sure you will agree, it would be difficult to reach agreement—not impossible, of course, but there would be certain problems.'

'From our point of view we should not wish to make a film which might be construed as propaganda.'

'We don't want you to do that. It would be a failure if you tried. We should expect you to deal with human relations and endeavour. Perhaps some day it will be possible—but not for a long time yet. . . .'

I still entertain the hope that this was not entirely a fruitless interview. Before I left, at Yang's request I outlined the subject-matter and treatment of several recent British films which I thought likely to appeal to prevalent Chinese taste, and he assured me that he would ask for copies to be sent.* Perhaps I shall do Wardour Street a good turn yet—and I pass on the following figures without comment to whomsoever they may concern: There are at present nine hundred cinemas in China—more than double the number in 1949. In that year the attendance figure was forty-seven million; in 1956 it had risen to thirteen hundred million. 'Proportionately, this is still too small,' said Yang. 'It means that each person on average goes only twice a year. At present, however, we can only produce forty feature films a year in our own studios, which means we have to import a hundred more from abroad. We plan to set up six new studios soon, but at the same time,' he hinted gently, 'we shall also build many more cinemas, and we shall still need the best foreign films we can get.'

* Whether he did or not I shall never know, but in the eighteen months since this interview took place British distributors have sold only five films, all based on Dickens' novels, for dubbing into Chinese. It would appear that the French not only make better films but also have a better sales technique —which meant in this case that they sent out a 'delegation'. The argument put to me by a British Legation official—that the Chinese fail to pay their bills—holds no water, for both the Rank Overseas Division and other British exporters to China say that they have had no difficulty of this kind.

25

Separate Viewpoints

OWN the main streets, on posters and hoardings, the anti-imperialist campaign was still in full swing. All the mass organisations had been well and truly mobilised. They had paraded, petitioned and protested, and the art students had been more mobilised than most. Every shop-window in the city centre was festooned with their work—some of it gruesomely brilliant. Eden and Mollet were shown battering stupefied heads against an accusing Sphinx or, with jack-boots and Swastika, they straddled a desert of Egyptian corpses. A burly, red-nosed Englishman and a grinning, rat-like Frenchman pinned an Egyptian woman to the sand with a bayonet down her throat. The unfortunate Mr. Dulles, who at that time was in hospital for a stomach operation, was shown raving in his sheets like a ghastly reincarnation of Hitler, or else gloating in an American bomber over a burning Egyptian village. Conversely, other posters showed handsome young Egyptian officers wringing the necks of monstrous fascist invaders.

Side by side with these, noble-looking young Russians repelled the counter-revolutionary hordes and charged with the red flag of freedom down streets bedecked with fascist banners. As a mass propaganda campaign it would have been hard to beat. There was some comfort in noting that none of the passers-by seemed at all interested in the posters, but after the episode in the apprentices' shop that was clearly nothing to go by.

There had been a colossal carry-on outside the British Legation two weeks back when the demonstrators had marched up to the gates with their petitions and banners. Although they had voiced their protest with customary courtesy, during the course of the meeting the rank and file had shinned merrily on to each other's shoulders and plastered banners, slogans and posters along the entire quarter-mile of the compound wall. The posters were still there: 'HANDS OFF!' 'DON'T AGGRESSIVE EGYPT!' 'STOP THE DIRTY WAR!' 'GET OUT FASCIST!', but now they hung, limp and tattered in the snow, and the streets of the Legation quarter were as deserted as they had always been since the old imperialist days when the Chinese were prohibited from entering them.

Arthur Boyd was waiting for me at the Hsin Chiao Hotel. He urged me to clear out of China on the first available plane. He was convinced that a major war was about to start. He had been living in almost complete isolation during the last few weeks, becoming increasingly depressed at each fresh news bulletin, and lashing himself into impotent fury when he compared it with the latest utterances in *The People's Daily*. 'Every time you find something good to write about this country,' he cried, 'you feel like tearing it all up as soon as you read this stinking paper!'

I spent several laborious hours working through the back numbers since the Hungarian rising began. They made an interesting Marxist serial.

At first the government had appeared to sympathise with the rebels. An editorial on 1 November welcomed the Nagy government and condemned 'past errors of big-nation chauvinism and incorrect thinking'. But all that changed overnight when Nagy demanded the abrogation of the Warsaw Treaty. 'The just discontent' of the workers became 'the White Terror'; 'fascists, counter-revolutionaries and Horthy elements' were crossing the Hungarian border 'arm in hand'. From then on the details of the revolt became blurred and submerged in the jargon of Marxist analysis.

'Celebrate the Great Victory of the Hungarian People!' sang *The People's Daily* on 5 November as Russian tanks rolled back into Budapest and 'the gallant Soviet people shed their own blood to save Hungary from fascist slavery'. A lengthy editorial, however, admitted how rampant the Terror had become, adding, with unconscious irony, 'This shows that there are indeed quite a number of counter-revolutionaries in Hungary, and a great many Hungarian people have not drawn a clear dividing line between friend and enemy'.

For the next ten days, as far as China was concerned, life in Hungary was 'returning to normal'. Then on 14 November *The People's Daily* launched out with an editorial of enormous length admitting for the first time the impact the 'counter-revolution' had made throughout the communist as well as the western world.

It was thought that the author of this declaration was Teng Hsaio-p'ing, the General Secretary of the Chinese Communist Party, so a few days before I left Peking I went with other delegates to interview him in the gilt-and-green splendours of the Hsin Hua Men.

It was an interesting occasion, for Teng is the dark horse of the Politbureau, having risen rapidly in the last few years to occupy sixth place in the hierarchy. Although his argumentative and somewhat arrogant disposition is said to make him unpopular with his colleagues, western observers believe that he now has more influence even than Chou En-lai.

Little is known about his early education, but after the First World War he travelled to France with other Chinese scholars on a work-and-study basis, joining the Communist Party in Paris, whence he returned about 1925 to take an active part in organising Party affairs. After the split between the Kuomintang and the Party he joined the communist base at Kiangsi, where he helped in organising the Seventh and Eighth Armies. In 1935 he took part in the Long March to the north-west and when the Red Army was reorganised after the Japanese invasion as the Eighth Route Army he became a divisional commissar. It was not, however, until 1950 that he began to emerge as a serious political contender. After heading various economic and financial committees he became Vice-Premier (one of ten), then Secretary-General of the Central Election Committee and, in 1953, Minister of Finance—although, despite this rapid rise, he was not appointed to the Politbureau until 1955.

Teng is still as little known to the majority of his countrymen as he is to the west (I was, I believe, the first western correspondent whom he had received). A compact, bullet-headed, highly articulate man, small even by Chinese standards, he looks a good twenty years younger than his estimated age of sixty. He told me little that had not already appeared in *The People's Daily*, but it was mildly instructive to be given the government's case from the horse's mouth. Although accompanied for the occasion by a group of government officials and Press and cultural representatives—including an extraordinary character whom I mentally labelled Laughing Boy, who sat with bedraggled black hair hanging halfway down his forehead, nodding and grinning ecstatically at every question I asked as though I were cracking a series of superlatively funny jokes—Teng elected to answer all my questions himself, and did so with suave authority and every appearance of enjoyment. 'Some people complain that we Party officials spend too much time in talking,' he said, after I had requested him to extend the interview beyond its scheduled two hours, 'so if you want to compete with us in this respect I think you will find we can last out a great deal longer than you.'

His attitude throughout was one of excessive cordiality: 'I know that the purpose of your questions is to improve mutual understanding, so you must speak with all frankness,' and it was difficult not to be charmed and at times distracted by the melodious intonations of his voice, a curious compound of singing and whining, as though he took a caressive kind of pleasure in words, a sensuous delight in the shapes and nuances of sound. Unfortunately the substance fell less agreeably on the ears than the sound.

I started with a general question on the basic principles of Chinese policy with regard to Hungary and Egypt.

'The principles have been repeatedly explained,' he said. 'They are the five principles of co-existence as stated in the joint declaration of the Bandung Conference.'

Now it so happened that the previous day the Bandung Powers, with the exception of China, had condemned Soviet intervention, a fact of which Teng clearly did not expect me to be aware.

'It has been reported by the B.B.C.,' I said, 'though not by your own newspapers, that the Bandung Powers have condemned Russia in the light of these five principles. How does your government justify its disagreement on this question?'

He hesitated for a moment and then tried to dodge the question altogether.

'Our stand on Hungary is as clear as our stand on Suez. It can be seen in *The People's Daily* editorial on 14 November: "Repudiate the viewpoint of the western powers!" '

'I read that editorial, but I would prefer to hear your personal opinion,' I said—not that I expected to be given it, but there was no harm in asking.

'My opinion is identical with that expressed in *The People's Daily*. The situation, of course, is too complicated to be covered in a brief answer, but since you seem dissatisfied with what has been said, I would simplify the issue in this way: from the viewpoint of the five principles, I believe there is no doubt about the Egyptian problem. Your troops were never invited to Egypt and their intentions were entirely aggressive. But with Hungary, Soviet troops are legally there by virtue of the Warsaw Treaty, for the benefit not only of the socialist camp but also of Hungary.'

I liked that 'but also'—like the deadly 'But yet, madam!' of Cleopatra's messenger.

'Surely you realise,' I exclaimed, 'that by abrogating the Warsaw Treaty Nagy was expressing the wishes of the Hungarian people for national independence?'

'It is too early to analyse events'—he conveniently forgot the lengthy analysis of the 14 November editorial in *The People's Daily*—'I agree, however,' he admitted in a deceptively conciliatory tone, 'that past errors in leadership and the dissatisfaction of the masses played a big part in causing the uprising. But the imperialist and counter-revolutionary forces took advantage of genuine grievances to instigate armed riots. Soviet troops were

stationed in Hungary at the request of the Hungarian government, so the intervention is obviously not of the same nature as
that in Suez. This is the essence of the matter, and it is more
important to look at the essence than to judge events simply from
a western viewpoint.'

'I am basing my questions not solely on a western viewpoint,
but on the criticism of Soviet intervention made by other highly
respected Asian countries. How do you reconcile your attitude
with theirs?'

'I wonder if your B.B.C. also reported that after the conclusion
of the Colombo meeting yesterday the Indonesian Prime Minister
told a Press conference that he condemned the aggression in
Egypt but thought that the Hungarian problem was different?'

It was my turn to dodge the question, for the B.B.C. report
I had quoted had been hurriedly passed to me by Arthur Boyd as
I was on my way to the interview, and this particular point had
not been mentioned. 'I find it difficult to interpret his speech as a
defence of Russian action,' I replied cautiously.

'You are entitled to your own viewpoint,' said Teng. 'But in
my opinion, support by the Soviet to Egypt and to the people of
Hungary are at one with each other. The relatively smooth
resolution of the Hungarian problem has enabled the Soviet to
offer more help to Egypt, and this has already produced an effect
on the problem. Many African and Asian countries think alike on
this, as shown in the United Nations voting.'

'Many English people think alike about it too,' I said, 'and have
openly protested against British policy. We wouldn't quarrel
with your attitude on Egypt if you showed a similar concern over
events in Hungary.'

'If you have read our editorials you will know that we have
been extremely concerned over these events.'

'Then how do you justify your continuing support for Russia?
Surely you are aware of the deep revulsion which many com-
munist sympathisers throughout the world have expressed at
Russian action in Budapest?'

'It is true that the Hungarian events have caused an upsurge of anti-Soviet feeling in certain quarters, and certain people have said that the Soviet are interfering in internal affairs. But we believe this to be a completely mistaken view. The people who feel this way have failed to look at the essence.'

'Might not the essence be simply that the Hungarian people want to run their own country in their own way?'

'That is a superficial view. The true essence was stated in a speech quoted in *The People's Daily* last week made by your own countryman, the Dean of Canterbury.'

For a moment I looked at Teng Hsaio-p'ing incredulously. Was this the best argument he could produce?

'I don't read the speeches made by the Dean of Canterbury,' I said. 'His views in no way represent those of the British people. I am surprised that a government as sagacious as yours has still not realised this.'

'Nevertheless,' said Teng, a little taken aback, 'Dr. Johnson stated the essence of the Hungarian problem, which is that reactionary forces want to turn a democratic country back into a fascist one, while at the same time certain imperialist elements want to take advantage of the situation in order to distract attention from the Egyptian problem.'

'I would rather hear your own views than Dr. Johnson's,' I said.

'These are my own views, and they have already been expressed in three editorials in *The People's Daily*. If Soviet troops had not intervened when they did then it can be definitely said that capitalism and imperialism would have been restored.'

'Isn't it possible,' I asked, 'that the Hungarian people preferred this possibility to that of communist dictatorship?'

'You are entitled to your separate viewpoint,' he said. 'As for the Chinese people, they complained bitterly that the Soviet delayed their intervention while imperialist planes were carrying counter-revolutionaries back into Hungary. Though many people may now blame the Soviet, many more would have done so if she had simply stood by with folded arms and allowed the counter-revolutionaries to triumph.'

It had become obvious, as Mr. Teng suggested, that we should have to keep our separate viewpoints; it was time to change the subject, although the other topic I wanted to discuss was hardly likely to bring us to a point of agreement.

'How do you interpret the term "freedom of the Press"?' I asked.

At first he did not see the drift of the question. 'I am not very clear about your implication. Do you mean, "Is there any freedom of the Press in China?" '

'Yes. And where is it in evidence?'

He still did not see exactly what I was getting at. He explained that ninety per cent of the literate section of the population enjoyed such freedom and that it was denied only to unreformed landlords, counter-revolutionaries, and 'those who are in prison or under surveillance'.

'I know that the foreign Press accuse us of "brainwashing",' he said, 'but you can't wash people's minds into socialism—you must show them all the facts first. Have you seen, for instance, the speeches by the Dalai Lama, which propagate religion, not materialism? Or the recent lectures by U Nu on Buddhism? We also print many criticisms of the government—although, of course, we should not print criticisms of our Taiwan policy, or articles saying that landlords should be restored. Are there any other implications to your question?'

'That is not quite what I mean by freedom of the Press. What freedom is there, for instance, to criticise your foreign policy or to outline the western viewpoint on international problems in which China is involved?'

'I know of no paper which can publish everything that is happening in the world,' he replied shrewdly—'or how many western newspapers have published our viewpoint on the Hungarian and Egyptian problems. Of course, my knowledge is limited, but I do know that we cover the western viewpoint in a factual sense—for instance, we have just published Eisenhower's recent correspondence with Bulganin. But our Press has the task of guiding our people's life in every field. We have a fixed responsibility to the people.'

'Don't you feel that part of this responsibility is to keep the people properly informed of the situation in Hungary and of the views expressed on this by the Asian as well as the western powers?'

'I feel it is better for everyone to have his separate viewpoint. As we're talking about freedom, I think each country should be free to choose its own methods. Political viewpoints should not impair mutual friendships and what is published in the Press should not impair relations between countries.'

'On the other hand,' I insisted, 'it might improve relations if the Press gave a more informed picture of what is happening in other countries. With this in mind, would you be willing to arrange a meeting with your Press representatives in which I could discuss their coverage of the western viewpoint with a view to improving mutual understanding between our two countries?'

'It is not a fact that we do not cover the western viewpoint,' he repeated. 'Perhaps we haven't covered it enough. What is enough and not enough is a matter of opinion. But as I have already said, I feel it would be better for us to keep our separate viewpoints.'

At least, I reflected, it was as polite a way of saying No as any.

26

Peace and Friendship

So we came to the last official dinner.

It was given, with an inspired sense of occasion, at the unpretentious Fong Tze Yuen restaurant, and it was memorable in more ways than one.

This restaurant is justly famed for its Peking duck and the meal was based entirely on this theme. Starting with the feet we worked meticulously through every edible aspect of the creature's carcass, from the brain to the testicles, a process which, accompanied by the usual subsidiaries of chicken, bamboo-shoots, rice, fish-soup and innumerable toasts in *mao-tai*, *bai-gar*, hot banana wine and Chinese brandy, took approximately three hours. The meal culminated in the breast and lacquered skin of the duck, carved at table by the chef in an operation of swift and surgical delicacy, the dish itself being a consummation too subtly satisfying to be adequately suggested in words. I had come a long way since my first exploratory sampling of the Chinese cuisine, but even the fabled delights of Hangchow and Canton had failed to arouse the exquisitely pleasurable sensations which the experts had assured me they would; there had been much to enjoy, to relish and admire, but nothing, I felt, that my palate would have been the poorer for missing; but now, in the Fong Tze Yuen restaurant, at the last delegation dinner, the lacquered duck of Peking proved the wondrous exception.

It was a curious, faintly melancholy evening, the end of a journey which had never seemed wholly real, an experience which could never be repeated. What the final verdict would be it was too early to say: the impressions were still either too vivid or too blurred and perhaps at the end they would resist any attempt at synthesis.

Most of the delegates would be leaving in the morning. Some of them I should miss: Carl, with his inimitable English and good-humoured wit; the hot-blooded Abou, with his sheik-like demeanour and civilised mind; the Malayan and the Sinhalese; poor dumb Pablo, even now singing a sad departing song; and Tamas, too, sitting at the table beside me—we had talked together a lot: as he had promised, he had never tried to sell me communism, nor had he attempted to make capital out of the Egyptian fiasco. More than anyone else he had kept the delegation together, taking in the process a good deal more mud-slinging than I had thought a communist could. It seemed illogical that he should be on that side of the fence—yet, if he had been in his Budapest office four weeks before, there was no doubt he would have been dragged out with the rest of the Federation staff to be shot in the street.

The dinner was more intimate than any given before, the only Chinese present being the leaders of the main youth organisations. The most important, or at least the most voluble of them, turned out to be the Laughing Boy of the Teng interview. With his drooping, uncombed hair and fixed smile he presided over the festivities like a thinner, bedraggled version of the Laughing Buddha; conspicuously a drinking man, he dedicated himself to the toasting of Peace and Friendship with increasingly raucous fervour.

It was difficult to join in the toasting game with the same spirit. The officials were, and had been, consistently excellent hosts; in consideration and courtesy, attention to detail and willingness to prepare or cancel arrangements according to the momentary whims of their guests, their efforts had defied reasonable comparison; you took for granted, of course—and they knew you took for granted—that they were out to please, an object which is not, after all, exclusive to hosts in a communist country; but they were also the very men who, for the past few weeks, through the medium of the Young Pioneers, the Youth League and *China*

Youth, had been engaged in selling to upwards of one hundred million young people the enormous lie of the fascist–imperialist plot in Hungary. Against this background the convivial exhortations to Peace and Friendship took on a dismal, ironic significance.

It was an unwritten rule at all these functions studiously to avoid saying anything that might be thought controversial, which is to say that you drank to a series of unimaginable abstractions: to Youth—in China—in Chile—in South America—in England—throughout the world; to Mutual Understanding: 'Our ideologies may be different but we must learn to trust one another!' To Prosperity and Happiness; to the Advancement of this and the Development of that. The real test of skill was always to think up something so comprehensively innocuous that it could not possibly be envisaged in any concrete shape whatever.

All this represented a form of social diplomacy which the Chinese have carried to its furthest pitch; consequently it must have been as shattering to them as it was to the guests when, on this of all occasions, one of their own number decided to break the rules. This happened late in the evening, somewhere about the twentieth toast. Who the gentleman was, what he represented, was not made clear, nor did it matter very much. Morose, pinch-faced, stiff-backed, he stood up to propose his toast. At first, none of the guests took much notice: he had a reedy, inaudible voice; the duck's liver had just been served with a superb dish of mushrooms and bamboo-shoots, and private little toasts were being proposed simultaneously around the circular tables; but when the interpreters took over, everyone turned to listen with a kind of appalled incredulity. For his speech, seemingly inoffensive in Chinese, amounted to a virulent tirade against Britain and France and a pledge of fiery solidarity with the youth of Egypt in their heroic struggle against the forces of aggression.

It was, of course, only an abbreviation of what the Chinese youth leaders had been bellowing at their flock for weeks, but that was not quite the point. The speech had to be challenged, even if it meant wrecking the dinner. The question was: were the English in a moral position to do the challenging?

While we shuffled and shifted and considered the matter, Carl pushed back his chair and settled it for us. In his halting, disjointed English, his face pale and drawn beneath his long blond hair, he proposed another toast. I cannot remember precisely what he said, but his speech was a brave and gallant gesture and this was the manner of it:

'In my country—small country—we not like see big country attack other small country—like Britain, France attack Egypt. This thing very wrong. All agree. But why you not say *also* very wrong when big country attack *Hungary*? Hungary people want freedom—*not* want Russia—*not* want communism. Want freedom in own country. So why do China not condemn also aggression of *Russia* imperialism? Give solidarity to *Hungary* people?'

After going through the circuit of translation the words, no doubt, lost much of their force, but what came through was sufficient to convulse the entire gathering; but he had not done yet:

'You toast tonight Peace and Friendship *all* peoples—but how can communist speak Peace–Friendship when blood of Budapest hot on communist hands? I say—if you believe Peace–Friendship *all* peoples, give toast to freedom *Hungary* peoples!'

The western delegates rose, grim-faced, to respond. The communists, rigidly seated, muttered angrily among themselves. The Chinese whispered together in an agitated huddle at the centre table.

We sat down tensely, and waited for the next move.

It came, not from the communist delegates, but from the ebullient Laughing Boy. His face suffused with smiles, head nodding slowly up and down, arms held out expansively in goodwill to all men, he burst suddenly into the centre of the room and proposed another toast:

'To the safe return of the delegates! To their happy reunion with their wives and families! To their future happiness!'

As the company rose to drink, he bounded over to Carl's

table and toasted, first Carl personally, and then all the guests around him in turn.

The tension eased. Tamas beside me had been on the point of challenging Carl but thought better of it: 'I will not pour oil on the troubled fire.' Littmarck drank to the Spirit of Greater Tolerance; on behalf of the women of England, Muriel toasted the three hundred million women of China; and in an unexpectedly witty speech, Stephen Tripp drank to the health of the interpreters.

Thus Peace and Friendship were restored; the lacquered duck was carved at table; and even the Chinese seemed visibly relieved when the dinner was over.

Early next morning the delegation set off for Moscow, leaving behind Muriel, Ricardo and myself, together with Vladimir, whose ears were still badly inflamed after the flight from Canton —so much so, in fact, that he had been unable to attend the farewell dinner.

I spent a forlorn kind of morning at the Summer Palace, where the lake was frozen and the willows bare; visited the university in the afternoon; and then, late that night, I walked into tragedy.

As I have mentioned earlier, the members of the Hungarian Army Ensemble were also staying in the Ch'ien Men Hotel. There were over two hundred of them, musicians, singers and dancers. They were often to be seen about the streets, in the department stores and bazaars. They wore their jack-boots and Russian-style uniforms with a cavalier air, but they kept strictly to themselves— silent, unsmiling, grimly aloof.

It seemed logical to suppose that their loyalties would lie with the regime which employed them, but there seemed no way of finding out; none of them seemed able to understand English and, even if they could, it was doubtful if they would care to talk.

But, as always, Ricardo's instinct in these things was truer than mine.

He met me at dinner in a state of great excitement. Going down in the lift during the afternoon he had spoken to one of the Hungarians in French—and got a reply. The man had invited him to his room. After a cautious beginning, he had decided to talk freely—'And not communist!' cried Ricardo. 'Hates communism—this man and nearly all Ensemble!'

It appeared that a number of them had a smattering of English. They would be glad to meet me; so after the performance that night I went with Ricardo to their room.

This meeting and those that followed are stark and vivid in my memory, but it is necessary to write of them without emotion, although they were as profoundly emotional as anything I have ever experienced; and it is necessary also, even at this distance of time, for what should be grimly obvious reasons, to omit much more than mere names.

The predicament of these men was agonising beyond words. They were living in the shadows of uncertainty and fear, enduring sleepless nights, and every day, in factory and theatre, stringing their nerves afresh to perform their parts in the empty charade of Peace, Friendship and Solidarity with the People's Republics. They had been given no news beyond official hand-outs and constant reassurances (which even Tamas Larincz had refused to believe) that their families were safe. They had no use for their own Embassy and no contact with anybody in Peking. If they had wished to seek asylum in a foreign embassy—which most of them, being married, did not—they would hardly have known where to go or whom they could dare to ask.

They believed that more than eighty per cent of the Ensemble were anti-communist, but even among those there were some they could not trust. Two weeks before, in Canton, they had held a secret meeting, but by the same evening the details of it had been reported to the Political Commander who was then in Peking, and they had been threatened with severe punishment on their return—'If we ever return!' they said. 'Many things can happen between here and Moscow. A hundred men can vanish and who is to know?'

The tour had been due to finish two weeks before, but now

nobody would say when it was likely to end. 'They tell us all is peace in Budapest—but they dare not let us go there.'

When I first went into their room they locked the door behind me and wrapped a blanket carefully round the telephone. They saw my look of surprise: 'This is not a game, friend,' they said. 'This is how we live. In England, perhaps, you would not understand.' They talked quietly and with difficulty—they had not used their English for years—and those who could not understand sat tensely waiting to be told what had been said. They spoke of life in Budapest under Rakosi and Geroe, of the methods of the Secret Police, of the bleeding of the uranium mines, the vicious system of communist privilege, their own living conditions—families of four and five crowded into one-room flats—of their conflicts with the Party—one had been expelled from college because his father had criticised Rakosi, another from school for refusing to learn Russian. They told of these things with a bitter and terrible hopelessness, knowing that they must all be endured again. 'Fascism or communism,' they said, 'we have had them both. We have found no difference.'

Their only interest each night was in hearing the news on the B.B.C. Hungarian service: all wireless sets had disappeared from the hotel on their arrival, but somehow they had rigged up a set of their own—they would not say where it was. The news came through each night at one o'clock and then, to reduce the margin of error, five of them would write it down simultaneously, then collate their separate versions and distribute a bulletin to their colleagues. For these men the B.B.C. was not merely the one service they trusted: it was their gospel and holy writ. They would not go to bed until the broadcast was over, and on nights when transmission failed some of them never went to bed at all.

Ricardo and myself were the first foreigners they had spoken to freely for years. We stayed with them until three o'clock, talking in hushed tones, with hiding-places prepared in case of unwanted visitors. It was not, as they said, a game; and before the night was through I found out exactly what they meant.

When we were ready to go they insisted first upon checking
s

that the way was clear. On the pretext of going to the lavatory one of them strolled down the corridor and came back to report that a serviceman was on watch at the far end. Our rooms were two floors higher up but theirs was conveniently placed against a back exit leading to the emergency staircase, and they thought we should be able to get out without being seen. We would still have to walk past our own serviceman whose room was opposite mine, but so long as he did not see us coming in through the emergency doors, he would be hardly likely to guess where we had been.

I thought at first we had got away with it. Three Hungarians whose rooms were in the opposite wing set off down the corridor to distract the serviceman's attention. Two others stood immediately outside the room and, covered by them, we slipped furtively through the doors. There was no light on the staircase and no sign of our own serviceman when we reached the fifth floor. We went down the corridor talking in casual tones and when, as we expected, he appeared in his doorway, we smiled politely and bade him good-night.

I went to my room feeling distinctly relieved—and then fell to wondering if the subterfuge had been really necessary. I had no doubt that this kind of thing was commonplace in Budapest, but Chinese communism was vastly different from the satellite variety. We were, after all, guests under the same roof; there was no reason why we should not meet as guests in each other's rooms.

But, as they said, it was not a game. With a sudden sharpness that jolted my nerves and stopped me in the act of undressing, the service telephone rang outside my room. The serviceman answered and I listened tensely while he jabbered into the receiver. His voice was startlingly audible in the hushed stillness of the night. He sounded excited, but you could never tell. After a few minutes he replaced the receiver and silence engulfed the corridor again.

I went on undressing and then lay awake apprehensively for some time. That telephone had never rung late at night before, and there was only one reason why it should ring now, shattering the sleep of other guests at something past three in the morning.

But nothing else happened: there was no abrupt knocking at the door, no tramping of feet along the corridor; no angry denouement; that, after all, would have been a sorry way for the Chinese to treat one of their guests.

It goes without saying that, having been nurtured in a society where the tapping of even a gangster's telephone may provoke more public indignation than the crimes he has committed, I found this situation strangely unreal—and also frightening, not so much for myself because, at the worst, I surmised, they could only order me out of the country—but what they could do to the Hungarians, or what might be done to them on their return home, was another matter.

It was another matter for Ricardo also. While he was manifestly anti-fascist he was nonetheless a subject of Franco's and, as such, more open to suspicion than most. Further, he had no embassy to turn to and, in any case, had come to China in defiance of Franco's ban. Although well versed in underground procedure he admitted in the morning that he felt distinctly uneasy; but he had no intention of giving up seeing the Hungarians unless they wished him to.

After breakfast I received a visit from Liu. We talked for some time about the Programme, but his manner was unusually frigid and at length he came to the point. 'There has been a change in the arrangements,' he said. 'You are to move today to another hotel.'

'Why is that?' I asked.

He explained apologetically that the rooms we were occupying were wanted for other guests; owing to an oversight they had not been booked beyond the date when the main body of the delegation had departed.

'But there are many other empty rooms,' I suggested.

'But only for today,' he said. 'Tomorrow new delegations will arrive.'

'But surely,' I said, 'they can't all be in use.'

'Deeply sorry,' he replied, 'we are putting you to such trouble, but we are in the hands of the Hotel administration. They say every room is full.'

It was, I suppose, possible; I remembered that when we arrived from Canton the Hotel had not been expecting us; but even so, with only four of us to accommodate, it seemed remarkably odd. Liu reiterated his apologies but urged me to get ready at once. 'You are to go to the Peking Hotel in the centre of the city. It will be more interesting for you there. Please pack your bags quickly.'

There was no further point in trying to preserve secrecy. I went down to see the Hungarians.

Two servicemen were sitting in the corridor in a position which commanded a view of the back as well as the front entrance. I brushed past them and went to the Hungarians' room. They were neither surprised nor alarmed to hear what had happened. They accepted the discovery of our meeting as one more charge which would be held against them, but they believed that their fate had been determined already; they were reconciled to whatever else might befall them, preferring to settle for all rather than for half. I felt, in watching their taut, strained faces that, having had no hand in the fighting themselves, they wanted to discharge their debt to those who had by walking into other dangers.

We agreed that we should meet openly from now on whenever possible and, to give a semblance of propriety to the relationship, they suggested I should attend their performance that evening and bring the other delegates with me.

It turned out to be a sombre, grimly ironic occasion. The programme consisted of Magyar dances and rousing national songs. I had seen the same sort of thing done in London by an Hungarian Ensemble a few months before, with a vitality and abandon which had brought cheers from the dress-shirted stalls, but here the dancing was mechanical, the singing tired and dejected. 'They have no spark,' said Vladimir. 'It is their mood.'

There was a large contingent of Russian technicians in the

audience and the ninety-strong male choir had to sing the *Song of the Volga Boatman* in their honour. They sang it with a desperate intensity, a kind of savage desire to have done, and when, at the end, the Russians rose and cheered for an encore, the singers stood stiff and unsmiling, eyes fixed rigidly on the conductor. For two or three minutes the cheering continued but the Hungarians never acknowledged it; the encores were shouted in vain. 'It was not true Volga Boatman,' said Vladimir afterwards, 'but song from empty heart.'

At the end of the performance the Russians marched on the stage to present them with bouquets. There were speeches and hand-shaking and excited applause from the audience. Some of the Hungarians smiled and relaxed, but most of them merely bowed their heads curtly, then stood tight-lipped and still. Later, they said that some of the Russians had tried to express their regrets over Budapest—as the members of the Moscow Circus, with whom they shared a hotel dining-room, had already done several times—but they did not want this kind of comfort. 'We know they are not to blame, so they have no need to remind us.'

Next day there was an orchestral concert which they were anxious I should attend. It was to be a special occasion; they had been waiting for it for days. They were going to play the *Eroica*. 'But for ourselves, not for the Chinese. They will not understand.'

I went with Ricardo. This time there were no Russians, only city workers and students. They listened, as they always did, relaxed but silently attentive, eager and generous in their applause, and never offering it in the wrong places.

The Orchestra played first a Mozart overture, then some Liszt, and the Grieg piano concerto; then they came to the *Eroica*. Whether they played it well or badly I could not say, nor did it matter; I only knew I had never heard it played like this before. For the first time since I had met them the Hungarians were *alive*. Before, they had played with a limp indifference; now their faces were eager and alert, their eyes aglow, and their instruments seemed to take fire in their hands. The great music swelled and surged in anguished exultation like a defiant requiem, a last burning anthem for the martyred soul of Budapest. When they had finished, they sat back with bowed heads, not looking at the audience or at each other, their cheeks flushed, and some with tears in their eyes.

The conductor turned and bowed, and they rose slowly to acknowledge the applause, their eyes still fixed on the ground. Ricardo jumped from his seat shaking with emotion. '*Vive l'Hongarie!*' he cried. '*Vive l'Hongarie!*' and one of the musicians turned towards him with a slow, grave smile of acknowledgment.

'I hope I did not embarrass them," said Ricardo later. 'But I had to shout it. I cannot go against my nature.'

We visited them now whenever we could, taking them old English newspapers and copies of the B.B.C. Bulletin from the Legation, in case they had failed to get their own. It was little enough, but they were as grateful as if we had brought news of their families.

Then we came to the last day of our visit and went to say goodbye. Arthur Boyd had offered to keep in touch with them after we left, but they felt it would be dangerous for him if he did. I offered them my London address but they refused to put anything on paper; they said they would memorise it instead: 'It is not difficult to remember once you have learned the habit.' They swore they would write eventually, however devious the route, to say if they were safe.

But even now I have still heard nothing whatever of them.

Back at the Peking Hotel my hosts were waiting for me. In accordance with modern Chinese custom, they had called to request my final 'criticisms'.

'And please be honest,' they said, 'so that we can discover our mistakes.'

I told them what I thought more bluntly, perhaps, than I should have done a week before. I admired—who couldn't?—their astonishing material progress, their industrial development, their hospitals and schools, their care for the health and welfare of their people, their preservation of their past heritage—and the tumultuous ferment of a nation moving to greatness—all this and more; but I deplored their limited conception of freedom, their ideological mania and, above all, the calculated hypocrisy of their attitude over Egypt and Hungary.

They answered me point by point, cogently and rationally, until they came to the last one. Then having justified their attitude on Egypt they shut up abruptly, ignoring Hungary altogether.

'And my last criticism?' I asked. 'What do you feel about that?'

'We have a different viewpoint,' was all they would say.

So we went down to dinner, where Ricardo was thumping the table, hammering the same point at another group of officials.

'Do you deny the Bandung statement? Do you admit there is a general strike in Hungary? Why? Why? Why do you shut your eyes to these things?'

'We have a different viewpoint,' came the discreet, echoing answer.

'Don't you realise,' I protested, 'that if you acted independently of Russia on this one issue the western attitude towards China would change overnight? If Chou En-lai stood up and condemned the Soviet intervention you might even find the Americans would clear out of Taiwan.'

'If Chou En-lai did that,' said one of them, 'the whole Chinese nation would rise up against him!''

27

The Long Night

WE left Peking on a snow-clad dawn, without fuss or formality. Everything had been arranged, even to the payment of excess baggage fares all the way home—an extraordinary little courtesy which I only discovered when I was taking off from Helsinki two weeks later.

Liu, Shen and a Federation official chivalrously turned out to see us off. We said little—all the relevant things had been said already—but they reminded me to report objectively on what I had seen and to send them anything I wrote.

There was a cold, bleak journey ahead and a long night to fly through as we aimed for the west. The morning sun gleamed deceptively as we flew out over the Great Wall—a jagged black crack cutting the ice-bound hills—and then on, over the frozen wastes of the Gobi desert, to the white peaks and crevasses of Mongolia, the land of the yaks and the felted yurts and the squat-nosed, brooding camel men. We came down briefly at Ulan Bator in an airfield sheeted with snow, then off again, westwards to Irkutsk, over the icy desolation of Lake Baikal, towards the stark forests of eastern Siberia, trailing far behind the sun, into a cold black abyss of lengthening night.

'Down below,' said Vladimir, 'is battle for virgin soil. New mining stations—pipelines—industries—young pioneers at work.'

'Good luck to them,' I said. 'Who wants to be a pioneer?'

'Ah! ah!' he laughed. 'Maybe no good for depraved bourgeois, but very important for men who look to future.'

The flight had set off the old pain in his ears although, as he explained in his new-found vernacular, the doctor had given him 'big pricks in arse' the night before. Muriel did not help matters much by chattering most of the way from Irkutsk to Novosibersk, for the most part comparing different aspects of the Russian scene with their English counterparts: 'We don't have forests as big as these in Siberia because there's no room, but we have woods instead.'

Conversely Ricardo was too cold to say anything for he had come on the trip with no overcoat or winter clothing of any kind (when he joined the delegation he had been on holiday in Paris 'dressed for summer'). The sight of his tall, spindly-legged figure crossing the Siberian airfields at twenty-five degrees below in a thin, canvas windcheater and light grey slacks eventually touched the heart of a young Russian sitting behind him; and, although the purple-faced Ricardo protested that the air was 'most good for the health', the young man forced his own overcoat upon him.

So we dozed and talked and lost all count of time as the long night dragged on. Between sleep and waking we staggered out of the plane at Novosibersk to find a blizzard blowing and gangs of tight-lipped women working with shovels and barrows to clear the runway of three feet of snow. Along the edge of the airfield squadrons of planes were bogged down nose-deep and buses lay derelict on distant roads. 'How does anyone last through the winter?' you wondered. 'How does anything *happen* here at all?'

We sat down to borsch and gritty chicken rissoles—supper or breakfast, who was to know?—beneath the stonily watchful gaze of Engels and Marx on one wall and Lenin and Stalin on the other. On an adjacent wall, in his Marshal's uniform, stood a solitary portrait of Bulganin.

'Tell me,' I asked Vladimir, 'what is Bulganin's military record?'

'He is Party general only,' he said. 'For dealing with political matters. Not same as military general.'

'In that case he shouldn't be in the Army at all.'

'Oh, yes.' He smiled darkly, enjoying the joke. 'Party general is for *before* fight. Military general is only for *during* fight.'

'But military general,' I suggested, 'may be shot by Party general without *any* fight.'

'I think,' he observed drily, 'there used to be some reason in what you say.'

We were joined by an elderly Canadian with a bluff, breezy manner who said he was a former missionary and had just been back to China for the first time since the War—as a guest of the government. Reports about communist treatment of the missionaries had been completely distorted, he said. People he had been told were shot were still alive: 'You can't trust your own friends even.' One old friend now in prison had told him that another mutual friend had died of dysentery in a labour camp, but when he himself had visited the camp there the man was, hale and hearty—'Not allowed out, of course, but with all the amenities he could need.'

There was something a shade synthetic about the Canadian's breezy self-assurance. He gave his name as Endicott, which meant nothing to me but registered immediately with Vladimir. 'He is very famous man,' he said. 'Very popular in my country.' A day or two later I discovered why; he was the leader of the Canadian 'Peace Committee'.

So we flew on for another three hours. Vladimir painfully held his head in his hands; Muriel chattered; Ricardo slept; and a young Swiss salesman sat beside me and for an hour and more, in fluent and highly audible English, expressed his contempt of everything Russian.

Then we climbed at last into the dawn, high above the dense black cloudbanks, and watched the morning sun forging up behind us in a pale, cold sky; then down again, beneath the murky ceiling of clouds, over drear white wastes and forbidding forests, through lashing snows, to the flat-roofed desolation of Omsk.

But now the undercarriage had frozen, and we flew seven times round the city while the pilot struggled in vain to release it, and we braced ourselves for the pancake landing we were sure would come. If the English keep cool heads in a crisis, the Russians can be said to have ice in their veins: they joked among themselves, shouted derisive suggestions to the pilot, or simply stared detachedly out of the window as though to admire the view; you would have thought they did this kind of thing every day—it may be, of course, that they did.

At length, with a mock gesture of farewell, the co-pilot ripped up a floorboard, shoved his head and shoulders through the opening, and dug about in the belly of the plane with a screwdriver. After a few minutes he came up again, frozen but cheerful, and announced with a grin, 'We land on the wheels!'

We came down to another meal (breakfast, for sure) of borsch and boiled goose. The goose was memorable; it had strength and hardiness in its favour, a life well spent, no doubt, among its kind, with some smatch of honour in it, but it seemed to have been captured in the last stages of senile decay. It startled even Vladimir, who promptly ordered a bottle of Caucasian wine to help alleviate the effects. The wine was as sharp and dry as a good Moselle, an unexpected treat, which delighted everyone except the young Swiss salesman.

'It is our best wine,' said Vladimir proudly. 'Look! Number One on bottle. That means *very* good wine!'

'I don't think,' sneered the Swiss, 'that the French put numbers on *their* bottles. Obviously I must tell them to do so.'

We came to Moscow just after four o'clock, with night closing in again. This time there was no reception party, no drinking to Peace and Co-existence—Kruschev had pronounced the death of *that* at the Polish Embassy a few days before—no caviare and vodka. No interpreters, even; nobody at all to own or chaperon us. For some time Vladimir busied himself on the telephone, then stood faithfully beside us until somebody chose to appear, although he was in torment with his ears and his one desire was to get to his doctor.

Ricardo could not sit still for long. When a contingent of Polish cavalrymen came clamping into the waiting-room in jackboots and full kit he was among them in a flash. He soon found somebody who could speak French. Poland was finding herself again—there was no doubt of that—you could read it in their proud and glowing faces. '*Vive Gomulka!*' cried Ricardo, and they danced jubilantly round together while the Russians in their thick black overcoats and astrakhan collars stood back astonished.

Eventually Igor arrived, the dark, Latin-featured young man from the Soviet *Komsomol*. He looked glum and morose, a vastly different Igor from the one with whom I had sung *Auld Lang Syne* at the send-off dinner. 'Things are not so good,' he muttered. 'It is a bad time for you to be here.'

Bad time or not, I wanted to see what impact the 'counter-revolution' had made upon the Russians themselves—if they would give me the chance. They did; but there was really little to report—I was able to go where I wanted and talk to whom I liked—but nobody had much to say. I sensed that people were bewildered and uneasy, but they would not commit themselves to an opinion, unless it had already been expressed for them in *Pravda*—except, that is, for the students. Some of them were only too pleased to talk freely to a foreigner.

Ricardo as usual was first off the mark. The day after we arrived he tracked down a group of Spanish students who had been brought to Russia as children during the Franco war and were now studying at Moscow University. They made no bones about condemning the Russian government. 'It was murder of the people!' they declared, and apparently they had been openly expressing this view since the intervention began. It seemed that twenty years of communist teaching had done nothing to impair their powers of reasoning. 'The government has never interfered with us,' they said. 'We have always said what we thought.'

Their Russian fellow-students were in a different case. They freely admitted that 'terrible mistakes' had been made in Hungary in the past—even that 'terrible crimes' had been committed, but, like Vladimir, they tended to lay the blame at Stalin's door, or, even more comfortably, at Beria's. It was one thing for them to condemn past methods but quite another to examine present motives: their attitude in fact was curiously analogous to that of those sterling English patriots to whom the only thing wrong with the Suez venture was that the troops had not gone far enough; but these students at least had some conscience about what their government had done.

Since the B.B.C. Russian Service was jammed those who could speak English listened regularly to the Home Service News and, when I asked if they had heard of Nagy's arrest or the latest U.N.O. resolution, they replied briefly, 'We have heard, but not read.' They knew, in fact, a good deal more about Hungary than I did, and it was useless to go on sniping at them as if they personally were responsible for their government's policy, although Ricardo never gave up the attack.

'Do you believe,' he asked one of them, 'that the general strike is still going on in Hungary?'

'Maybe, and maybe not,' said the student cautiously.

'But *Pravda* has not reported it?'

'*Pravda* does not say it is still going on.'

'Do you believe that *Pravda* printed the whole of Tito's speech?'

'It printed most of it.'

'But not the important part. Not the same as in *Borba*. *Why* didn't it print the whole of it?'

'I am not the government,' said the student testily. 'You had better ask them.'

'But you support the government!' cried Ricardo, thumping his fist on the table. 'Why do you sit there and defend such things? *Why? Why? Why?*'

The student refused to reply. 'I cannot argue with a firework,' he said; but later his friends told me that he was one of many who for weeks had been agitating against the *Pravda* and radio censorship.

Yet on certain subjects, where careful reticence might have been expected, *Pravda* was surprisingly communicative. On the charge of deportations, for instance, it printed fervent denials from the members of the Lithuanian Catholic Church and the Trans-Carpathian clergy 'resident on the Soviet-Hungarian border'. One issue even reported that, in the British Trade Union movement, while 'the rank and file, factory workers and office employees, hail the victory of the Hungarian people over the fascist counter-revolution,' the National Miners' Union, 'drawing on bourgeois information sources,' had condemned Soviet action— 'an attitude which hardly reflects the broad mass of the British people. . . .'

It snowed continually for three days while snow dredgers and gangs of dour-faced women worked round the clock to keep the streets clear. All through the day the inevitable queue, more than a quarter-mile long, curled round the walls of the Kremlin to the mausoleum in the Red Square. I had little inclination to play the official tourist, but one evening I dutifully took my place in the queue. Gazing at the stony face of Stalin, I asked Igor why he was still allowed to remain in this beatified state. 'Maybe he will not be here for long,' he replied curtly.

Every day, around and about the city, familiar but un-expected social problems were apparent. In the middle of the afternoon a drunk staggered into me in the street and then pro-ceeded to kick impotently at the mudguard of a stationary car. In the Moscow Hotel, while the orchestra ground out incessantly Gershwin's *Love Walked In*, serious-faced young couples had their verbal love-making interrupted by the arrival of uninvited gregarious louts; and sometimes there were brief scuffles as gangs of *stilyagi*, wearing drain-pipes, long jackets, and bobbed hair styles distinctively their own, upset the tables or smashed their glasses on the floor.

For Igor, these Moscow editions of the Teddy boy were outside the bounds of Marxist analysis. They came mostly from well-to-do homes, he said, and were 'no good to anybody'. If he had his way they would be thrashed without mercy as 'spoilt children, enemies to decent society'.

Meal times in the Moscow Hotel regularly presaged a battle of wills between Igor and the staff. Even when the restaurant was empty it was often necessary to wait twenty minutes and more before the meal could be ordered—and as long again until it actually appeared on the table—while the waiters in their pre-revolution monkey suits loitered vaguely about the kitchen or gazed dreamily out of the windows as though recollecting halcyon days of yore. Igor attributed all faults to 'bureaucratic delays in the kitchen', but eventually admitted that the waiters were trying to bludgeon us into tipping them, a practice which his communist principles would not allow.

He was an ideal chaperon, not least because he always sensed when he was not wanted and, in fact, seemed glad of the excuse to take himself elsewhere. At first he explained that he had other business to attend to, but as we got to know each other better he admitted that it was of a strictly amatory kind.

Most nights we went together to the theatre: plays of Shaw, Sartre and Genet, as well as three Shakespearean productions, were running concurrently, and *Dial M for Murder* had just gone into rehearsal at the Pushkin. At the Mali there was the best production of *Macbeth* I have ever seen, directed by Stanislavsky's old pupil, Zubov, and at the Mayakovsky an extraordinary one of *Hamlet* which lovingly revived the decorative vulgarity and declamatory excesses of the English classical style at the turn of the century. Samoilov, the idol of the Moscow bobby-soxers, played the name part with a grinding fury which would have done much credit to Ivan the Terrible in his most demented moments; and the production culminated in the dropping of a vast orange canopy beneath the folds of which Hamlet and Claudius writhed and wrestled, invisible to the audience, like pillow fighters under the sheets of a gigantic bed.

The play had been cut more than any *Hamlet* I have seen but, owing to Samoilov's obsession with the dramatic pause, it still contrived to last over four and a half hours; indeed, there were times when his pauses seemed longer than his speeches and, during the 'Woo't fight, woo't fast, . . . woo't drink up eisel' in the graveyard I actually nodded off to sleep, woke up and nodded off again in the space between two consecutive lines.

This style, however, was not universally approved; next day, when I told students at the Foreign Language Institute that I thought the production 'utterly reactionary' they roared their agreement.

By this time living on the communist circuit had begun to take its toll. I felt tired in a way I had never done since the War: too tired to keep awake in the theatre—I dozed one night through most of *Romeo and Juliet* at the Bolshoi—and once fell asleep in the Moscow Hotel in the middle of dinner; too tired to think much about anything that had happened on the way. Muriel and Ricardo had left for Prague already but I was going back via Scandinavia; it would be good to relax for a while and hear the hard-drinking Finns retelling their stories of the Winter War; it would be good to spend a few aimless nights amongst people on the same ideological wavelength as myself.

Yet I liked the Russians I had met. They had never attempted to hamper my movements or to curb what I had to say; I had criticised them frankly and I think they had been frank with me. In happier times, perhaps, with Vladimir and Igor, I should try to pick up the broken strands of friendship—unless they had already been swept away forever on the tide of political necessity.

Vladimir had been ill in bed ever since we returned to Moscow, but he turned up on my last evening with a parting present of a bottle of vodka. 'For special bourgeois friend,' he said simply. 'To drink with depraved friends in London, in memory of distant friend in Moscow.' He smiled as he spoke but the words had a frosty, elegiac sound.

I left Moscow at dawn the next morning.

Red carpet days were over; no more interpreters and State-paid chaperons; no more buckshee cigarettes and civic receptions; no more deliberations over the Programme; no more toasts to Peace and Friendship; for better or for worse, no more Solidarity with anyone or anything. Ahead lay the grey Gulf of Finland and the desolate pine forests; beyond them, the friendly streets of Helsinki: the gay advertisement boards and familiar petrol signs, the neon-lit shop windows and American cars—the garish symbols of the bad old bourgeois world.

Never before had I cared for it so much.